CLASSI

Learning the Joy of Prayer

Pray in the Spirit

Praying Together

ISBN 0 85476 793 2

Designed and produced by Bookprint Creative Services
P.O. Box 827, BN21 3YJ, England for
KINGSWAY PUBLICATIONS
Lottbridge Drove, Eastbourne, E. Sussex BN23 6NT
Printed in Great Britain.

Reproduced from the original typesetting
of the single-volume editions.

Learning the Joy of Prayer

LARRY LEA
WITH JUDY DOYLE

KINGSWAY PUBLICATIONS
EASTBOURNE

Contents

Part Seven: Praise
'Yours is the kingdom and the power and the glory for ever'

Part Eight: Prerequisites, patterns, participation

Part One

Preparation

His name is not Henry

I was seventeen years old in 1968 when the heavy doors of the psychiatric ward of Mother Frances Hospital in Tyler, Texas, closed and locked behind me.

I had a brand new convertible and a beautiful girl-friend; I was an all-state golfer with a scholarship; I lived in a large house. (The entire second floor was mine — two bedrooms, two bathrooms and a study.) I had a lot of 'stuff'. But I went stark-raving crazy in that environment because I had everything on the outside and nothing on the inside.

Weeks before, I had sought help from my dad, who had made his money in the oil and gas business in Texas.

'Help me, Dad!' I begged.

But my father was an alcoholic who didn't know Jesus; his heart was as empty as mine. All he did was stare at me for a moment in disbelief, then exclaim in exasperation, 'Larry, any kid who has everything you've got and is depressed has got to be on drugs.'

My mother, who was a Christian, rushed to my defence. 'My son wouldn't get on drugs,' she retorted, shocked by my father's accusation. 'He must have a brain tumour or something.'

During this terrible time of depression, I went to church one Sunday morning looking for something real. I needed help so badly that at the end of the service I walked to the front of the church — watched by all my friends seated on the back row. I said to the pastor, 'Sir, have you got anything for me? I'm losing my mind, and I don't know what's wrong.'

Do you know what the pastor did? He just patted me on the shoulder and whispered reassuringly, 'You'll be all right, son. You're a good boy. Here, fill out this card.'

All Dad had to offer me was money, and all the church had for me was a card to fill out. I didn't know anywhere else to turn, so when my mother kept insisting that something must be physically wrong with me, I gave in and went to the doctor. After extensive tests revealed no physical reason for my deep emotional problems, I was admitted to a hospital psychiatric ward, and the rounds of psychological examinations began.

Soon the doctor walked into my room and said in an understanding tone, 'You're depressed, aren't you? These will help.'

He handed me four tranquillisers, and the next thing I knew, every four hours someone brought me four little pills. That did it: I lost it. The last lights of reality flickered out, and the fog rolled in. The doctors called it a nervous breakdown, but in reality it was a 'transgression breakdown'. I was a sinner who didn't understand Christ's atonement for sin. I didn't know life could have purpose.

For six weeks in that ward I didn't even see the sun. Part of the time I lay in a drugged stupor with my eyes rolled back in my head. When I would come to, I thought the black lady cleaning the floor was my mother and that the patient across the hall was the doctor. There I was, the heir to a fortune, and I had lost my mind.

My grief-stricken parents reluctantly made reservations at the state mental hospital so I could be committed.

But before I could be transferred, one day I strayed out of my room into the hall, where I noticed a crucifix. Being somewhat curious, I removed it from the wall and managed to focus my eyes and thoughts long enough to make out its Latin inscription, *INRI*. Confused, I wandered along the corridors of that Catholic hospital, collecting crucifixes and pondering those puzzling letters.

Of course, when the nuns spied me with the crucifixes clutched to my chest, they rushed forward to retrieve them. With the sisters in hot pursuit, I broke into a run, and my befuddled muttering amplified into a bewildered wail, loud enough for the whole world to hear: 'His name is not Henry . . . . His name is not Henry! His name is Jesus!'

In my room several days later, I seemed to come to my senses. I fell to my knees and began to cry out, 'Jesus! Jesus! Merciful Jesus!' It was not a very religious prayer. I just called out to God over and over, pleading, weeping, sobbing out his name.

Suddenly, I heard an inner voice speak in my spirit. He said, 'Now you are my son. You will take my message to this generation. You will be my mouthpiece and my minister.' Then the voice told me I could get up and go home.

I was well, but I couldn't leave because they had me locked up. The doctor came in the next day and asked routinely, 'How are you doing, Larry?'

'I'm better now,' I answered.

Puzzled, the doctor hesitated, then asked matter-of-factly, 'Why do you think you're better now?'

Returning his steady gaze, I said, 'Because yesterday I talked to God.'

The doctor raised his eyebrow and muttered sceptically, 'Yes, right.' But unable to deny the peace that had replaced my inner turmoil, he soon discharged me from the hospital.

That psychiatric ward was a strange place to begin my walk with the Lord. But when I cried out to him, Jesus came through the locked doors and barred windows: he walked right into my heart and placed

a call on my life to serve my generation. Like a
newborn colt on weak, wobbling legs, I walked out of
the hospital and back into life. But this time I didn't
walk alone. Since that hour, I've never been out of his
care.

Why am I willing to open the dusty pages of my life
and share that story with you? Because my misery is
forgotten — passed away — and in its place abides
steady peace and divine purpose. I believe *you* are part
of that purpose. God has drawn us together in order
that you might partake of the grace he has extended
to me.

I don't know at which juncture my experiences will
interface with yours or at what point the word of the
Lord will come to you, but it will happen — and the
truth will set you free. Constraining habits that keep
you from God's best, obsolete ways of seeing yourself
or others, lifeless traditions that exert control over you
even though truth long ago overpowered them — all
will be defied by the Spirit of God who makes all things
new.

I invite you to partake of my grace and to learn, from
the Holy Spirit's gentle, friendly instruction, what I
have learned through the painful yet precious
experiences of my life.

How about you? Is your situation as desperate as
mine was? Are you in a place where you can't talk
or buy your way out, and there's no back door?
Perhaps you're not there; perhaps you're just in the
spiritual doldrums. Nothing seems new anymore. You
were saved years ago and now you're sure you've
'heard it all'.

'Since when,' you say sceptically, 'has God said
anything new to anybody?'

Well, let me give you some advice: stop trying to
think your problem through or wait it through. Pray
it through.

Your *situation* may or may not be desperate, but only

when *you* are desperate enough to get down on your knees, confess your needs to him and call on his name will he speak peace to you and your problems. That's your next step. Take it now, my friend. Take it now.

And when you call out to him, remember: his name is not Henry. His name is Jesus!

2

A radical change

Almost two decades have passed since that day in the psychiatric ward when I wept my way into Christ's presence and his peace flooded my being.

I know now what healed me. For the first time in my life I comprehended that God saw me right where I was and knew me, that he needed me and had a purpose for my life and that I needed him.

These same three needs are basic to every human being, including you. You need *somebody to see you;* you need *somebody to need you;* you need *something to give your life to.* Giving your life to another human being is not enough. Pouring yourself into a career and buying material things will not feed the gnawing need in your heart. There will always be a 'vacancy' sign flashing in the window of your soul.

When I discovered Jesus, life seemed to pulse with purpose and meaning. I couldn't keep it to myself. I had to share what I had discovered. But there was a problem. Pastors wouldn't let me preach in the churches because they thought I had 'nuthouse religion', so I preached at the ice-cream parlour or wherever anybody would listen.

I finally got my chance, though, when they agreed to let me preach just once at First Baptist Church in Kilgore, Texas, my hometown.

That Sunday a hippy sat listening to me preach. I knew by his vacant stare that either his brain was fried or he was stoned out of his mind right there in church. Sometime during the service I realised that the hippy was Jerry Howell, the keyboard player for a rock band called The Mouse and the Traps. (Jerry was one of the Traps.) The group had a number-one song on the Dallas charts at that time. The local kids idolised Jerry, but their parents thought he was the scourge of the earth.

At the end of the service, Jerry walked up to me and remarked casually, 'I really related to what you said today.'

'Jerry, what are you doing in church, man?' I asked as I shook his outstretched hand.

He sighed. 'Well, my dad died six months ago, and I promised him on his deathbed that I'd drive back from the University of Texas every weekend and take my brother to church. I'm just keeping my word to my dad.'

Jerry paused and lowered his voice. 'What you had to say is the first thing I've heard here in the last six months that's made any sense to me.'

Later, I couldn't get Jerry off my mind. I knew he was reaching out for help, so I phoned and asked him to go to church with me.

'Jerry,' I began hesitantly, 'er . . . this is Larry Lea.' Dead silence on the other end of the line.

'Er, Jerry . . . I'm a youth director now at the First Baptist Church in New London.' (I didn't add that it was the only Baptist church in the tiny town.)

'Jerry,' I continued more confidently, 'why don't you come out and play the organ for me? You can play *Amazing Grace*, can't you? I'll sing and you can play, and we'll have church with all these young people.'

'*Me?*' he answered. 'You want *me* to play organ in a *church?*'

Little did I know that every day for four years Jerry Howell had been high on drugs. I later learnt that when the phone rang, Jerry had been out in his back garden counting the blades of grass, trying to keep his head on his shoulders.

'Look, Jerry, I need your help,' I assured him. 'You

have a great talent, and God can use you. He loves you, man, and he has a plan for your life. I'll drive by and get you this evening. I'll even get you a date,' I added, waiting for his reply.

'A date!' he blurted. 'With a church girl?'

At seven o'clock I went to pick up Jerry for the service. He was dressed in his faded blue jeans and a tee-shirt. He had blond hair flowing down to his waist but was bald on top. And his old van — the kind with drawn curtains on the windows and an elaborate stereo system blaring Jimi Hendrix and Led Zeppelin rock — was in the driveway.

Here I sat with my short-back-and-sides haircut, my tape of Jim Nabors singing *The Lord's Prayer* and the family Bible on the dashboard. When Jerry climbed into my car, his eyes darted from the family Bible, to me, back to the Bible, then straight ahead. Boy, was he quiet. We drove and picked up the girls, but Jerry hardly said a word to anybody.

As we stepped inside the church, I nodded my head towards the platform and said, 'Jerry, there's the organ. You know what to do.'

Jerry played *Amazing Grace* in a way it's never been played before or since! I sang and preached, and we had church.

It was about eleven-thirty when we pulled into his driveway after dropping the girls off. Jerry spoke for practically the first time all evening.

'Larry, is there anything to this Jesus?' he asked earnestly.

I hardly knew how to respond because Jerry was confused, in the middle of a nervous breakdown and bound with drugs, but I breathed a prayer for help.

During the first part of our conversation that night, Jerry asked a lot of questions that I didn't have the answers to. Sometimes I honestly replied, 'I don't know, Jerry.' But God filled my mouth, and I just kept giving him Jesus.

When we got through talking, it was three-thirty in the morning. Jerry stared straight ahead, heaved a deep sigh and asked, 'Well, how do I get it?'

So I — deep Christian and experienced soulwinner that I was — said, 'What you do is, you open your Bible to Matthew five, six and seven [because that was the only part of the Bible I knew], then you get on your knees and start hollering, "Jesus! Jesus! Jesus!" and when it hits you, you'll know you've got it.'

That night Jerry Howell did just that, but before he could hit his knees, God had saved him, delivered him from a four-year drug habit and called him to preach.

When it was over, Jerry walked to the home of his best friend, Max, the drummer for their band. It was six o'clock on the fourth of July, and Max was out in the back garden feeding his rabbits. (These were strange people.)

When Jerry came around the corner of the house, Max took one look at him and gasped, 'Man, what happened to you?'

Jerry grinned and explained, 'I met this weird little dude named Larry Lea, and we talked all night about Jesus.'

'Hey, man, how do I get it?'

Jerry gave it to him straight. 'You get your Bible and you read Matthew five, six and seven, then you get down on your knees and . . . .'

At seven-thirty that morning my phone rang. It was Jerry.

'Larry, I got it, I got it! And I came down here and told Max about it, and he got it, too. But you know how strange he is. You'd better come over here and check him out.'

That wasn't the only phone call Jerry Howell made that day. The local barber shop was closed for the holiday, but Jerry called the barber at home.

'Mr Buck,' he said hesitantly, 'this is Jerry Howell. Would you cut my hair?'

Mr Buck didn't stutter. Quick as a flash, he answered, 'Sure, son. Come on over.' He couldn't resist adding, 'I've been wanting to cut your hair for a long time.'

Six weeks later, a clean-shaven Jerry Howell with a short-back-and-sides haircut went off to Bible college with the weird little dude named Larry Lea. One day Jerry announced, 'Larry, God has called me to preach, and I'm supposed to go hold an evangelistic campaign.'

And that's exactly what he did. Within six months after his own conversion, Jerry Howell had led a thousand people to God!

Jerry is now pastor of Church on the Rock in Kilgore, Texas, the very place where he was once considered the offscouring of the earth. How did that radical change come about? You see, Jesus came along and said, '*I see you*, Jerry Howell, hiding there behind your walls, and *I need you* for a special task. I've got something you can give your life to. All I need to hear you say is that *you need me.*'

Now I want to ask an important question. How about you, my friend? Do you need a radical change in your heart? In your home? In your relationships? Are you sick of your doubts and unbelief? Jesus sees you right where you are. He needs you for something special that only you can do. And you need him.

Jesus changed Larry Lea, a seventeen-year-old boy in a psychiatric ward. Jesus changed a Texan hippy named Jerry Howell. And he can change you, too. You don't even have to read Matthew five, six and seven. Just get down on your knees and call on Jesus.

And don't worry: when it hits you, you'll know you got it!

3

Read the red and pray for the power

Jerry Howell and I, two growing, newborn converts, were room-mates at Dallas Baptist College. Besides attending class, about all we did for three years was 'read the red' and pray for the power. We devoured the words of Jesus that were printed in red ink in our black Bibles.

Jerry and I were captivated by Christ's miracles, compassion and power to help the helpless. We craved what he had. We longed to do what he did. We hungered and thirsted for more of Jesus.

One night I left the dorm and went for a walk. It was a still, clear night, and the view of the lights, mirrored in the lake in the valley below the college, was serene and soothing. I strolled along the edge of the hill and talked to God.

After a time, I paused and stared up at the stars, but the consuming desire in my heart stretched far beyond those shimmering pinpoints of light.

'Oh, God,' I pleaded, my face wet with tears, 'I want all you have for me. Please, Father, if there's power in this gospel, give it to me! Give it to me, Lord . . . .'

I guess you know it's dangerous to pray a prayer like that. The next thing I knew, my startled ears heard my stammering lips speaking a language I had never learned. Shocked, I clamped my hand over my mouth and gasped, 'But, God, we don't believe in this!'

Does that blow your theology? Don't worry; it blew mine, too. I didn't understand what had taken place, but it sounded an awful lot like what the disciples experienced in the book of Acts.

I didn't let it happen again for a while. But one evening I visited the home of a minister who prayed over me. Sure enough, my new prayer language came bubbling out again. This time I just let it flow. I knew this was the Holy Spirit and that he had filled and flooded my being in answer to that honest, desperate prayer. God also baptised Jerry in the Holy Spirit.

Although we tried not to be divisive or to make a big deal about our experiences, word about the two guys with the funny prayer languages soon got round to most of the four hundred budding Baptist preachers in our dorm. Their reactions were mixed: icy aloofness, warm interest, red-hot hostility and all in between.

At night when we knelt beside our beds and began to pray, we would hear doors creak open all along our hall. We would listen as scurrying feet stopped abruptly outside our door. One night Jerry rose quietly to his feet, crept stealthily across the floor and threw open the door. There, crouched at our threshold, were several surprised, embarrassed fellow-students.

We all had a good laugh about it, and the guys learned that even though Jerry and I, in the privacy of our room, sometimes prayed in prayer languages other than English, we weren't in there swinging from the light fixture or rolling on the floor. We were just experiencing praise and intercession in a powerful new dimension. And the guys who were interested soon discovered that we were willing to talk about our fulfilling new experience if they cared to risk it.

For a while it seemed that Jerry and I were going to get along well with most of those other Baptist preacher boys. But one of my professors at the college learned of my baptism in the Spirit and tried to reason with me.

'Son,' he said, 'it's all right if you want to speak in your prayer language in your private devotions. Just don't go around broadcasting your experience and telling other people how to receive it.'

My eyes brimmed with tears as I quietly replied, 'I can't do that, sir.'

His jaw tightened and his careful, deliberate words cut my heart like a knife. 'Then in that case, Larry, you have no ministry.'

That professor wasn't the only one concerned about my baptism in the Holy Spirit. When my father learned of my new experience, he warned, 'Larry, you're gonna wind up out under a tent somewhere with a bunch of snaggle-toothed people who foam at the mouth.'

For a while, it looked as if he might be right.

But 1972 was a big year for me: I graduated from college; I married my wife, Melva Jo; and Howard Conatser, pastor of Beverly Hills Baptist Church in Dallas, surprised me with a generous invitation to become his youth minister.

I appreciated his offer, but I really didn't want to be a youth minister. My desire was to become an evangelist like TV evangelist James Robison, and I told Pastor Conatser so.

He wasn't upset in the least. 'Just pray about it, Larry,' his raspy bass voice drawled confidently.

So I prayed, and to my astonishment, the Lord directed me to accept the position.

Back then I wasn't one to beat around the bush when a head-on confrontation would do just as well. When I learned that the youth group at Beverly Hills existed on a steady diet of skating parties, barbecues, bad-taste parties and trips to the amusement park, I strolled in before the critical stares of fifty pairs of young eyes and announced, 'Y'all, we're not gonna do all that stuff anymore. We're gonna read the red and pray for the power.'

The response was tremendous. Overnight the youth group went from fifty to fourteen. Phenomenal growth!

And to top it all, a girl sauntered up to me with a smirk on her face and fire in her eyes and threatened, 'Listen, if you don't do what we want you to do, we're gonna run you off just like we ran off the four youth directors before you!'

I sucked in my breath, commanded my little ol' insides to stop shaking, prayed she wouldn't notice the quiver in my voice and offered her an option.

'Sister,' I said as I stared her right in the eye, 'you can't run me off, because you didn't run me in. I'm here because God told me to be here, and I'm not leaving. It'll be a lot easier for you to move your membership to another church than for me to move my furniture!'

That was the end of that conversation and the beginning of a new day for many young people.

That group of fourteen began meeting on Tuesday, Wednesday, Thursday and Sunday nights. By the end of the first summer, we had grown from fourteen to a hundred and forty. By the end of the second year, we had a thousand teenagers in our youth services, and many more flocked to the Christian concerts we sponsored. God honoured my obedience to his call and the zealous witness of those young people. (Many of those same people are now members of Church on the Rock.)

But one of the most dangerous things that can befall any minister happened to me. I became a successful preacher without developing my own personal prayer life. Don't get me wrong; I sometimes prayed fervent, earnest prayers, but my prayer life was sporadic and inconsistent.

Outside, everything looked great. I preached to crowds of kids every month. We had a concert ministry which drew thousands of teenagers weekly and was telecast nationally for five years. But something was happening on the inside of me. My own preaching was convicting me. Again and again after ministering to a congregation, I found myself alone in a back room of the church, crying out to God and repenting over my prayerless life.

Those were some of the most miserable days in my memory. But God was getting ready to give me a chance to obey another call — the highest call of all.

4

The highest call of all

After Howard Conatser died in 1978, I was called to be the pastor of his three-thousand-member church. That was a very tempting offer to a twenty-eight-year-old youth minister, but right away God let me know that it wasn't for me.

A man on the committee approached me with an offer that went something like this: 'Son, we're gonna triple your salary, put you on television and make you rich and famous. You just preach sermons that bring people down the aisle and play your cards right, and we'll make you a success.'

This was another of those heart-to-heart, eye-to-eye conversations that I was becoming accustomed to, so I squared my shoulders and replied forthrightly, 'Sir, I quit playing cards when I got saved.'

Well, that bought me a ticket back home to Kilgore.

Although I was graduating from Bible college and my wife and I had three small children by this time, I moved back into the same bedroom I had slept in as a teenager in high school. My future seemed to have fallen into one glorious heap. God knows how to motivate us to pray, doesn't he!

At about that time I met Bob Willhite, pastor of the First Assembly of God Church in Kilgore, Texas, and he invited me to hold a mission in his church. Something about this soft-spoken, grey-haired gentleman captured my attention. I knew immediately that this man was to be my pastor, and I told him so.

I conducted the mission for him and his praying people. It lasted seven weeks, and we saw five hundred

teenagers saved. We witnessed the conversion of the
entire senior class of one of the local high schools. But
the greatest thing that happened during the revival was
my personal conversion from being a preacher in the
pulpit to becoming a man who was more interested
in prayer than anything else in life.

It came about like this. One evening I remarked,
'Pastor Willhite, I understand you're a man of prayer.'

'That's right,' he said. 'I pray. I've been rising early
in the morning to pray for over thirty years.'

My pulse quickened and I said to myself, 'Oh, Jesus,
this is a real one.'

Masking my excitement I asked, 'While the mission
is going on, would you let me come and pray with you
in the mornings?'

'Why, yes,' Pastor Willhite agreed. 'I'll pick you up
in the morning at five.'

I might as well confess that when four-fifteen rolled
around the next morning and that screeching alarm-
clock went off, I didn't feel one ounce of anointing to
pray. No angel stood by my side and commanded,
'Come, my son. Let us journey to the place of prayer.'
All I wanted to do was pull the covers over my head.
But I managed to stagger to the shower and to be
clothed and in my right mind when Pastor Willhite's
car pulled into the driveway.

As we rode to the church that morning before dawn,
I didn't have any idea what God was going to do in
my life, but I was absolutely certain that I was
answering the most vital call of my ministry — the call
to pray.

That call will haunt each of us until we answer it.
It had haunted me for six years. But when I obeyed
it, that choice marked the turning-point in my
ministry. From that day on, I rose early every morning
to pray. Of course, I sought God's *hand*, praying,
'Lord, do this for me. Do that for me.' But more and
more I also found myself seeking God's *face*, thirsting

for his friendship and communion, hungering for his holy, loving, compassionate nature to be formed within me.

I felt like a little child who didn't know my right hand from my left. I knew there was so very much to learn about prayer and communion with my Father. The cry of my heart became: 'Teach me how to pray, Father. Teach me how to pray.'

And one morning during that two-year period of travelling as an evangelist, while I was in prayer, the Holy Spirit began to reveal truths about the Lord's Prayer that I want to share with you later in this book.

I was in Canada conducting a youth mission when the Lord impressed upon me, 'Go to Rockwall and establish my people there.' Rockwall, a town with a population just under eleven thousand people, is perched on a ridge overlooking Lake Ray Hubbard, some twenty-five miles east of Dallas. It is a small town in the smallest county in Texas.

If God had commanded, 'Fall off the face of the earth,' I don't think I could have been any more astonished. Actually, at the time, the two orders would have appeared to be somewhat synonymous.

But I moved my family to Rockwall and began to apply the principles God had taught me about growing a church. We began Church on the Rock (COTR) in 1980 with thirteen people. We rapidly outgrew the house where we met and moved to the Rockwall Skating Rink, where we had about two hundred people on our first Sunday.

We soon overflowed that facility, so the church began holding services in the Rockwall High School cafeteria. Growing rapidly, we knew we desperately needed our own building, so we began saving every dollar we could.

One day P.J. Titus, a native of India and a long-time friend with a proven ministry, walked into my office with an urgent need. The Lord had placed upon his heart a burden to begin a Bible college in India, and it would take twenty thousand dollars to accomplish that task.

My thoughts went immediately to the twenty thousand dollars in the church's savings account that was designated for our new building, and a struggle began within me. Knowing I had something critical to pray about, I asked Titus if he could return the next day for my decision.

As we sought the Lord's will, the Holy Spirit directed us to sow, not save, our last seed. But I was not prepared for Titus's reaction. The next day when he returned to my office and I handed him a cheque for twenty thousand dollars, he burst into tears, the sobs shaking his small frame.

When he was able to speak, he told me why the cheque meant so much to him. 'I told the Lord that if you would give me the twenty thousand dollars to begin the Bible college, I would leave the United States where I've lived these past few years, return to India and spend the remainder of my life ministering to my people.'

Titus is now doing just that. Because we dared to sow our precious seed instead of eating it or hoarding it for ourselves, the Lord has given Church on the Rock the second largest Bible college in all of India, and Titus is training men and women to reach their nation for God.

But when he walked out of my office with our last twenty thousand dollars in his hand, I didn't know how it would turn out. We were still having church meetings in a rented cafeteria, and now we were back to zero financially. I believed that God would provide, but I wasn't quite prepared for the instrument he chose to work through!

One Sunday after the meeting, an honest-to-goodness Texan cowboy sidled up to me and drawled, 'You're either straight out of heaven or straight out of hell. I don't like preachers, but I like you. God told me you are to be my pastor.'

Then he took me out to his truck where he thrust an old work-boot into my hands. Seeing the bewilderment on my face, he explained, 'I've been a Christian for a long time, but being on the rodeo circuit for the last couple of years has kept me from having a church home. I've just been puttin' my tithes into this old boot. Now God says I should give it to you.'

There was over a thousand dollars inside that boot. When I peered inside, the Lord immediately nudged me that he was going to use the incident for his glory.

Taking the boot to the next service, I shared with the congregation what had happened. Spontaneously, they began to stream forward and stuff into the boot money to construct the building we needed so desperately. Sunday after Sunday, the miracle continued.

The building was finished without borrowing any money for its construction: we moved in debt-free.

Because the crowds overflowed the new auditorium the first Sunday we gathered there, we immediately increased to two Sunday services — then three, four, five — to accommodate the people. We also had to add Tuesday and Thursday night midweek services because the Wednesday evening service could not hold the crowds.

Our records reveal that the church has grown from thirteen people to over seven thousand members with a thirty-two-member pastoral staff and more than four hundred and sixty home cell-groups. To house the phenomenal harvest, it became necessary to construct a church building that would accommodate eleven thousand people.

And if all of this were not enough to thrill the heart of any thirty-six-year-old pastor, in the spring of 1986, Oral Roberts asked me to become the vice president of Oral Roberts University (ORU) and serve as dean of theological and spiritual affairs. When I protested that I could not leave my church, that sixty-eight-year-old American Indian leaned forward and said, 'I don't want you to leave your church. I want you to bring the spirit and life-flow of your church into ORU.'

My elders freed me from the administrative and counselling duties which can consume a pastor's time and released me to pray, preach in our church, direct the national prayer revival which God has called me to lead and, until recently, prepare spiritual leadership through ORU.

Have you ever stopped to reflect upon the magnitude of a simple, yet life-changing choice you made years before? I think about my choice often, and I always thank God that I answered the call that is higher than my call to preach — the call to pray.

Every believer may not be called to preach, but every Christian is called to pray. Prayer is our duty. Prayer is our privilege. Prayer, like air, water and food, is necessary for our survival and growth. But many believers regard prayer as an optional activity.

Corrie ten Boom, the beloved author of *The Hiding Place*, sometimes posed this question to believers: 'Is prayer your *spare tyre* or your *steering-wheel?*'

Meditate on that question in the privacy of your own heart and remember: There is a higher call — the call to pray. Have you answered it?

5

A divine progression

People heard God's voice yesterday, and that was good. But it is also essential that we hear his voice today. *'Today,* if you hear his voice . . .' (Hebrews 3:7).

Today the Holy Spirit is speaking a word to the church. God is calling his church to pray, and we had better listen because the bottom line on all that will take place from now on is: '"Not by might nor by power, but by my Spirit," says the Lord Almighty' (Zechariah 4:6).

It is important for us to understand that the desire to pray is not something we can work up in our flesh; rather, the desire to pray is birthed in us by the Holy Spirit. If he has already implanted that divine desire in your heart, pause right now and thank God for it. If not, ask him to put it there. Then pray that God will help you transform that divine desire into daily discipline. As the discipline to pray is formed within you, discipline will 'change gears'. Prayer will no longer be duty or drudgery. It will become a holy delight.

God longs to see your heart transformed into a house of prayer. Why? Because there is so much he longs to do for you and through you. Therefore, as you begin to pray, a divine progression will take place within you. Let me explain what I mean.

It was a normal business-as-usual day in the temple at Jerusalem until the moment Jesus walked in. His grief joined hands with holy anger. After fashioning a whip from small cords, Jesus strode purposefully towards the money-changers and the buyers and

sellers of oxen, sheep and doves, forcefully driving
them and their mooing, cooing, bleating wares out of
the temple.

Before the amazed onlookers could react, Jesus was
back, this time to overthrow the tables and seats of
the money-changers and dove-sellers. The scattered
coins still spun and rolled across the floor as he
thundered, '"My house will be called a house of
prayer," but you are making it a "den of robbers"'
(Matthew 21:13).

Aware that only the guilty had anything to fear, the
blind and lame thronged to him in the temple, and he
healed them there amid the laughter and happy
hosannas of children. When the chief priests and
scribes angrily demanded that Jesus quiet the
children's joyful cries, he calmly countered, 'Have you
never read, "From the lips of children and infants you
have ordained praise"?' (see Matthew 21:12-16).

Take a moment to observe the beautiful progression
in these verses. First, Jesus cleansed the temple,
causing it to become a house of *purity* (v12). Then he
pronounced that it would be called a house of *prayer*
(v13). Next the temple was transformed into a house
of *power* as the blind and the lame came to him and
he healed them there (v14). And finally, the temple
became a house of *perfected praise* (v16).

Shouldn't this same progression take place in the
church and in the individual believer today? To echo
the words of Paul, 'Don't you know that you yourselves are God's temple and that God's Spirit lives in
you?' (1 Corinthians 3:16). You and I are part of the
church that is the habitation of God through the Spirit
(Ephesians 2:20-22). But sadly, our temples, too, are
often polluted by grasping greed, manoeuvring motives
and selfish sins.

It is a mockery for believers to talk one way and
live another. God will not bless an impure church.
His church will not become the house of power and

perfected praise until it allows the Holy Spirit to purify its sanctimonious soul and transform it into a house of prayer.

Listen to God's solemn warning to his church: 'Today, if you hear his voice, do not harden your hearts as you did in the rebellion, during the time of testing in the desert' (Hebrews 3:7-8). These verses indicate that because the children of Israel heard but did not heed, their mission to possess the land of Canaan was thwarted.

God had promised that land to the children of Israel. But when ten out of twelve men sent by Moses to spy out the land returned fearful and faint-hearted because the land seemed unconquerable, an entire generation died in the wilderness. Although two of the spies, Joshua and Caleb, confidently affirmed, 'We should go up and take possession of the land, for we can certainly do it' (Numbers 13:30), when the vote was in, the tens had it over the twos.

God does not operate on our timetables. He was ready to march them across the Jordan River, but the people were caught up in petty daily routines.

A self-seeking leader remarked smugly, 'Have you noticed? Moses just isn't anointed anymore.'

A dissatisfied wife nagged her weary husband, 'You've got to get more manna for our kids!'

A well-meaning elder warned, 'Joshua and Caleb are off on a "hyper-faith" tangent. How can they run around proclaiming, "We're able to overcome," when everybody knows that the enemy is stronger than we are?'

They feared the giants instead of God. They focused on the problems instead of the promises. They saw walled cities instead of the will of God. And because they missed what the Spirit was saying, they wandered in the desert forty years. They died there and their bones bleached in the wilderness.

It's no different today. We're here to possess the

land, my friend, but instead we're busy redecorating
the house, watching Saturday night football, trying to
pay the mortgage and worrying about our 'stuff'. All
the while, the interceding Holy Spirit is calling us to
pray, and we aren't listening.

The contemporary church is far from biblical
Christianity. Mediocrity has invaded the body of
Christ, and we think it's normal. God is accelerating
everything in these last days, yet ninety-nine per cent
of us are lagging behind. We long to see God's power,
but before the power of God can be revealed, we must
develop the discipline of prayer.

I don't know if you have ever uttered a prayer like
this, but I have: 'God, I want you to take everything
out of my life that's not like Jesus. I don't want
anything in me except that which glorifies and
magnifies Jesus Christ the Lord.'

In order for that prayer to become a reality, things
that *can* be shaken *must* be shaken so that 'what cannot
be shaken may remain' (Hebrews 12:27).

After I shared that thought in a sermon, a teenager
remarked, 'Sounds to me like you're talking about a
whole lot of shaking goin' on.'

The girl was right. There is going to be a lot of
shaking.

If you could talk to me right now, would you confide,
'Larry, a whole lot of shaking has gone on in my life
these last few years'? Some of you might say the same
thing about the churches you've attended. A lot of
stirring, a lot of shaking, a lot of changes have taken
place. Why? In order that we can take the next step
in this divine progression.

Today if you hear his voice calling you to pray, don't
harden your heart. Ask the Holy Spirit to give you
no rest until your prayer life moves from mere desire
to daily discipline and on to holy delight. Let Jesus
drive out and overturn the things in your life that are
preventing your temple from becoming a house of

prayer. Smelly oxen, bleating sheep, cooing doves and tarnished coins are poor substitutes for the satisfying, holy presence of God.

Face the facts. If you do not begin to pray, you will not be any further along with the Lord next year than you are right now. There is always the agony of choice before the promise of change. So what will it be: business as usual or are you ready to take your next step with God?

Jesus is waiting for you to pray, 'Lord, make my temple a house of purity, prayer, power and perfected praise for your glory.'

He is ready to begin that divine progression in your temple right now. Are you?

6

Lord, teach us to pray

After his father's funeral, my friend Bob Tyndall thumbed through the worn Bible that had been one of his dad's closest companions. His glance fell upon this handwritten notation in the margin: 'Jesus didn't teach us how to preach. He didn't teach us how to sing. He taught us how to pray.'

Robert Tyndall Sr was right. Prayer was a priority with Jesus. Regarding the beginning of Christ's ministry, the Gospel of Mark says, 'Very early in the morning, while it was still dark, Jesus got up, left the house and went off to a solitary place, where he prayed' (1:35). Regarding the middle of Jesus' ministry, after he miraculously fed the five thousand, Matthew 14:23 says that Jesus went up alone into a mountain to pray. Regarding the end of Jesus' earthly ministry, Luke tells us Jesus went out, as was his habit, to pray (Luke 22:39-41).

Jesus made a habit of prayer, and he taught others to pray by his words and example. In the gospels we discover that the most exacting work Jesus did was to pray; then, overflowing with anointing and compassion, he went from those places of intercession to receive the fruits of the battles he had won in prayer — mighty miracles, authoritative revelations, wonderful healings and powerful deliverances.

Because prayer was a fixed habit of his life, it is not surprising that, even as he faced the jeers and curses from scoffers at the foot of his cross, the first words he uttered as he hung there were a prayer (Luke 23:34).

Jesus faced death as he had faced life: unafraid. As he died, he committed his spirit into his Father's keeping and said, 'It is finished' (John 19:30).

But we must not think that Christ's death marked the end of his prayer ministry. The writer to the Hebrews says that Jesus' ministry in heaven today is intercession: 'He is able to save completely those who come to God through him, because he always lives to intercede for them' (Hebrews 7:25). Jesus' continuing ministry in heaven is prayer. I am on his prayer list, and so are you.

Jesus would never do anything that was worthless or dry or dull, and he would never ask you to, either. Right now he is extending to you the highest call of all. He is repeating to you what he said to his disciples in the Garden of Gethsemane: 'Could you men not keep watch with me for one hour? . . . . Watch and pray so that you will not fall into temptation. The spirit is willing, but the body is weak' (Matthew 26:40-41). Jesus wants you to learn how to spend time with him, how to tarry with him one hour in prayer.

I think I know how you feel. I had said yes to him so many times. I had the desire, but not the discipline.

I remember an evening when I preached at a place called the Bronco Bowl in South Dallas. (That's the bowling-alley where Beverly Hills Baptist Church met after we outgrew our church building.) Three thousand teenagers were in the auditorium that night, and when I gave the invitation we saw five hundred come forward for salvation.

I'll never forget it. As I stood before that sea of earnest faces and commanded, 'Get right with God,' something inside me asked, 'When are *you* going to get right with God?' As I left the platform, others thought I was slipping away to talk to the converts, but I was actually going into a back room to lie on my face before the Lord.

I was frustrated about this matter of prayer. Looking

back, I believe it was *holy* frustration. The Spirit of God simply would not let me settle for anything else than the ministry of prayer.

I don't want to leave the wrong impression. We prayed at Beverly Hills. Sometimes we prayed all night. We prayed in a great harvest. The church grew from four hundred to well over three thousand in four years! But God was asking me to make a practice of rising early in the morning, praying through to the place of victory and walking in the authority and anointing of God. I needed a day-by-day walk — not a frantic race to get 'prayed up' for some special event.

During those days when I was minister of youth at Beverly Hills, I was invited to hold a youth mission in Hereford, Texas. Ever since my conversion, I had longed to be an evangelist; I was delighted by their invitation to come. All but one denomination in town was co-operating so each service was to be held in a different church.

The mission didn't start off too well. That first night, we went to the Church of God. It was cold outside, and it was cold inside, too. I preached as well as I could and gave the invitation, but nobody came forward for salvation.

The next night we went to the Assemblies of God church. We had a good praise and worship service, but the preaching and call for salvation were a repeat performance of the night before. I felt as if everybody was wondering, 'When's he going to do something? When's it going to happen?' That's certainly what I was thinking.

The third night we went to the Methodist church. I made sure I arrived a little early so I could get alone with God. Just as I was looking for a place to pray, two Catholic nuns with a guitar walked through the back door. They made a beeline for me and asked, 'Brother Lea, would you tune our guitar for us?'

Startled by the strange request, I just stared at them

and said, 'Well — I — er — yes, I will.' (How do you say no to two Catholic nuns?) So we slipped away to a side room where I tuned the guitar.

Sensing my nervousness as my preparation time before the service slipped away, one of the nuns put her hand on my arm and said reassuringly, 'Don't worry, Brother Lea. We've prayed for you today for eight hours.'

I could hardly believe what she had said, but nevertheless felt grateful, even relieved. She laid her hands on me and began to speak in tongues. The other one began singing in tongues. Within a few seconds I didn't know if I was terrestrial or celestial, but I knew I was with two women who really knew God!

When they had finished, one of them said to me, 'Does the phrase "It is finished" mean anything to you, Brother Lea?'

Chills went all over my body, because that was my text for the evening.

The service began, and I preached from one of those right-handed Methodist pulpits way up high in the air. At the end of the sermon I gave the invitation, and a hundred young people walked forward!

The next night I was to preach at the Catholic church. I got there early and breathed a sigh of relief when I saw the two nuns walk in the back door carrying their guitar. This time I ran right up to them and asked, 'Could I tune your guitar for you?' My heart hadn't been in it the night before but it really was this time.

We went through the little guitar-tuning ritual, and I got down to business. Without batting an eyelid, I said, 'Let's do it again; you know, what we did last night.'

So they laid their hands on me, and it happened again. Then the nun who had never spoken a word of English in my presence asked casually, 'Brother Lea, you remember the woman who had the issue of blood and reached out to touch the hem of Jesus' garment?' (You guessed it. That was the text I had chosen for my sermon that evening!)

I preached, and a hundred more people found God that night. By the end of the week, five hundred people had been saved in that small town.

As I flew back to Dallas, I tried to figure out just exactly how, in my most humble way, I would announce at the staff meeting what God had done through me. 'How did the youth mission go?' 'Oh, not too bad — we had five hundred saved. It was a pretty good week.'

I had always wanted to be an evangelist. Now I *knew* I was an evangelist, and it felt wonderful. I was gloating over the number of people saved, thinking about how I could report it meekly, when the Holy Spirit abruptly interrupted my musings.

'Son,' he said, 'let's get one thing straight. You had nothing at all to do with that mission.'

My mouth dropped open, but I shut it fast.

The voice inside me continued: 'What happened was simply that somebody *prayed the price.*'

Those words rang in my ears for years afterwards. Prayed the price! Somebody prayed the price.

By 1978 when Pastor Conatser passed away and I was extended the call to become the pastor of Beverly Hills Baptist Church, my holy frustration had reached a climax. I was at the place where nothing mattered anymore except the call to pray. I had to answer this call, this call which was higher than the call to preach. That's when I took my little family and went back home to Kilgore, Texas. That's when I met B.J. Willhite and my desperate *desire* to prayer shifted into holy *discipline.*

It was during those days, while I searched for wisdom as a person would search for lost money or hidden treasure, that the Lord began to reveal to me new things, hidden things about prayer that I had not known before. As I continually cried out to him, he poured revelation into my spirit.

By the time he commanded me to go to Rockwall and establish his people there, I had been delivered from the theology that says, 'Big is better.' I went to Rockwall with one thought in mind, and that was to equip some people and teach them how to pray. I did not know I was moving right into the taproot of the very thing that blossomed into the outpouring of the power of God in the first century. I just knew I had to pray and I had to teach other people how to pray.

Our church was about a year old in 1981 when I went to New Orleans to hear Paul Yonggi Cho, pastor of Yoido Full Gospel Church in Seoul, Korea, the largest church in the world. The Lord helped me get in to see him, and we met in a small back room of the church hosting the seminar. As my eyes met his, I felt as if I were looking right into the man's soul.

I knew we had only a minute and my one-liner had better be good, so I blurted out something like, 'Dr Cho, how did you build such a great church?'

He smiled back at me and, with no hesitation, replied, 'I pray, and I obey.' And then he laughed.

I chuckled with him, but inside I was rehearsing his words. 'That's the key,' I muttered to myself. 'That's it right there. Pray and obey, Larry. Pray and obey.'

I will never forget his words. You see, there are a lot of people who want to obey, but they don't pray. And there are some people who pray, but don't have the courage to obey. But prayer and obedience must go hand in hand if we are to move into the power and anointing of the Spirit of God.

I'm convinced that the disciples weren't much different from you and me. Like us, they had to beat their brains out against one brick wall after another before they came to Jesus and said, 'Lord, teach us to pray.'

That's the way it was for me. I tried to pray on my

own, but I knew there was something missing. I kept crying out to God, 'Lord, teach me how to pray. Teach me how to pray.' And one day, no sooner were those words out of my mouth, than the lessons began.

7

Could you not tarry one hour?

When I asked the Lord to teach me how to tarry with him an hour in prayer, I remembered that Jesus instructed his disciples, 'This . . . is how you should pray' (Matthew 6:9). I opened my Bible to the verses we have come to call 'the Lord's Prayer' and pondered those sixty-six words:

'Our Father in heaven, hallowed be your name, your kingdom come, your will be done on earth as it is in heaven. Give us today our daily bread. Forgive us our debts, as we also have forgiven our debtors. And lead us not into temptation, but deliver us from the evil one, for yours is the kingdom and the power and the glory for ever. Amen. (Matthew 6:9-13 margin).

I was puzzled, and I said so. 'Lord, I can say that in twenty-two seconds, and I can sing it in a minute and a half. How is this ever going to help me tarry with you an hour?'

The Spirit of God answered: 'Say it really slowly.'

Like an obedient child, I began reciting the familiar words, pausing after each short phrase: 'Our Father in heaven . . . hallowed be your name . . . .' Just as those words were out of my mouth, the Spirit of God began to drop into my heart a series of revelations and visions that planted me once and for all in the discipline of prayer and shifted my prayer life into holy delight.

I hope it doesn't upset anybody when I admit that I saw a vision. I can almost see the eyebrows going up. Do you know what's wrong with believers today? We've studied the counterfeit for so long, we don't even recognise the original anymore. It's a shame that a boy who had attended church off and on for seventeen years wound up in a psychiatric ward before he found out God could talk!

If only I had known someone like those two little Catholic nuns I told you about. One of them came up to me some time ago and asked with a smile, 'Do you know how I know things?'

I returned her grin and asked, 'How?'

She replied matter-of-factly, 'I know 'em in my "knower"!'

If you are a believer, you, too, have a 'knower'. It is the witness of the Holy Spirit.

After I asked the question, 'Lord, how can I learn to tarry with you one hour?' the Lord made me a promise.

'When you learn to tarry with me one hour,' he pledged, 'something supernatural will happen in your life.' And then he showed me that what we call 'the Lord's Prayer' is actually a prayer outline.

You see, the first-century rabbis usually taught by giving topics of truth. They listed certain topics and then, under each topic, the rabbis provided a complete outline. In his model prayer, Jesus enumerated topics and instructed: 'This . . . is how you should pray' (Matthew 6:9-13). We have memorised, quoted and sung the Lord's Prayer, but we have not seen it as a group of six topics to be followed in prayer under the guidance of the Holy Spirit.

My friend Brad Young, author of *The Jewish Background to the Lord's Prayer,* says that certain ancient writings contain prayers of early Christians which are based upon the Lord's Prayer and require about one hour to pray through.

Young also made a fascinating observation based on Acts 1:14. You remember that the disciples, along with Mary the mother of Jesus, Christ's brothers and other believers, gathered in the upper room after Jesus' ascension, in obedience to his command to wait for the Holy Spirit? Scripture records: 'They all joined together constantly in prayer.' Young pointed out that the Greek does not read 'in prayer'; rather, this verse actually states: 'They all joined together constantly in "the Prayer".' He said that ancient literature often refers to the Lord's Prayer as 'the Prayer'.

Today a new generation of disciples is discovering the principles, purpose and power behind the familiar words of the Lord's Prayer. And, as we rediscover the power and necessity of prayer, our prayer lives are moving from desire to discipline to delight.

As you discipline yourself to take this prayer outline and come into God's presence, prayer will become your life flow as it was the life flow of Jesus and the early church. But I should sound this warning: This is no little ten-watt truth; it's a powerful two-hundred-and-forty-watt revelation that can illuminate your temple with the glory of God and transform your house of prayer into a house of power and perfected praise.

If you're ready, plug in.

Part Two

Promises

*'Our Father in heaven,
hallowed be your name'*

8

Appropriating God's names

Discipline is a dirty word to many of us. When most people think about discipline in prayer, they get a grim, determined look on their faces, grit their teeth and vow, 'I'm going to do it if it kills me!'

That's the look my young son, John Aaron, put on his face when I told him to eat his spinach. 'Daddy,' he said in his most man-to-man voice, 'I don't *like* it, but I can *eat* it.'

How many times have you said that to God: 'Father, I don't *like* to pray, but I can *do* it'? Prayer doesn't have to be a duty; it can be a delight.

Have you ever noticed that the Lord's Prayer begins and ends with praise? We are to enter his gates with thanksgiving and his courts with praise (Psalm 100:4). Jesus knew this when he instructed, 'When you pray, say: Our Father in heaven, hallowed be your name' (Luke 11:2 margin).

Love says 'our' and faith says 'Father'. The omniscient, omnipotent Creator-God dwelling in eternity invites believers to call him Father.

The word 'hallow' is not a common word, but it means 'to sanctify or set apart; to praise; to adore'. The phrase should be translated, 'May your name be sanctified.' It is the expression of an intense desire that God's name be recognised, set apart and adored.

We don't stop to realise that the name of the Lord can be either sanctified or profaned by our conduct. But ancient documents record that, because a martyr's sacrificial death would frequently cause others to glorify God, the Hebrew idiom 'to sanctify the name' was often understood to mean to give one's life for his faith.[1]

What a powerful truth! We can sanctify God by the example of our righteous lives, as well as by our words of praise and adoration (Matthew 5:16).

As we learn to follow Christ's prayer pattern and to set apart, praise and adore the name of God, prayer will shift out of frustrating desire and determined discipline and move right on into holy delight.

The discipline I am talking about will lead you into God's holy presence and cause you to walk in kingdom priorities. It will help you learn how to 'pray in' what you need and will enable you to get along with everybody all the time. It will help you face the devil and leave him sitting in the dirt. It will cause you to be the head and not the tail, to be above only and not beneath. It will enable you to walk in victory every day of your life.

But in order to hallow our Father's name, we must understand that God's character and will for his children are revealed in his names. Our Father's names reveal what he has promised to be *in* us and what he has promised to do *for* and *through* us.

Blessings brought by Jesus' blood

As God was revealing the prayer outline to me he gave me a clear vision of what God has given us. I saw Jesus picking up a large basin and walking towards what I perceived to be a huge rock altar behind which shone a great light. As I watched, the Lord emptied the contents of the basin upon the altar, and I realised that the living, swirling liquid poured out upon that altar was his own blood.

The Word of God flooded my mind: 'You know that it was not with perishable things such as silver or gold that you were redeemed from the empty way of life

[1] Brad Young, *The Jewish Background to the Lord's Prayer*, Centre for Judaic-Christian Studies, Austin, Texas, 1984

. . . but with the precious blood of Christ, a lamb without blemish or defect' (1 Peter 1:18-19).

Suddenly it all came together: 'God sent his Son . . . to redeem those under law, that we might receive the full rights of sons. Because you are sons, God sent the Spirit of his Son into our hearts, the Spirit who calls out, *"Abba*, Father"' (Galatians 4:4-6).

I looked at that blood and exclaimed, 'Father, Father!' for into my 'knower' there came a warm and wonderful witness that, when I received Christ's forgiveness, I was adopted into the family of God and accepted as his child and heir. God was my Father by virtue of the blood of Jesus.

Then it seemed as if the living blood upon that altar spoke of the covenant blessings it had bought for me.

First, it testified that all my sins are forgiven, and I remembered, 'He was pierced for our transgressions, he was crushed for our iniquities' (Isaiah 53:5). I looked at that blood and wept both for sorrow and for joy, because I knew he had washed me from my sins in his own blood (Revelation 1:5), and sin no longer had dominion over me (Romans 6:14).

Then the blood testified that because of the blood of the Lamb, I can boldly enter into the Most Holy Place (Hebrews 10:19-20). My body has now become the temple of the Holy Spirit, who lives in me and is God's gift to me (1 Corinthians 6:19). I praised God that the blood of Jesus has opened up a new and living way in order that I might experience the fulness of the Holy Spirit.

Next, the blood testified to me that by Christ's wounds and sufferings I am healed and made whole (Isaiah 53:5; 1 Peter 2:24; Matthew 8:16-17) — healed spiritually and physically, mentally and emotionally. Jesus is the Great Physician, the sympathising Jesus.

And then the blood testified that Christ has made me free from the law of sin and death (Romans 8:2). Jesus took the curse of my failure and insufficiency

(Galatians 3:13), and now he always causes me to triumph in Christ (2 Corinthians 2:14).

Last of all, the blood testified that in my covenant relationship with God my Father, I am free from the fear of death and hell. Jesus Christ has abolished death and has brought life and immortality to light through the gospel (2 Timothy 1:10).

As the Spirit of the Lord revealed what the blood has done for us, I suddenly recalled the Hebrew names of God compounded with the name *Jehovah* in the Old Testament.

You see, when God wished to make a special revelation of himself, he used the name *Jehovah*. In that name, he revealed himself as the true and eternal God, the one who is absolutely self-existent, the one who is unchangeable.

The significance and origin of the name *Jehovah* are especially brought out in God's revelation of himself to Moses at the burning bush (Exodus 3:13-15). Through four centuries of oppression in Egypt, the children of Israel had believed in God's existence, but they had not experienced his presence. God proclaimed to Moses that he had personally come down to deliver his people from bondage and to lead them into the promised land. But before his servant Moses could lead God's people, Moses had to learn who God was and is.

When the Lord first proclaimed to Moses, 'I AM WHO I AM,' the name he used for himself was considered by Hebrew translators too sacred to be spoken aloud. So they used the consonants YHWH or JHVH, which we can read as *Yahweh* or *Jehovah*.

Yahweh implies more than just God's *existence;* it implies his personal, intimate *presence.* God's name *Jehovah* reveals his readiness to save his people and to act for them. Thus, the name *Jehovah*, or 'I AM WHO I AM', can be rendered, 'I am with you, ready to save and to act, just as I have always been.'

In the Old Testament, there are eight names compounded with the name *Jehovah: Jehovah-tsidkenu, Jehovah-m'kaddesh, Jehovah-shammah, Jehovah-shalom, Jehovah-rophe, Jehovah-jireh, Jehovah-nissi* and *Jehovah-rohi.* Each of these names is a revelation of the character and nature of God.

In Exodus 6:3-4, God links his name Jehovah to his covenant with Abraham, Isaac and Jacob. But the eight compound names of God in the Old Testament also correspond to the five-fold promise God makes to his people in the new covenant or New Testament. While God's names reveal different dimensions of his character they also point to their fulfilment in the person and work of Jesus Christ.

What are the five promises or benefits in the new covenant with which the eight compound names of God correspond? Of what five things did the testifying blood on the altar speak?

The benefits we enjoy in the new covenant deal with five vital areas. To make the areas easy to remember, I will begin each with an *s:* 1. sins — forgiveness of sins and deliverance from sin's dominion; 2. Spirit — the fulness of the Holy Spirit; 3. soundness — the promise of health and healing; 4. success — freedom from the law's curse of failure and insufficiency; 5. security — freedom from the fear of death and hell.

As the Spirit of the Lord revealed what the blood has done for us, I began to understand what it means to pray, 'Our Father in heaven, hallowed be your name.' Let's look at the five benefits given to us by virtue of Jesus' death.

Forgiveness of sins and deliverance from sin's dominion

The first benefit you enjoy in the new covenant because you are a child of God by virtue of the blood of Jesus is the *forgiveness of sins.*

How can a sinful person be acquitted of unrighteous-

ness and become righteous before God? In the Old
Testament, the penalty of death incurred because of
sin had to be borne by an innocent sufferer whose
righteousness would be reckoned to the sinner.

But no human being is innocent and righteous, and
the blood of animals cannot take away sin. Therefore,
there had to be a divine remedy. The provision of
righteousness was made in Jesus Christ, God's only
Son, who died in our place (2 Corinthians 5:21; 1 Peter
3:18).

The compound name of God, *Jehovah-tsidkenu*
(sid-kay-noo), means 'Jehovah Our Righteousness'
(see Jeremiah 23:5-6). This name reveals the facet of
God's character that transacts the redemption by
which humankind is fully restored to God.

Jesus Christ, our *Jehovah-tsidkenu,* was substituted
for us (Romans 5:17-19). The name 'Jehovah Our
Righteousness' reveals the method of our acceptance
before God ('God made him who had no sin to be sin
for us') and the measure of our acceptance ('that in
him we might become the righteousness of God') —
2 Corinthians 5:21.

Therefore as you pray, 'Hallowed be your name,
Jehovah-tsidkenu,' thank God that he has already made
a decision about your sins. In his mind he already says,
'I forgive you.' All you have to do is come and
appropriate that forgiveness, for the Bible says, 'If we
confess our sins, he is faithful and just and will forgive
us our sins and purify us from all unrighteousness' (1
John 1:9).

Do you get it? *Righteousness equals Jesus Christ
plus nothing.* 'You have been given fulness in Christ'
(Colossians 2:10). Remember the words of the old
hymn *Rock of Ages:* 'Nothing in my hand I bring, Simply
to thy cross I cling'? That's it! Let me share a story
to illustrate this profound truth.

Some years ago I was away from home preaching
in a black church. (I don't believe in reincarnation, but

I sometimes jokingly say that if I did, I'd ask to come back as a black preacher. Talk about liberty!) My dad, who was saved about two-and-a-half years before this time after having been an alcoholic for fifteen years, came to the motel where I was staying to drive me to the church.

I was eager to see him, but as I answered his knock at the door, my heart sank.

It wasn't raining, yet there he stood dripping wet. His dark hair was plastered to his scalp and his expensive blue suit and leather shoes oozed water that made puddles on the concrete balcony outside my door.

My first thought was, 'Oh, no! Dad got drunk and fell in the pool.' But I didn't want to confront him without hearing some kind of explanation. I invited him in, handed him a towel and asked very calmly, 'Dad, are you all right?'

As he mopped the water off his face, he explained what had happened.

He had been on his way to my room when he glanced down from the second storey balcony and saw the body of a small child lying motionless at the bottom of the pool. Without a second thought, he jumped off the balcony, hurdled the chain-link fence that enclosed the pool and dived into the water. He hauled the boy's limp form out of the pool, gave him artificial respiration, got him breathing and carried the frightened child to his grateful mother.

I was so proud of my dad that day. And I'll never forget that incident because that's what *Jehovah-tsidkenu*, 'the Lord Our Righteousness', did for me — and you. We were dead in the water, dead in trespasses and sins, but he jumped into the pool and saved us. He who knew no sin was made to be sin for us that we might be made the righteousness of God in him (2 Corinthians 5:21).

If you can swim your way out or buy your way out

or confess your way out, you don't need a Saviour. But if you're dead in the water, you've got to have Jesus. You must exchange your sin and guilt for his righteousness and grace if you hope to obtain eternal life.

I don't know about you, but when I remember how Jesus carried my sin and died for me on the cross, I don't have any trouble hallowing his name, *Jehovah-tsidkenu*, 'the Lord My Righteousness'.

But Jesus is more than our righteousness. He offers not only forgiveness for our sins; he offers deliverance from sin's dominion, because Jesus is our sanctifier. Now what does that mean? The primary meaning of the Hebrew word *sanctify* is 'to set apart for God's service'. Believers are to be different from, set apart from, the world by obeying God's commands.

God is holy, separate from his people, yet he sanctifies us and makes us holy in order that we might have fellowship with him. In Leviticus 20:8, he is called *Jehovah-m'kaddesh* (ma-ka-desh), 'the Lord Who Sanctifies'. But because this name has not been transliterated in our English Bibles as have his other names, it has often escaped notice as one of the compound names of Jehovah.

God's Holy Spirit indwells believers and empowers them to live holy lives and to be spiritually and morally pure (see 1 Corinthians 6:11; 1 Thessalonians 4:3-4; 5:23). Therefore, as you meditate upon God's name, 'Jehovah Who Sanctifies', praise him because the blood of Jesus not only takes away your sin; it breaks the power of sin in you. Thank him that the blood of Christ does not overlook sin; it overcomes (see Romans 6:17-18; Hebrews 13:12; 1 Corinthians 6:9-11).

Hallowed be your name, *Jehovah-m'kaddesh*, 'the Lord Who Sanctifies'.

Spirit: The fulness of the Holy Spirit

Because God is your Father, the second benefit you enjoy in the New Covenant is *the fulness of the Holy Spirit*. The compound name of God, *Jehovah-shalom* (sha-lom), means 'Jehovah is Peace' (see Judges 6:24). The Hebrew word *shalom* is most often and most appropriately translated 'peace' and represents wholeness and harmony with God and contentment and satisfaction in life.

Christ's atonement is the basis for peace with God. Before humankind could be reconciled to God, someone had to pay the price of sin, which was death. Jesus Christ paid that price, and the fellowship between God and man which sin broke was atoned for by his blood (see Colossians 1:20-22). 'The chastisement needful to obtain peace and well-being for us was upon him' (Isaiah 53:5 Amp).

As Jesus died and his blood broke down the barrier of sin separating us from God, something supernatural occurred in the Jerusalem temple. The inner veil separating the Holy Place from the Holy of Holies (God's presence chamber containing the ark and the mercy seat stained by the sacrificial animal blood which was brought in by the high priest once each year) was torn from top to bottom, opening the way for us to enter into the Holy of Holies — into the very presence of God himself (see Hebrews 10:19-22).

Josephus, a first century Pharisee and historian, reported that this four-inch-thick veil, which was renewed every year, could not be pulled apart by horses tied to each side. It barred all but the high priest from the presence of God. But when it suddenly ripped apart from top to bottom at the death of Jesus (Mark 15:37-38), access to God was made available to all who come to him through Jesus.

Hallowed be your name, *Jehovah-shalom*, 'the Lord is Peace'. Thank you for restoring humankind to that peace with God which was lost through the fall.

Another compound name of God, *Jehovah-shammah* (sham-ma), means 'Jehovah is There' (see Ezekiel 48:35). *Shammah* is the Hebrew word meaning 'the overflowing, ever-present One'. This name is the promise of a holy God dwelling in the midst of his people. It is the promise of his presence.

The presence of God himself is in believers, who are the living, growing, holy temple of God, through the Spirit (see Ephesians 2:19-22). The word used for 'temple' in verse 21 does not refer to the temple in general, but the 'sanctuary'. In the sanctuary stood the altar of incense, and in the holiest place of all was the mercy seat above which the divine presence or the Shekinah glory hovered. Now, through Jesus, we are temples of clay filled with the glorious presence of God.

Thank God that because your sins are forgiven you can be filled and flooded with God himself: you can be filled with his Holy Spirit. And that's not all. Jesus promised, 'Never will I leave you; never will I forsake you' (Hebrews 13:5). He has sent the comforting, strengthening, interceding, communing Holy Spirit to your side.

Hallowed be your name, *Jehovah-shammah*, 'the Lord is There'.

Remember, you are hallowing God's name because of who he is and because of what he has done for you. As you meditate upon the various names of God your Father, affirm your faith by turning your thoughts into declarations of faith and praise.

'Father, you are *Jehovah-tsidkenu*. You are my righteousness. I stand before you righteous and forgiven because of the blood of your dear Son.

'You are *Jehovah-m'kaddesh*, 'the Lord Who Sanctifies'. You conform me into the image of your Son and break sin's power over me.

'You are *Jehovah-shalom*, my peace. Jesus made peace by the blood of his cross and reconciled me to you. Now your peace which passes all understanding keeps my heart and my mind.

'You are *Jehovah-shammah*. You have filled me with your overflowing presence, and you will never leave me nor forsake me. Thank you for living in me, Lord.'

That is an example of what it means to hallow God's name and to make faith declarations based upon who he is and what he has done for you. But there is much more for which you should hallow your Father's name.

9

Appropriating God's promises

Don't get me wrong. Prayer is not magic, nor is it easy. But prayer works. As we acknowledge him in all our ways, God really does give us the desires of our hearts.

Some time after I became a Christian, my mother confided to me that she planned to leave my dad. 'Larry,' she sighed, 'your dad and I have lived together all these years, and it's been a terrible life. I just can't take his drinking anymore. I can't keep living this way.'

Crushed, I pleaded, 'Mum, please don't leave him.'

But Mother countered, 'You're gone now, and your sister has grown up and left home. Why shouldn't I leave?'

'Because, Mum,' I answered, 'I've been reading the red part of my Bible.'

'Well, what's that supposed to mean?' Mother asked wearily, a note of exasperation in her voice.

'It means that Jesus said in Matthew 18:19, "If two of you on earth agree about anything you ask for, it will be done for you by my Father in heaven." I'm one, Mother, and you make two. We can agree and it can be done.'

But Mother didn't share my excitement. She just took a deep breath and admitted, 'I don't even have enough faith to believe, Larry.'

'That's okay,' I said. 'It doesn't say, "If two of you agree and believe." It just says, "If two of you agree." If it takes believing, then I'll believe for both of us.'

I put my arm around her, and we prayed a prayer of agreement.

Do you know what happened after that conversation?

Things got worse! Has that ever happened to you? Did you ever pray for something really hard, but things just got worse?

One night after Dad got drunk and wrecked his car, I knelt down beside him and tried to talk to him about God, but he levelled me with the back of his hand and snarled, 'Don't tell me about that Jesus stuff!'

That night I prayed a puddle of hot tears on my bedroom floor. Jesus had kindled a burning desire in my heart for my dad's salvation, and I refused to give up. You see, I had his promise: 'Delight yourself in the Lord and he will give you the desires of your heart' (Psalm 37:4).

That doesn't mean I could have a Cadillac this week, a Mercedes next month and a new house next year. I'm not talking about carnal craziness. I'm talking about losing your life in Jesus and letting him plant his desires in your heart.

The next week I walked into the kitchen and found my mother sitting at the kitchen table crying. My first thought was that something terrible must have happened. 'Mother!' I exclaimed in alarm. 'What's happened?'

She dabbed at her tears and replied, 'I don't know exactly. All I know is that your dad pulled over by the side of the road today, got out of the car and prayed, "Jesus, if you can do anything with an old drunk like me, I'll give my life to you."'

Within the next few days, I received a call from a hospital in Dallas where my dad had been admitted because his body was totally devastated by alcohol. My father's familiar voice ordered, 'Son, bring me a Bible.'

Astonished by his request, I said, 'Dad, what's happened to you?'

Embarrassed, yet proud of his new commitment, he replied sternly, 'You *know* what's happened to me.' But his tone softened as he repeated, 'Bring me a Bible.'

With a Bible under my arm I rushed down to the

convalescent centre. As I walked into his room, Dad embraced me. The first words out of his mouth were: 'Would you pray for me?'

Together we fell on our faces and cried and prayed. That was over fifteen years ago. My dad has remained sober ever since, and he's the best friend I've ever had. He and my mother are members of my church, driving seventy miles each way every Sunday to attend services. It all happened because my faithful Lord planted a holy desire in my heart to see my dad healed and made whole in spirit, soul and body. That's the third benefit we enjoy in the new covenant: health and healing.

Soundness: Health and healing

The compound name of God, *Jehovah-rophe* (ro-phay), means 'Jehovah Heals'. The word *rophe* means 'to restore, cure or heal not only in the physical sense but also in the spiritual and moral sense'. That's what God did for my dad.

In my systematic theology class at Bible college, professors tried to tell me that Jesus doesn't heal in our day; then they attempted to convince me that this new covenant was better than the old. I didn't buy it, and neither should you! He is still 'the healer God'.

Do you or does someone you know need healing? Then begin to thank the Lord that by his stripes (or wounds) we are healed (see Isaiah 53:5; Matthew 8:16-17). Healing is already a finished work in the mind of God (1 Peter 2:24).

Make that faith declaration. Concentrate on the blood, not on yourself or how you feel. Concentrate on who he is and what his blood has purchased for you. As you praise him, he will be what you need him to be — he will be *Jehovah-rophe*, 'the Lord Who Heals'.

Put yourself in a faith position before God. Remember, the greatest faith words ever spoken are 'thank you'. Therefore, stir yourself up to give thanks for the stripes he took on his back for your healing. Hallow his name, *Jehovah-rophe,* and thank him for the health and healing that are yours through Jesus Christ.

Success: Freedom from the curse of the law

The fourth benefit you enjoy because of the covenant relationship with God your Father is *freedom from the curse of the law.*

When I was growing up, my home environment wasn't too positive. My dad used to shake his head at me in disgust and mutter, 'I'll probably have to support you for the rest of my life.'

I half believed him. I felt doomed to failure; I really didn't expect to succeed in life. The real Larry Lea never seemed to measure up to anybody's expectation.

I thought it was just me. I didn't know Paul plainly declared in Romans 3:23: 'All have sinned and fall short of the glory of God.' Our sins condemn us to failure. All men and women fall short continually in every area of life: morally, emotionally, financially, socially, spiritually and physically. No mortal has ever fulfilled all the requirements of the law.

I was preaching on this subject once when I uttered the worst preacher 'blooper' of my entire ministry. Waxing eloquent, I exclaimed, 'All have sinned and fall short of the glory of God.' Then, pointing towards the congregation, I asked, 'How many of you are tired of always falling short? Well, I've got good news for you. Christ has redeemed us from all our falling shorts.'

Christ had redeemed us, but there was no way for me to redeem that situation! My wife laughed so hard she almost fell out of her chair. But the fact of the matter is, Christ truly has redeemed us from all our 'falling shorts'.

In Galatians 3:10 we read, 'Cursed is everyone who does not continue to do everything written in the Book of the Law.' However, Romans 8:2 states, 'Through Christ Jesus the law of the Spirit of life set me free from the law of sin and death.' And in Galatians 3:13, Paul declares: 'Christ redeemed us from the curse of the law by becoming a curse for us, for it is written: "Cursed is everyone who is hung on a tree."'

What is this curse of the law from which Christ has redeemed us? To answer that question, we must return to the book of Genesis and its account of the fall of humankind.

Adam and Eve's decision to disobey God, a decision resulting in the fall of our first parents, had far-reaching effects. By their act of disobedience, sin and all its dreadful consequences entered into the world. God's image in humankind became distorted and marred, human beings became alienated from their Creator and all humankind came under a sentence of death.

Through Moses God gave men and women his law that set forth the only standard of righteousness acceptable to God. The Mosaic Law, a covenant of works, established a model for humankind's everyday conduct; however, lacking power to conform to that perfect standard, men and women always fell short. The curse of the broken law meant humanity was doomed to a frustrating, hopeless lifestyle of failure.

But when we fell into sin, we also fell into God's arms of redeeming mercy. Jesus Christ, God's only Son, and the only perfect human, voluntarily offered himself up on the cross, bore the death penalty of the curse for us, satisfied every demand of the law, and gave us a new and better covenant.

New covenant believers are free from the law's condemnation because Christ's righteousness has been imputed to them. In addition, as a result of Christ's atonement, the commandments of the law become, not impossible standards, but gracious duties and privileges willingly and effectively carried out by a

redeemed people possessing the power of the Holy
Spirit.

But that's not all that Jesus Christ accomplished for
us when he took away our curse. Through Jesus,
God's riches belong to his covenant people, riches that
cover every conceivable need on this earth.

According to Galatians 3:14, Christ redeemed us
from the curse of the law in order that the blessing
of Abraham might come on us. What was the blessing
of Abraham? Genesis 24:1 tells us that the Lord
blessed Abraham in all things. Paul reasons, 'He who
did not spare his own Son, but gave him up for us all
— how will he not also, along with him, graciously give
us all things?' (Romans 8:32).

Deuteronomy 28 details the blessings God has
ordained to overtake obedient believers, blessings
which are ours through Jesus Christ. Let me list some
of them. God's blessings will be upon you, your family
and your material possessions (v4). God will cause
your enemies to be defeated (v7). The Lord will
command his blessing upon your storehouse (your
treasury) and upon all you undertake (v8). He will
open his treasury to you in order that you might lend
and not have to borrow from others (v12). You will
be successful, for God will make you the head and not
the tail. You will be above and not beneath (v13).

However, if God's covenant people do not obey him
and walk in his ways, God promises to rebuke every
enterprise to which they set their hands and to allow
them to be overtaken by curses, confusion, poverty,
failure and devastating diseases (Deuteronomy 28:
15-45).

Thus Jesus, as we have seen, took the curse of our
failure and insufficiency and became our source of
success and blessing, our *Jehovah-jireh* (pronounced
'yeer-a' in Hebrew, but commonly pronounced 'ji-ra').
The name *Jehovah-jireh* means 'the Lord Who Sees'
or 'Jehovah's Provision Shall be Seen' (see Genesis 22,
especially v14).

God our Father sees our needs beforehand and makes provision for them. His name, *Jehovah-jireh*, is a revelation of God's willingness and ability to make provision for our sin and need. Because Jesus has taken the curse away, we are free from moral, financial, emotional, social or spiritual failure, for God has *ordained* our success. We can do all things through Christ (see Philippians 4:13).

Therefore, as you hallow his name, *Jehovah-jireh*, thank God that you are free from the curse. Make the praise declaration that Jesus, who was made a curse for you, has freed you, and you do not have to live under the curse of the law. The writer of an old hymn made such a declaration: 'Though earth hinders and hell rages, all must work for good to thee.'

Sing it! Say it! Believe it!

Security: Freedom from the fear of death and hell
The fifth benefit you enjoy in your covenant relationship with God your Father is *freedom from the fear of death and hell*.

The compound name of God, *Jehovah-nissi* (nis-see), means 'Jehovah My Banner' (see Exodus 17:15). The word for *banner* might also be translated 'pole, ensign or standard'. Among the Jews, it is also a word denoting 'miracle'. As an ensign or standard, it was a rallying-point to kindle hope and efforts, a signal raised on an elevated place on a special occasion. The banner represented God's cause, his battle, and was a sign of deliverance and salvation.

Isaiah predicted that a rod would come forth out of the stem of Jesse which would be an *ensign* (flag or banner) of the people (Isaiah 11:10). That stem of Jesse is Jesus Christ (Romans 1:3). Jesus, our banner of redemption and warfare, was lifted up on a rugged cross on Mount Calvary. He has gone before us and conquered the world and its power to harm us (John 16:33 Amp).

God has exalted Christ far above all other rulers, authorities and powers, put all things under his feet and appointed him the head of the church (Ephesians 1:18-23). Now Jesus goes into battle before believers, gives us the victory and makes us conquerors (1 Corinthians 15:57).

When Jesus Christ, our banner, was resurrected from the dead, he abolished death and brought life and immortality to light through the gospel (see 2 Timothy 1:10). Now we no longer have to fear death, for Jesus Christ's death and resurrection rendered powerless him who had the power of death, Satan (Hebrews 2:14-15). Christ's banner over us is love, and love never fails.

Another compound name of God, *Jehovah-rohi* (ro-ee), means 'Jehovah My Shepherd' (see Psalm 23). The primary meaning of *rohi* or *ro'eh* is 'to feed or lead to pasture, as a shepherd does his flock'. It can also be translated 'companion' or 'friend'.

Jesus is the shepherd of his people (John 10:11; Hebrews 13:20), and he feeds, leads, protects and cares for his sheep. Because he is our shepherd, we do not have to fear death (see Psalm 23:1, 4, 6; 1 Corinthians 15:55-57).

As you meditate upon the cross, praise the Lord that you are free from death and hell because your sin was taken away at Calvary. Praise him because you will never perish, but will have eternal life. Focus on Jesus who was crucified and declare: 'I have been crucified with Christ and I no longer live, but Christ lives in me' (Galatians 2:20).

Consider this: If you are a believer, and someone took a gun and shot you right now, your earthly body would slump in death, but your living spirit would go immediately into the presence of the Lord (see 2 Corinthians 5:8). Once your spirit grasps the truth that you are an eternal creature who will never die, you will live differently, talk differently, walk differently.

You are an eternal being, already experiencing eternal life.

Thank God that he is your banner who has conquered death, hell and the grave. Praise the Lord because he is your shepherd who will lead you through the valley of the shadow of death and into the house of the Lord, where you will dwell for ever.

Hallowed be your name, *Jehovah-nissi,* 'the Lord My Banner'. Hallowed be your name, *Jehovah-rohi,* 'the Lord My Shepherd'.

Philippians 2:9-10 says: 'God exalted him to the highest place and gave him the name that is above every name, that at the name of Jesus every knee should bow.' The knees of every foe must bow and acknowledge Christ's supreme authority, power and dominion. The full character and nature of God the Father are found in the name of Jesus. The *Jehovah* names of God apply to Jesus, who said, 'I have come in my Father's name' (John 5:43). 'In Christ all the fulness of the Deity lives in bodily form,' states Paul in Colossians 2:9.

By believing on Jesus' name we are born again (John 1:12-13), and by believing on his name we live in victory. We must submit to the lordship of Jesus and to the dominion of that name in every area of our lives, for Paul said, 'Everyone who confesses the name of the Lord must turn away from wickedness' (2 Timothy 2:19).

If we allow anything in our lives that is not his nature and will, we are misusing his name. We are not sanctifying his name; we are profaning it. Therefore, we must submit to the lordship of Jesus and to the dominion of his name in every area of our lives, for God has commanded, 'You shall not misuse the name of the Lord your God' (Exodus 20:7).

In the great Azusa Street revival of the early 1900s, this altar invitation was given: 'Everyone interested in pardon, sanctification, healing and the baptism in the Holy Spirit, rise and come.' The speaker was right. Jesus is our righteousness, sanctifier, peace, healer, provider, banner and shepherd, and he is the overflowing one present within us.

Our Father in heaven, hallowed be your name. Help us, Lord, not to misuse your name.

Review questions

1. Why can we call the God of the universe 'Father'?

_____

_____

_____

2. Draw a line connecting each Old Testament Hebrew name for God with its correct English translation:

Hebrew	Translation
Jehovah-tsidkenu	Jehovah My Shepherd
Jehovah-shalom	Jehovah is There
Jehovah-shammah	Jehovah Who Sanctifies
Jehovah-m'kaddesh	Jehovah is Peace
Jehovah-jireh	God's Provision Shall be Seen
Jehovah-rohi	Jehovah My Banner
Jehovah-nissi	Jehovah Heals
Jehovah-rophe	Jehovah My Righteousness

3. Match the letter of each word on the left with the benefit in the New Covenant with which it corresponds:

Word		Benefit
a. Spirit	_____	The promise of forgiveness of sin and deliverance from sin's dominion
b. Soundness	_____	The fulness of the Holy Spirit
c. Sin	_____	The promise of health and healing
d. Success	_____	The promise of freedom from the curse of the law
e. Security	_____	Freedom from the fear of death and hell

4. Cursing and using God's name as a swear word is one way in which people misuse his name. Explain another way we can misuse his name. _____

_____

_____

_____

_____

Prayer Outline

1. Our Father in heaven
   a. Form a mental picture of the blood shed by Jesus on the cross
   b. Thank God that you can call him 'Father' by virtue of that blood

2. Hallowed be your name
   a. Benefit 1: Sin — forgiveness of sin and deliverance from sin's dominion
      - [ ] Hallow his name
      - *Jehovah-tsidkenu:* Jehovah Our Righteousness
      - *Jehovah-m'kaddesh:* Jehovah Who Sanctifies
      - [ ] Make your faith declarations
   b. Benefit 2: Spirit — fulness of the Holy Spirit
      - [ ] Hallow his name
      - *Jehovah-shalom:* Jehovah is Peace
      - *Jehovah-shammah:* Jehovah is There
      - [ ] Make your faith declarations
   c. Benefit 3: Soundness — health and healing
      - [ ] Hallow his name
      - *Jehovah-rophe:* Jehovah Heals
      - [ ] Make your faith declarations
   d. Benefit 4: Success — freedom from the curse
      - [ ] Hallow his name
      - *Jehovah-jireh:* God's Provision Shall be Seen
      - [ ] Make your faith declarations
   e. Benefit 5: Security — freedom from the fear of death and hell
      - [ ] Hallow his name
      - *Jehovah-rohi:* Jehovah My Shepherd
      - *Jehovah-nissi:* Jehovah My Banner
      - [ ] Make your faith declarations

3. Am I misusing the Lord's name?
   a. Ask the Holy Spirit to reveal areas in which you may be misusing the Lord's name
   b. Submit yourself to the lordship of Christ

4. Pray in the Spirit, worshipping and making melody in your heart to the Lord

Part Three

Priorities
*'Your kingdom come,
your will be done'*

10

God's kingdom in you and your family

The *Mekilta*, an ancient manuscript that includes a commentary on most of the book of Exodus, includes this parable:

A man came to a province and asked the people if he could reign over them.

They said, 'What good have you done for us? Why should we accept your reign?'

In response, the man built them a wall. He brought them water. He fought battles for them. Then he asked the question again, 'May I reign over you?'

They responded, 'Yes, yes!'

The parable continues: Thus it was with the Omnipresent. He redeemed Israel from Egypt. He parted the sea for them. He brought them manna. He provided them with a well. He sent them the quail. He fought the battle of Amalek for them. He said to them, 'May I reign over you?'

They replied, 'Yes, yes!'[1]

The parable stops there, but its application does not. God our Father comes to us and asks, 'May I reign over you?'

Often our audacious reply is, 'Who are you and what good have you done for us that we should accept your reign?'

God need not reply, yet out of love he does: 'I am your Father, the Creator God, who so loved the world that I gave my one and only Son, that whoever believes in him shall not perish but have eternal life. His shed blood brought you righteousness and sanctification,

[1] Brad Young, *The Jewish Background to the Lord's Prayer*, Centre for Judaic-Christian Studies, Austin, Texas, 1984

peace and brought you righteousness and sanctification, peace and access into my presence. With the
stripes on his back you were healed and made whole.

'He has redeemed you from the curse of falling
short. He sees your needs ahead of time and makes
provision for them. He is your banner who goes into
battle before you and breaks open the way. You do
not have to fear death or hell because he is the Good
Shepherd who laid down his life for his sheep,
abolished death and brought life and immortality to
light.'

Then once more God asks, 'May I reign over you?'

God reigns over us when we obey him, accept his
rule and authority in our lives and become active in
Jesus' kingdom movement to defeat evil, redeem
sinners and bring to humankind the blessings of God's
reign. This, essentially, is what we are earnestly
desiring when we declare, 'Your kingdom come, your
will be done.' We are submitting to God and calling
upon him to perform his will on earth.

Consider the verbs in these two statements: 'Your
kingdom come, your will be done on earth as it is in
heaven.' In the Greek, the verbs are placed at the
beginning of these two statements for emphasis. I
cannot translate the meaning in any better way than
to say that it is like a man firmly, decisively putting
his foot down. 'Come, kingdom of God! Be done, will
of God!'

Let me illustrate. In a business transaction or in a
relationship, have you ever said, 'I'm drawing the line
right here. This is the way it's going to be. I'm putting
my foot down!'? That is the idea in these two
statements. Therefore, it is neither arrogant nor
presumptuous to declare boldly, 'Come, kingdom of
God! Be done, will of God!'

God has a will for each day of your life; therefore,
put your foot down in prayer. Instead of constantly
mouthing weak little prayers such as, 'Oh, Jesus, help

me,' begin boldly declaring God's promises. Stand in the victory that Christ has won for you. Refuse to let Satan's puny attempts to intimidate you hinder God's mighty purposes. Declare that God's will shall be done, that his kingdom shall come.

And what is the kingdom of God? Paul tells us, 'The kingdom of God is not a matter of eating and drinking, but of righteousness, peace and joy in the Holy Spirit' (Romans 14:17).

We want God's priorities to become established in our lives, but so often 'the tail wags the dog'. Someone has called it 'the tyranny of the urgent', meaning that we allow many things that cause us anxiety and trouble to crowd out the important things, things that should be given top priority.

For example, have you ever buttoned up your jacket and missed the top button? You glanced down, saw everything was out of line and realised you would have to unbutton it and start all over again. Life is like that. If you don't have God as your top priority, nothing else will line up as it should. Your health, emotions, goals and relationships get off centre.

How well I know! In the early years of my marriage and ministry, my time priorities were all out of line. I was a student at a Bible college thirty-five miles away from home, minister of youth and evangelism at Beverly Hills Baptist Church, a husband and the father of three little kids.

When it came to time management, my priorities went something like this: the church came first, my studies came second, my family came third, and prayer and communion with God came last. I knew that Jesus commanded, 'Seek first his kingdom and his righteousness, and all these things will be given to you as well' (Matthew 6:33), but I did just the opposite. I was busy seeking 'all these things' instead of seeking first the kingdom.

But when I put Jesus first, he began to put all the

other things into their proper places, and the confusion and disorder were replaced by the soothing peace of God.

As the years passed by and my schedule became busier and more complicated, it became necessary for me to be away from my family much of the time, but Melva and I knew what to do. We made our schedules a matter of prayer, and God showed us unique solutions for our particular way of life.

What works for me will work for you. As you give priority to prayer and seek God's wisdom, the Lord will begin to correct and realign your schedule, revealing the solutions to your time management problems.

Ordering your *time* priorities is important, but next you must establish *prayer* priorities. As you pray, you must declare that God's kingdom come and his will be done in these four major areas: 1. yourself; 2. your family; 3. your church; 4. your nation. How do you pray over these four important areas?

Just as the set of its rudder determines a ship's course, so the tongue sets the course of one's life, for the tongue is the rudder of life (see James 3:3-5). Although aimless confessions will not accomplish much, when the tongue agrees with the Spirit of God and declares with sincerity and faith, 'Your kingdom come, your will be done,' the correct course of life is set. So every day as you pray, declare that God's kingdom shall come and that his will shall be done in these four major areas.

Yourself

Begin with yourself. James 5:16 says, 'The prayer of a righteous man is powerful and effective.' Unless you are right before God, your prayer will not be effective. Each day pray that God's kingdom — his righteousness, joy and peace — be established in you and that his will for you that day be set in your spirit.

You need divine wisdom and revelation if you are properly to administrate your home, business, resources and so forth. When you pray, 'Your kingdom come, your will be done,' invite Jesus to assume his rightful place on the throne of your heart and to rule your spirit, soul and body. Then pray over the particular concerns in which you will be involved throughout the day.

Ask the Holy Spirit to empower you with ability, efficiency and might. In the words of Jude, 'Build yourselves up . . . make progress, rise like an edifice higher and higher' by 'praying in the Holy Spirit' (Jude 20 Amp). Stay before the Lord until the course of your day is set and the Spirit of God is functioning in you. This is vitally important, for if Jesus is not Lord in *you,* he will not be Lord in your second priority — your family.

Your family

If you are married, pray for your partner. Pray that righteousness, peace and joy will rule your partner's life. Making the declaration of faith 'Your kingdom come, your will be done,' pray over the needs of your partner until the Spirit releases you to move on in prayer. This is vitally important because if you lose your own house, your work for the house of God will be greatly hindered.

A young evangelist on the verge of losing his wife seemed more concerned about his reputation and the evangelistic meetings he had scheduled than in wooing his wife and seeing their marriage restored. As he knelt to pray about the great ministry he wanted to do for God, the Lord put a piercing question to his young servant: 'What makes you think I want to entrust *my* Bride to you when you won't even take care of your own?'

Our families must come first. Some of the most remorseful people I know are individuals who tried

to win the world for God but lost their own families
in the process.

How should you pray for your family? If you have
children, declare, 'Your kingdom come, your will be
done,' in each of their lives. Make specific petitions.
Listen to what the Spirit of God speaks to you
regarding your children.

The Lord began speaking to me about our son, John
Aaron, while he was still in his mother's womb, and
everything the Spirit of God said to me is coming to
pass in his life.

When he was eleven, John Aaron said, 'Dad, do you
remember Mike, the boy at school whom nobody likes
because he's dyslexic? He can't read, and the kids say
he's stupid. Well, today I led him to Jesus.'

Do you know why that happened? Because every
day of John Aaron's life I have declared, 'Your
kingdom come in him, Lord. Will of God, be done in
him!' Every day I pray over my son and my two
daughters, Joanna and Joy Elizabeth, and make that
declaration over them.

I also pray over the individuals each of them may
eventually marry and pray that they will not get out
of the perfect will of God for their lives. Why? Because
I've seen that it pays to pray like that.

Here's the best illustration I know of praying for
your children and those whom they will marry:

My wife, Melva Jo, has her master's degree in music;
she is an operatic soprano, an incredible vocalist who
has sung all over the world. We met when we were
in college. She was Miss Dallas Baptist College, and
I was a 'mole in a hole'. (I was busy reading the red
and praying for the power, remember?)

Here she was, the socialite of the campus, singing
for the president of the Southern Baptist Convention,
and here I was, just a little old guy who couldn't match
my socks. We were both in the college choir, so I had
noticed her, of course. But I was dating a girl back in

my hometown, and Melva was engaged to a guy in Mississippi.

Our choir travelled all over the world that year, and Melva and I became friends. One evening she and I were in my car heading for a concert when she casually announced, 'Well, I'm gonna get married.'

I grinned and said, 'You ought to marry that poor guy, Melva. You've been engaged to him for three years.'

Melva was silent for a minute, then answered quietly, 'Yes, but I'm not going to marry *him*.'

Something in the way she said that made something inside of me go 'Doi-yoi-yoi-yoing!' I didn't say a word and neither did she, but it must have hit her, too, because she didn't want me to drive her back to the college that night. Actually, she did something really mature: here she was a senior in college, and she hid in the bathroom so I couldn't find her.

And the next day? Well, then she wouldn't go to class because she didn't want to face me. But I knew where she worked, so I did something really mature, too. I went there and hid behind a tree. When she finished work, I jumped out in front of her and commanded, 'Melva Jo Bryant, don't you go anywhere.'

She smiled, ducked her head and said softly, 'I'm not going anywhere.'

We went to a quiet hillside to talk. The sun was setting, and it was so romantic. Like Simon Peter not knowing what to say on the Mount of Transfiguration, I blurted out, 'Do you realise we could get married?' (That was one of the first serious things I had ever said to her.)

Returning my gaze, she said thoughtfully, 'Yes, I guess so. Larry, if this is really the Lord, my fiance will call and break up with me.'

You guessed it. Three days later that dude called her. 'Melva,' he confessed, 'I've been wanting to call for several weeks now, but I didn't want to break your heart. You see, I'm going out with a girl here in Mississippi, and I want to break my engagement to you. I don't think we should get married.'

He must have been shocked by the tone in Melva's reply. 'Good!' she said, breathing a prayer of thanks. 'Good!'

Melva came to me and told me what had happened, adding emphatically: 'This is the Lord's will.'

I thought, 'I'm too young to die!'

Then Melva announced, 'We've got to talk to my dad.'

'Your dad?' I mumbled, trying not to choke.

So we drove off to the hills of Arkansas where Melva had grown up. Late that night we arrived at her parents' home, where they greeted us at the door. Melva introduced me and announced proudly, 'Dad, this is the man I'm going to marry.'

Mr Bryant stared at me and sputtered, 'That? That? That's what I've prayed for — for almost forty years?' (That's not the whole truth, but it went something like that.)

Then he sat me down at their breakfast table and told me a story I'll never forget.

'Son,' he began kindly, 'Melva's mother was told that it was medically impossible for her ever to bear a child. But we cried out to God as Hannah did for Samuel. For twenty years we prayed, "God, give us a child. Your will be done over our child." After twenty years of marriage, we made a vow to God. We promised, "God, if the child you give us is a boy, we will dedicate him to the ministry. If it's a girl, we'll dedicate her to be a pastor's wife."'

Mr Bryant paused, and I thought, 'I never even had a chance!'

Then Melva's dad continued the story. 'When my wife was forty years old, she conceived for the first time. For seven of the nine months of pregnancy she lay flat on her back in bed. But when she gave birth to a healthy girl, we held our baby up before the Lord and vowed, "Jesus, every day of her life we will declare that the will of God be done in our child."'

Don't you see? Melva's decision, 'I'm not going to marry him,' was the forty-year composite of her parents' putting their foot down in prayer and declaring, 'Your will be done in the life of our daughter, Lord.'

That's why I urge you to intercede for your children and to pray that they will not get out of the perfect will of God for their lives. While your children are young, ask God to reveal his plans for their futures in order that you can train them up in the way they should go. Treasure in your heart those things the Lord speaks to you about each child, and claim God's wisdom daily in guiding and training your children.

Petition the Lord to lay other family members upon your heart. Allow the circle of your concern and compassion to be enlarged.

At times you are sure to get 'hung up' in prayer, unable to leave one person. When that happens, be sensitive to the Holy Spirit because he knows that the person needs prayer that day. Make sure you don't rush through some little prayer formula, but pray until the Holy Spirit gives you release.

If your prayer time is gone and you haven't prayed through all the topics in the Lord's Prayer, stop and then pick up the prayer outline where you left off at the first opportunity later in the day — driving your car, working around the house, before going to sleep. Let your life become a life of prayer. Learn to 'pray the price' for what you need.

And every day as God asks, 'May I reign in you?' joyfully declare: 'Yes, yes! Your kingdom come, Lord. Your will be done. I call upon you to perform your perfect will in me, in my partner and children and in my loved ones. I place your will before my own desires.'

There are other important priorities yet to be established and maintained. Let's consider these next as we, with intense inward yearning, continue to pray this powerful plea: 'Your kingdom come, your will be done!'

11

God's kingdom in your church and nation

In 1974 I interviewed Richard Wurmbrand, a Jewish Christian who had spent three years in a Romanian dungeon where he was tortured for his faith.

'Mr Wurmbrand,' I asked, 'do you think American Christians are going to experience what you experienced?'

His reply startled me. 'No,' he answered thoughtfully, 'I don't think it's *going* to come. I think it's already here. In America, I experience ten times more demonic spiritual oppression fighting to make me draw back than I ever experienced in a dungeon.'

It is an indisputable fact. As believers, you and I are part of God's army, and it is at war. It's time we realised that God's army was formed to fight, not to show off our shiny brass buttons and polished boots. God has called us to be warriors — to be an anointed, delivering army with healing in our hands. We can lose by default, but we *cannot* lose if we will fight.

Paul, one of God's generals, commanded us to 'fight the good fight of the faith' (1 Timothy 6:12). Notice that Paul didn't say, 'Fight if you feel like it. Fight if you have that sort of personality.' Every believer must fight the good fight of faith. Satan has declared war on believers, and he doesn't fight fair.

The devil doesn't bat a bloodshot eye at attacking the harmless, the innocent or the inexperienced in battle. You and your family are just as much Satan's prey as your church and your nation are. Therefore, it is of critical importance that you learn how to pray daily over four vital areas and declare, 'Come, kingdom of God! Be done, will of God!'

We have talked about how you can establish and maintain godly priorities in yourself and your family. Now turn your attention to two other critical areas, your church and your nation, and let's discover how to defeat the devil there.

Your church

Your third prayer priority is your church. Pray for the pastor, the leadership of the church, the faithfulness of the people and the harvest.

Pastor

As you pray for your pastor, ask God to anoint him, speak to him and direct him. Petition the Lord to give your pastor a shepherd's heart, to impart wisdom to him as he spends time in the Word and in prayer, and to make him a pure channel through which the gifts and power of the Holy Spirit can flow.

Leadership

Say the leaders' names in prayer. As you pray for them one by one, the Holy Spirit will often show you specific needs. Pray for the people in the church who are ministering in ways which touch your own life directly. Pray that the Lord will make the various groups and organisations in the church healthy. Ask the Lord to show them how to breathe in through fellowship and breathe out in evangelism.

Faithfulness

Pray that the people of the church will be faithful to their families, to the vision God has given your church, and to Jesus. Entreat the Holy Spirit to plant them in the house of the Lord so that they will bring forth fruit as soulwinners and intercessors. Pray that they will be faithful in bringing their tithes and offerings into the storehouse and that they will serve God as he deserves to be served.

Harvest

God gave me a passage from Isaiah to claim when praying in the harvest for the church: 'Do not be afraid, for I am with you; I will bring your children from the east and gather you from the west. I will say to the north, "Give them up!" and to the south, "Do not hold them back." Bring my sons from afar and my daughters from the ends of the earth — everyone who is called by my name, whom I created for my glory, whom I formed and made' (Isaiah 43:5-7).

Therefore, as I pray over my church, I speak to the powers and principalities of the air who work in the children of disobedience (see Ephesians 2:2). These powers and principalities hold the reins over certain areas, so I speak to the area north of my church as if it were a person and say, 'North, you have people whom God wills to become a part of my church. I command you in the name of Jesus to release every person who is supposed to become a part of this body.'

Then I speak to the south, east and west, and in the Spirit I look them right in the face. I command them to release *every* one — not every other one — that God has ordained to be saved, planted, strengthened and established in my church.

I tarry there in prayer until I have a release in my spirit that the evil powers are listening and relinquishing what belongs to me. Through the Spirit, I face those geographical areas and challenge them until they drop the reins of control. Then in Jesus' name, I ask God to dispatch angels to minister to the heirs of salvation (see Hebrews 1:13-14).

Now that may sound 'far out' to some people. But let's not fall into the habit of labelling every slightly out-of-the-ordinary approach we run up against as the sure sign of a counterfeit; it may be the real thing. Remember how unorthodox Jesus' methods seemed to the Pharisees who perceived themselves to be spiritual experts.

As Donald Gee, a wise British pastor and Bible teacher for many years, once said, 'Those who pretend to pass judgment in spiritual matters must be prepared to show their credentials of personal spiritual experience.'[1] Unfortunately, many people condemning manifestations and experiences birthed by the Holy Spirit have had little personal experience with either.

How many of you know that Jesus Christ is the same yesterday, today and for ever? And how many of you also know that the Pharisees are the same yesterday, today and for ever! Let's not be spiritually ignorant and naive. Let's desire to be balanced, not embalmed. Now get a good grip on your theological hat, because I've got something else to say!

One day when I was praying intently in the Spirit and commanding the north to give up everyone who belonged to my church, I saw a vision of a huge, black, moss-covered, Darth-Vader-looking creature. He stood at least nine feet tall, and he held a chain. The demonic creature sneered at me in contempt, beckoning to me, mocking me, as if to say, 'Are you really serious? Are you willing to fight me over this?'

Something stood straight up in my spirit, and I knew how David must have felt as he faced Goliath. I heard myself backing him down, declaring that he *would* release every soul the Holy Spirit was drawing to become a part of God's church. He stared at me as I resisted him in the name of Jesus, then he slowly dropped the chain and backed off.

Close to that time, something else happened. One morning I was speaking to the north, south, east and west, commanding them to give up. Just then, I saw a vision of a huge, marching army. I'm talking about tens of thousands! They were wearing battle fatigues and marching in perfect time.

[1] *Concerning Spiritual Gifts*, by Donald Gee, Gospel Publishing House, Springfield, Missouri, 1972

Amazed, I asked, 'Lord, what's that?'

The Lord replied, 'Son, that's your church.'

At that time, our church had only about three hundred people, so I gasped incredulously, 'My church?'

Later, the Lord spoke again and explained, 'Larry, when you pray that the east will give up, you're thinking about the Texas towns of Greenville and Sulphur Springs, less than fifty miles away, but when I say east, I'm thinking about Germany. I'm talking about Jerusalem. I'm the God of the whole earth.'

I laughed and really got a kick out of that. I even shared it with the intercessors in our early morning prayer meeting, and we all laughed about God thinking of Germany when we declared, 'East, give up! Don't keep back!'

The next Sunday as I gave the invitation at the close of the service, I said, 'All week I've prayed over you people, and I know you are here from the north, south, east and west, because we've prayed you in. The Bible says the Lord added to the church daily such as should be saved. How many of you feel today that the Lord is adding you to this church? Will you please raise your hand and then come down to the front here so I can pray over you?'

Among those who walked down the aisle was a handsome six-foot-four man with his beautiful blonde wife and two cute little boys. The Spirit of God whispered to me, 'Ask him where they're from.'

Obediently, I singled out the man and enquired, 'Sir, would you tell me where you're from?'

He almost clicked his heels together and saluted! He said, 'Two years ago while I was serving in Germany as a major in the US Army, I heard one of your tapes about praying over the north, south, east and west. The Lord told me to resign my commission in the army, move to Rockwall, Texas, and join the army of God here.'

Folks, this is real stuff! We must learn to pray and obey, as Paul Yonggi Cho said years ago, and God will take care of the details. It wasn't a beautiful building or some perfectly orchestrated programme that added over four thousand new members to Church on the Rock in 1985. In one three-month period in 1986 we saw over five hundred people born again. That spiritual momentum continues to build. That's not Larry Lea; that's God.

God has taught us first to pray and command the north, south, east and west to give up. Then we ask the Holy Spirit to draw souls to Jesus, and we release angels to minister to the heirs of salvation. We pray, 'Don't let the people have accidents while they're on their way to church. Don't let things provoke families to arguments and prevent their coming to God's house. Minister grace to the people as they're driving here.' And last, we declare the faith level given to us by God.

What do I mean by that? When I speak of faith levels, I'm not referring to 'hype', 'positive mental attitude' or man-made and man-motivated objectives. I'm talking about Spirit-imparted goals. You see, the Spirit of God puts into my spirit a specific number of souls I'm to ask God for. I share it with my staff, and we begin to ask for that specific number of additions. Each morning as we pray, we set ourselves in agreement with God for that particular number of souls to be added to the church.

Through the years, we have noted a marked correlation between the number of faithful intercessors in our early morning prayer meetings, the amount of tithes and offerings given and the number of people added to the church.

For instance, in 1984 we had about twenty faithful intercessors at morning prayer. (We had more people praying, but I'm talking about faithful prayer warriors.) Our offerings were around twenty thousand dollars weekly, and about twenty people joined the church each week.

The number of intercessors grew, and about midway through 1984 God said, 'I want you to believe me for sixty new members and sixty thousand dollars a week.' We began having about sixty faithful intercessors, the offerings grew to sixty thousand dollars weekly, and we averaged sixty new additions to our church each week.

The number of faithful intercessors climbed, and in 1985 our faith level was for a hundred additions to the church and one hundred and ten thousand dollars each week. God brought it to pass, and this spiritual correlation continues.

Today we have many more prayer warriors. Entire families come to the church for morning prayer, and many members of our church who live too far away to drive to Rockwall each morning for prayer have begun morning prayer meetings in their homes.

I'm not promising that the same thing will happen in your church, but I'll tell you this: if I were you, I would ask the Holy Spirit to purify my motives. Then I would help begin an early morning prayer meeting in my church if it didn't already have one, and release God to do what he wants to do in your midst.

Make prayer for your church a priority. Pray for the pastor and leadership. Pray for the faithfulness of the people and for the harvest, and declare, 'Come, kingdom of God. Be done, will of God!'

Your nation

Your fourth prayer priority is your nation. Pray that the Prime Minister will have the wisdom of God; that spiritual leaders will walk in wisdom, be people of prayer and be kept by the power of God. Pray specifically, naming your local and national leaders. Intercede for the UK. Pray for revival.

The Lord also commands us to pray for the peace of Jerusalem (Psalm 122:6), so pray for the nation of Israel.

You may wish to ask God to lay another nation of the world upon your heart — communist nations, countries experiencing revolution or famine, and so forth. Allow the Spirit of God to enlarge your borders of concern and compassion.

At this point, you will have prayed through the first two topics in Christ's model prayer: 'Our Father in heaven, hallowed be your name'; and 'Your kingdom come, your will be done on earth as it is in heaven.' There are four remaining demarcations.

Perhaps you now realise how simple it is to pray one hour. You are learning how to pray for multitudes of things that once caused you fear, worry and frustration. And now instead of thinking, 'How could I ever pray for an entire hour?' you may be wondering, 'How can I ever get through it in only one hour?'

You see, our problem has been simple. Not knowing what to say or do when we prayed, we wore ourselves out in about ten minutes. But Jesus said, 'This is how you should pray,' and he gave us a prayer outline to follow.

In the context of this prayer are the five major themes that have been restored to vitality in the church in our time. They are praise and worship, kingdom authority, prosperity, relationships and spiritual authority. Each of those themes is there, and each is in perfect balance.

Yes, in the context of this prayer is everything you need in order to live full and free in spiritual victory!

Review questions

1. The _____ is the rudder of life (James 3:3-5).

2. What is the kingdom of God? Romans 14:17 declares, 'The kingdom of God is not a matter of eating and drinking, but of _____ , _____ and _____ in the Holy Spirit.'

3. What are four major areas in which God's kingdom should be established?

   a. _____

   b. _____

   c. _____

   d. _____

4. Unless you are right before God your prayer will not be effective, for the Bible says, 'The prayer of a _____ man is powerful and effective' (James 5:16).

5. Your third priority is your church. What four specific areas should be covered when you pray for your church?

   a. _____

   b. _____

   c. _____

   d. _____

6. As a reminder to yourself, in the space provided below list specific people and topics for which you personally want to pray when you come to the fourth priority, your nation:

   _____

   _____

   _____

   _____

7. Can you think of time you spend doing unimportant, unnecessary things during the course of your day that could be devoted to prayer? If so, list those times here and ask the Holy Spirit to help you and remind you to redeem that time.

   _____

   _____

   _____

Prayer outline

1. Make a declaration of faith: 'Your kingdom come, your will be done — not simply willed — but done'

2. Four major areas to establish his kingdom

   a. Yourself

   ☐ Be sure you are right before God

☐ Ask Jesus to be seated on the throne of your life and to rule in every area

☐ Abide before the Lord until the course of your day is set and the Spirit of God is functioning in you

b. Your family

☐ Partner

☐ Children

☐ Other family members

c. Your church

☐ Your pastor

☐ Leadership of the church

☐ Faithfulness of the people

☐ The harvest

d. Nation

☐ Local and national political leaders

☐ Spiritual leaders

☐ Revival

3. Ask the Spirit of God:

a. To implement your priorities

b. To help you live them out

Part Four

Provision
*'Give us today our
daily bread'*

12

Being in God's will

A third-year Bible college student rarely dines at the exclusive Petroleum Club in Fort Worth, Texas, but I was in those elegant surroundings at the invitation of the wealthy gentleman seated across the table.

After grace, I reached for my fork, then paused in surprise. He was crying. This distinguished, respected, sixty-year-old millionaire bowed his head, and hot tears dripped off his chin, staining his expensive silk tie.

'Sir,' I said softly, 'what's wrong? Can I help?'

Several seconds elapsed as he struggled to regain his composure. Taking a deep breath, he confided, 'I was nineteen years old when God called me to preach, but I said no. I wanted my own way, wanted to make a lot of money. So I refused to take my hands off my life.'

His voice broke, and more tears trickled down his face. 'But I don't have any peace,' he sobbed brokenly. 'I missed God's purpose for my life.'

I can't help imagining that the scene I witnessed that day was a repeat performance of a similar role that might have been played by another wealthy aristocrat in his latter days — the man whom we have come to know as the 'rich young ruler'.

You remember the story. Jesus was on his way to Jerusalem when a well-dressed young man came running up and fell at Jesus' feet. 'Good teacher,' he asked earnestly, 'what must I do to inherit eternal life?'

Mark records the momentous decision that took place in the next few moments: 'Jesus looked at him and loved him. "One thing you lack," he said. "Go, sell everything you have and give to the poor, and you will have treasure in heaven. Then come, follow me." At this the man's face fell. He went away sad, because he had great wealth' (Mark 10:17-22).

The rich young ruler was a good man, a religious man, but there was something amiss. Jesus knew what it was, and he put his finger on it: the love of money. When he instructed the young man to sell out and follow him, Jesus wasn't trying to rip the guy off. He was trying to prevent him from trusting in his riches. Jesus was offering the man the soundest investment counselling he would ever receive, but he refused it and walked away.

God's principles are diametrically opposed to those of the world. God says, 'Give, and it will be given to you.' The world cautions, 'Get all you can, and can all you get!' But man's ways are not God's ways.

Have you ever noticed the beautiful balance in the Lord's Prayer? The first concern is *his name;* the second is *his kingdom and his will.* Then he tells us to pray, *'Give us* today our daily bread.' If we seek first God's kingdom and his righteousness, all the other things will be added to us. We must understand that Jesus wasn't trying to transform the rich young ruler into the poor old beggar. He was trying to break the power of the greed and poverty that bound this young man's soul.

The rich young ruler's purpose was to count his money at night. He built his life around his money. A lot of people are like that. They have their security cushions, but they can't sleep at night or enjoy their slap-up meals. God wants to free his children from that suffocating mindset.

It is no surprise that God's four basic requirements for successfully praying in what we need are not what the natural man would guess readily. What are those requirements? First, you must *be in the will of God.* Second, you must *believe it is God's will to prosper you.*

Third, you must *be specific* when you pray daily for what you need. And fourth, you must be *tenacious*.

Be in the will of God

Being in the will of God implies four things: 1. fellowship with Jesus through prayer and reading the Word of God; 2. fellowship with God's church; 3. diligent, balanced work habits; 4. obedience in giving.

Fellowship with Jesus

To be in the will of God, daily fellowship with Jesus in the Word and in prayer is essential.

If, like the rich young ruler, you have religion but not a relationship with God, you will not experience God's peace, purpose or power. But as you fellowship with Jesus, the Holy Spirit empowers you with divine ability, efficiency and might to do the will of God (see Acts 1:8 Amp).

Fellowship with one another

The story is told of a woman who walked up to Dwight L. Moody at the conclusion of a service and said, 'Mr Moody, I want to sing in your choir.'

Moody enquired, 'Who is your pastor? Where is your local church?'

The woman stuck her nose in the air and replied smugly, 'I don't have a local church or a pastor. I'm a member of the great universal church.'

Moody thought about it for a second and said, 'You go and find the pastor of the great universal church and sing in his choir.'

Now Moody wasn't being rude; he was being realistic, for the Word of God commands: 'Obey your leaders and submit to their authority. They keep watch over you as men who must give an account. Obey them so that their work will be a joy, not a burden, for that would be of no advantage to you' (Hebrews 13:17).

It is God's will that we be rightly related to our

brothers and sisters in a local church. We should also be committed and submitted to our pastor. We are commanded not to forsake the assembling of ourselves together; instead, we are to exhort one another (see Hebrews 10:25 RAV). *Exhort* means 'to admonish, to urge one to pursue some future course of conduct'. Isn't it wonderful to have fellowship with believers who can impel us morally, encourage and urge us forward and stimulate us to good works?

Balanced, diligent work habits

The next prerequisite to being in the will of God is to have diligent, balanced work habits.

Paul gave instructions regarding work (see 1 Thessalonians 4:11-12). We are to earn our living with our own hands and command the respect of the outside world as we are self-supporting and have need of nothing. Paul warned us not to be neglectful of duty and pass our lives in idleness, being busy with other people's affairs instead of our own, thus doing no work (see 2 Thessalonians 3:11-12). As a matter of fact, Paul commanded: 'If a man will not work, he shall not eat' (2 Thessalonians 3:10).

As pastor of a church, I've noticed that we human beings seem to be divided into two groups: givers and takers. I know for a fact that there are seasons when God may lead a believer to live by faith, and then he will even send ravens to feed that believer if necessary. However, far too often, the brother or sister who asserts, 'God told me to live by faith,' is actually saying, 'I want to live on *your* faith.'

That's one side of the coin. But the other side of the coin is also a problem. Too many believers are working two jobs in order to keep up with the Joneses and dress their kids in designer jeans. We need to be real! We sing, 'When we've been there ten thousand years, bright shining as the sun', without a thought that the material things for which we neglect the kingdom of God and work so hard will be vapour in ten thousand years.

Some believers are workaholics who allow the cares of this life and the deceitfulness of riches to choke out the Word of God and render their lives fruitless (see Matthew 13:22). Pride, fear, worry and insecurity drive us to overwork, but when we realise that God our Father is our source — not ourselves or paycheques or savings accounts — we can be content to do the possible and let him do the impossible.

Obedience in giving
The fourth prerequisite to being in the will of God is obedience in giving.

In Malachi 3:10, God promises that if we bring our tithes into the storehouse, he will open the windows of heaven and pour out so many blessings we cannot contain them. Acknowledging God as our source and giving unselfishly back to him helps destroy the root of all evil, the love of money (see 1 Timothy 6:10). If we take care of the *root* of evil, we will not have the *fruit* of evil in our lives.

God promises that if we bring our tithes into the storehouse, he will pour out blessings upon us. On the other hand, in Malachi 3:8-9, he promises curses if we rob him of tithes and offerings. God will not bless something he has cursed. Obedience in giving is essential if we are to receive God's best.

We also need to realise that there is a proper order to giving and receiving. First, we give that there may be meat in *God's* house; then he blesses *our* house. First we give; then it is given to us (see Luke 6:38). As we seek first the kingdom of God and his righteousness, all these things will be given to us as well (Matthew 6:33).

When we give to God first, rather than hoarding our limited resources, we acknowledge that he is our source. Remember: we cannot claim God's blessings if we are violating this basic principle of prosperity.

We must also obey God when he asks us to give the unusual or unexpected. I learned that one the hard way. Perhaps you can learn from my mistakes.

I was a twenty-four-year-old married man when I went to India to minister. While there I prayed for a seventeen-year-old girl who had been blind for ten years. God instantly healed her, and the entire village turned to God because of that miracle.

I had the privilege of ministering in villages where the people had never heard the gospel preached. One day as I walked along a dusty road, the Holy Spirit asked, 'What would you say if I told you, just as Jesus told the rich young ruler, to sell everything you own? Would you do it and give the money to missions?'

I replied glibly, 'Lord, I'd do anything you tell me to do.' (Let me urge you never to tell God you will do something unless you mean it.)

I just assumed it would be one of those 'Abraham and Isaac' deals where God tested me to see if I was willing and then just dropped the matter. Instead, God commanded, 'Go home and do it!'

At that time, Melva, baby John Aaron and I lived in a tiny second-storey flat. Right beneath us lived seven illegal aliens. I mean, this was no high-class joint. We worked for a church, and all we had was a bed, a sofa, two hundred dollars in savings and a car that wasn't worth repairing.

But when God asked me to sell what we had and give the money to missions, I discovered that people who don't have anything can be just as hung up on their 'stuff' as people who have everything.

When I told Melva what the Lord had told me in India, she didn't feel a confirmation at all. As a matter of fact, she said, 'I don't believe that's God, Larry. Let's pray some more about it.'

So instead of obeying God, we prayed a little about it, and I enrolled in Bible college. But I became physically sick, emotionally sick, and I was so depressed for six months that I hardly made it.

One Sunday morning I was too ill to go to church, so I sat at home watching evangelist James Robison on television. Suddenly, James whirled around, pointed at the camera and announced emphatically: 'There's a man listening to me who wants to be a prophet of God. God has already told you what to do, and you haven't obeyed him. Mister, you will remain sick and stay at home until you do what God told you to do.'

His long, skinny finger seemed to point through the screen right at me! So do you know what I did the next day? I got myself a Loadlugger trailer and loaded up everything we had in the house.

My father-in-law met me at the front door. (You remember him and the tremendous first impression I had made on him?) Making every effort to stay calm and uninvolved, he stuffed his hands in his pockets and asked, 'What are you doing, son?'

I replied, 'I'm loading up all our furniture, and I'm going to sell it and send the money to India.'

His eyes widened and he choked out, 'What did you say?'

But I had made up my mind. I was tired of not doing what Jesus had told me to do. Melva cried a little as she helped me load it all up, bless her heart, but we obeyed.

It wasn't easy. Melva and John Aaron and I slept on the floor for a while. Before you shake your head and mutter, 'What a fanatic,' let me tell you the rest of the story.

Two years later, while we were still working on that same church staff, we made our final payment on a home costing forty-nine thousand dollars. It happened supernaturally. Why? Because God said, 'Give, and it will be given to you. A good measure, pressed down, shaken together and running over, will be poured into your lap. For with the measure you use, it will be measured to you' (Luke 6:38). That's the perfect way to describe God's abundant provision for me and my family through the years.

And if you're wondering about my relationship with my father-in-law, let me assure you that we share a mutual love and respect for each other. He and Melva's mum moved to Rockwall so that they could be near us and their grandchildren, and the two of them have won a special place in the hearts of our congregation at Church on the Rock.

It's really very simple. The requirements for being in the will of God can be reduced to one element: the lordship of Jesus Christ in your life. If he is Lord, you will have fellowship with him in a personal prayer life and in the Word. You will have fellowship with his church. You will be diligent and balanced in your work habits, and you will be obedient in giving. If these basic prerequisites to being in the will of God are established in your life, you can depend on God to supply all your needs.

That's the first requirement for praying in God's provision. There are three more. As we discuss them, mentally 'grade' yourself and look for weak areas you may need to strengthen in order to pray more effectively, 'Give us today our daily bread.'

13

Meeting God's requirements

My father made a fortune in oil and gas in Texas, so I grew up surrounded by luxury. But because 'stuff' had never satisfied, I reacted against wealth and concluded that anybody who had money and 'stuff' couldn't be right with God.

But the more I studied the Bible, the more it defied my philosophy. When I opened the Bible, I thought I would find a bunch of impoverished ascetics. Instead, I read about wealthy Abraham (see Genesis 24:35). I read about Abraham's son, Isaac, who sowed and reaped a hundredfold during a time of famine and accumulated great possessions (see Genesis 26:1, 12-14). As I studied the lives of King David and his son, Solomon, I shook my head in amazement at their tremendous wealth.

Then I read about Job and how he lost everything, and I thought, 'Now we're getting on the right track.' But Job 42:10 reveals that God turned the captivity of Job and gave him twice as much as he had before.

I read the words of Moses in Deuteronomy 8:18: 'Remember the Lord your God, for *it is he who gives you the ability to produce wealth,* and so confirms his covenant.' I studied the promises in Malachi 3, referring to the giving of tithes and offerings.

Then I got into the New Testament and saw the promise of Jesus: 'Give, and it will be given to you. A good measure, pressed down, shaken together and running over, will be poured into your lap. For with the measure you use, it will be measured to you' (Luke 6:38).

And I discovered his pledge to those who sacrifice for the sake of the gospel: 'No-one who has left home or brothers or sisters or mother or father or children or fields for me and the gospel will fail to receive a hundred times as much in this present age (homes, brothers, sisters, mothers, children and fields — and with them, persecutions) and in the age to come, eternal life' (Mark 10:29-30).

At about that time, I discovered the second requirement for praying in God's provision. You must believe that it is God's will to prosper you.

Believe it is God's will to prosper you

Where did we ever get the idea that it was Jesus who came to steal, kill and destroy? 'The blessing of the Lord brings wealth, and he adds no trouble to it' (Proverbs 10:22). Paul promised, 'My God will meet all your needs according to his glorious riches in Christ Jesus' (Philippians 4:19).

Some people have taken these truths concerning prosperity and gone off on a selfish 'bless-me' tangent. But that doesn't negate God's promises. Our Father has made this promise to his faithful children who seek his blessings in order that they might be able to stretch out filled hands to the needy:

'God is able to make all grace (every favour and earthly blessing) come to you in abundance, so that you may always and under all circumstances and whatever the need, be self-sufficient — possessing enough to require no aid or support and furnished in abundance for every good work and charitable donation . . . . And [God] who provides seed for the sower and bread for eating will also provide and multiply your [resources for] sowing, and increase the fruits of your righteousness [which manifests itself in active goodness, kindness and charity]. Thus you will be enriched in all things and in every way, so that you can be generous' (2 Corinthians 9:8, 10-11 Amp).

God doesn't bless us so that we can tear down our old barns and build bigger ones. Believers sometimes misunderstand the purpose of God's blessings and drown in their own gravy.

God knows that money is a necessity. Would it shock you to learn that the Bible says more about money than anything else? The Scriptures are replete with instructions on how to make, save, give and manage money. You see, God wants his children to be givers, not takers; to be the head, and not the tail; to be lenders, not borrowers.

If you aren't already obeying God's command to tithe, why not begin right now? Don't be like the rich young ruler who walked away sorrowful. Sell out to Jesus, and watch him rebuke your devourer. Get the doubt out. Believe that it is God's will to prosper you, then claim his promises for your needs. Daily ask for your allotted portion necessary to fulfil God's plan for your life.

What have we discussed so far? First, in order to pray in God's provision, you have to be in the will of God. Second, you must believe that it is God's will to prosper you. These are extremely important requirements for 'praying in' what you need, but they are incomplete without two additional steps. You must be specific when you pray, and you must be tenacious.

Be specific

A third aspect of praying in God's provision is making specific requests. Do you bring specific needs to God each day, or do you just expect the answers to come in? Jesus instructed us to pray, 'Give us today our daily bread.' By this we know we are to pray daily over our specific needs.

Immediately after Jesus gave his disciples the Lord's Prayer in Luke 11, he related a parable illustrating the importance of asking specifically. Pay close attention to his words: 'Suppose one of you has a

friend, and he goes to him at midnight and says,
"Friend, lend me three loaves of bread, because a
friend of mine on a journey has come to me, and I have
nothing to set before him"' (Luke 11:5-6).

Did you catch it? Did you notice that the man asked
specifically for three loaves of bread? When you pray,
'Give us today our daily bread,' ask specifically!

If you had to have over a hundred and twelve
thousand dollars every week to meet your budget,
would it make you nervous? That's what I face every
Monday morning, but I don't worry about it. Why?
Because over a thousand members of our church are
daily agreeing with me in prayer, asking specifically
for that amount to come in.

First you must pray specific prayers over the needs
of the house of God, then pray specifically for the
needs of your own house. When you have sown your
financial seed into his kingdom and have been faithful
to God and to your church, you can confidently ask
for your specific needs.

Be tenacious

In Luke 18:1-8, Jesus told the parable of the unjust
judge and the widow who repeatedly, persistently
begged, 'Grant me justice against my adversary.'
Because of the woman's tenacity, the unrighteous
judge granted her request. Jesus emphasised this point
to his disciples when he asked, 'Will not God bring
about justice for his chosen ones, who cry out to him
day and night? Will he keep putting them off?' (v7).

It takes tenacity, shameless persistence, to recover
what Satan, our adversary, has stolen from us, but
today many believers are not aware of that fact.
Instead, they search for spiritual shortcuts. Of course,
there may be times when we can 'name it and claim
it'. But there are also times when we must intercede
fervently, for many needs and situations require
earnest tenacity before victory comes.

In his valuable book *The Art of Intercession,* Kenneth Hagin, the well-known faith teacher who in his lifetime has spent untold hours in intercession, urges believers to intercede. He explains:

'Here is where some people miss it. They don't hear everything you teach, and they grab some little something and run off with it. There are some things you can pray the prayer of faith on — and you pray one prayer and that's the end of it. You don't have to pray anymore; you just thank God for the answer . . . . But there are other things you cannot pray the prayer of faith on . . . . For God to accomplish what he desires to accomplish . . . the art of intercessory prayer will have to be resurrected.'[1]

Though your answer may be long in coming, be tenacious. When God hears your prayer of faith, the answer is conceived at that moment (see Daniel 10:12-14). If God's response is delayed, continue to carry the petition in your heart. Don't allow yourself to grow weary as you bear the burden. Don't lose heart and give up, for by doing so you will miss the answer God has prepared.

There can be miscarriages in prayer. That thing conceived in the Spirit can be aborted if we cast away our confidence and refuse to wait on the Lord.

The Amplified Bible translates Matthew 7:7: 'Keep on asking and it will be given you; keep on seeking and you will find; keep on knocking [reverently] and the door will be opened to you.' Jesus told his disciples that 'they should always pray and not give up' (Luke 18:1). Remember: God is a rewarder of those who diligently seek him (Hebrews 11:6).

To summarise, in order to appropriate God's provision you must first be in the will of God. Next, you must believe that it is God's will to prosper you. Then you must be specific and tenacious in prayer.

[1] *The Art of Intercession,* by Kenneth Hagin, Kenneth Hagin Ministries, Tulsa, Oklahoma, 1980

This is how Jesus taught us to expect and experience God's provision.

Review questions

1. True or False? In the following blanks write 'T' if you believe the statement to be true, 'F' if you think it is false

a. _____ Being in the will of God is a basic requirement for successfully praying in what you need

b. _____ To be in the will of God, fellowship with Jesus in a consistent personal prayer life and in the Word of God is essential

c. _____ If we are in God's will, we will be rightly related to our brothers and sisters in a local church and be committed and submitted to our pastor

d. _____ Diligent, balanced work habits are important if a person desires to be in the will of God

e. _____ God says we should take care of the needs of our own house first. Then if there is anything left over, we should help take care of the needs of his kingdom

f. _____ To appropriate God's provision, it is important that you believe that it is God's will to prosper you

g. _____ God knows what we need before we ask. Therefore, it is not necessary to ask daily and specifically for what we need

h. _____ We should only ask God for something once. If he wants us to have it, he will give it to us without our having to keep asking

i. _____ There is copious evidence in God's Word that it is his will to bless his people

2. a. In order to appropriate God's provision it is important that we be in the will of God, believe that it is God's will to prosper us, ask God specifically for our daily needs and be tenacious. In which two of these things have you been weakest?

_____

_____

b. What will you do to correct those weaknesses?

_____

_____

Prayer outline

1. Be in the will of God

a. Ask the Holy Spirit to help you develop a consistent, daily personal prayer life and time in the Word where you fellowship daily with Jesus

b. Pray that the Lord will plant you in your local church and make you a contributing, functioning, healthy part of that body

c. Examine your work habits. Are you slothful? A workaholic? Ask the Lord to give you ability, efficiency, might and balance

d. Examine your giving. Are you obeying the Lord in bringing your tithes and offerings into the storehouse? Or are you greedy, stingy or a poor manager? Do you pay your bills and have a reputation as a fair and honest person who keeps your word? Take time to pray along these lines

2. Believe that it is God's will to prosper you.

a. Memorise Scriptures such as Luke 6:38 and Philippians 4:19 to use as faith declarations as you pray in your provision

b. Meditate upon the Word of God until you truly understand and believe that it is God's will to bless you

3. Be specific

a. Bring specific needs daily before God

b. Decide to pray instead of worry

4. Be tenacious

a. Repossess lost ground that the devil has stolen from you. Discouragement and unbelief have robbed you of answers to prayer. Take up those petitions again and persevere until the answer comes

b. Praise the Lord because he is *Jehovah-jireh:* he sees your need beforehand and makes provision

Part Five

People

'Forgive us our debts,
as we also have forgiven
our debtors'

14

Getting along with everyone

'You'll never play basketball for me again!' the coach
threatened angrily as he marched me off the court
towards the sidelines. But the fury on his face and the
determination in his voice let me know this was more
than a threat; it was a fact.

Why hadn't the coach asked to hear my side? Hadn't
he seen the other kid throw the first punch? And why
hadn't he just suspended me for a game or two instead
of taking me out of play altogether? Those questions
clouded my mind for the rest of the year as I 'rode the
bench', but I consoled myself with the thought that I
would get to play for another coach in my next
academic year.

But it wasn't to be. The coach was promoted right
along with me, and I sat on the bench during my first
year, and on into my second year. Finally, we got a
new coach and I was allowed to play again, but the
damage had been done. By that time, tangled roots of
bitterness had established themselves deeply in the soil
of my heart.

Years later when I was a Bible college student, the
Lord convicted me of that bitterness, and I wrote to
that coach asking him to forgive me for the grudge I
had carried against him.

Why was it so important to ask his forgiveness? As
Christians, you and I are in the process of becoming
full grown in God. Part of the process of spiritual
growth is learning to forgive one another because our
relationship to our fellow-men and -women affects our
relationship to God. God will not extend mercy to

those who refuse to forgive (see Mark 11:25-26 margin).

If husbands and wives learn to say, 'I'm sorry. Please forgive me,' their marriages keep growing. If not, the marriages die. This is true of any relationship; learning to forgive is an essential element of growth.

May I ask you a personal question? Does a dark cloud rise up on the inside of you when you think of certain people? If so, you need to understand that God uses those who sin against us to teach us how to forgive. And we can never forgive others until we know that we ourselves have been forgiven. Because we are forgiven, for Jesus' sake we forgive others.

Can you see why forgiveness is an important key to spiritual liberty, victory and joy?

As you pray, 'Forgive us our debts, as we also have forgiven our debtors,' there are certain things you must do if you want to get along with everyone all the time.

Ask God to forgive you

Often as you thank God for the blood of Jesus, the Holy Spirit puts a finger on some sin you need to confess and forsake. So when you pray, 'Forgive us our debts,' ask God to look into your heart. If unconfessed sin surfaces at this point, confess the sin to God and claim his promise, in 1 John 1:9: 'If we confess our sins, he is faithful and just and will forgive us our sins and purify us from all unrighteousness.'

In that verse the word *confess* means 'to speak the same thing'. In other words, we must agree with what God says about our sin and be willing to turn away from it.

But the debts Jesus refers to when he instructs us to pray, 'Forgive us our debts, as we also have forgiven our debtors,' encompass more than just our sins. The term also refers to personal debts or moral obligations connected to our relationships with others. That brings us to the second thing we must do if we expect to get along with everyone all the time.

Forgive as often as you want to be forgiven

Take a moment to study this question which Peter put to Jesus: 'Lord, how many times shall I forgive my brother when he sins against me? Up to seven times?' How would you have answered?

Listen to Christ's reply: 'I tell you, not seven times, but seventy-seven times' (Matthew 18:21-22). What was Jesus saying? He was teaching: Forgive as many times as you are offended. Why would Jesus make such a statement? Because that is how many times he is ready and willing to forgive us.

Next, Jesus told Peter a parable which reveals tremendously important truths about forgiveness. This familiar story is found in Matthew 18:23-35, and it teaches a great deal about forgiveness.

First, Jesus uses the parable to teach us that God has forgiven our great debt of sin — a debt so huge that it would be absolutely impossible for us ever to repay it. The servant in this parable owed the king ten thousand talents, approximately £7 million. But the king forgave the servant and cancelled his enormous debt.

That's not the end of the story, though. A fellow-servant owed the forgiven servant a debt of a hundred denarii (about £13), and the forgiven servant made a moral decision not to forgive the debt of his fellow-servant; instead, he had him thrown into prison.

What is the truth conveyed here? That our debt against God is greater than any debt a person will ever owe us and that when we refuse to forgive another person, we place that individual in bondage.

When the king heard what had happened, he asked the forgiven servant a question which is one of the most pivotal in the New Testament, for it is God's question to each one of us: 'Shouldn't you have had

mercy on your fellow-servant just as I had on you?'
(v33). This tells us that we are to forgive at the same
level as we are forgiven by God.

Once we realise how much *we* have been forgiven
by God, we can freely forgive others. If you have
trouble forgiving, ask God to give you a revelation of
Calvary and the price his Son paid for your
forgiveness.

Jesus concludes the parable by describing the king's
anger towards the unforgiving servant. The king
delivers the servant to the tormentors. The lesson? If
we don't forgive, God will deliver us to tormentors
until we choose to forgive others.

You might as well get this straight. If you do not
forgive, you will live with tormenting memories and
demonic oppression until you release the person and
forgive. If you don't forgive, Oral Roberts, Billy
Graham, Kenneth Hagin and James Robison could
agree in prayer and dump two five-gallon buckets of
twenty-forty oil on you, but you would remain in
torment. Why? Because deliverance will not come
until you choose to forgive.

Maintain a right attitude towards others

How is it possible to have a right attitude towards
everyone all the time when some people are hovering
around like vultures waiting for you to fail?

The meaning of the Hebrew word translated 'enemy'
in the Old Testament is 'observer' — someone who is
critically watching. There are always people waiting
to point out your faults, hoping you will fail. So how
do you maintain a right attitude?

The key to a right attitude is preparation. Don't put
off deciding how you will react to those who wrong
you until the hot breath of the enemy is steaming up
your glasses. Each morning before you walk out of
your door, make a wilful decision that you will
respond with love and forgiveness towards those who

offend you. Decide that you will not allow unforgiveness to rob your spirit of victory, joy and peace.

That simple decision can save you a lot of grief. How
do I know? Because I have let unforgiveness rip me
off, and it was no fun.

After my room-mate Jerry Howell and I were filled
with the Holy Spirit at Dallas Baptist College, things
didn't run too smoothly. We lived in a dorm with four
hundred and thirty Baptist preachers, and most of
them didn't like what we had. It wasn't that Jerry and
I were running around trying to promote our
experience as the ultimate doctrine in the theological
world; it was just that it was apparent to all that
something fulfilling and exciting had happened to us,
and that irritated some people.

One day the spiritual leader on campus confronted
me. He was thirty-five; I was twenty-one. He was six-
foot-seven; I was five-foot-seven. He weighed in at
about eighteen stone; I tipped the scales at nine and
a half. Thank God the confrontation was verbal and
not physical.

So this guy scowled down at me and growled, 'Larry,
if you lay your hands on and pray for anybody else,
I'm gonna pray that God will chop your arms off right
at the elbows.'

The Lord gave me grace and I was able to reach up,
put my hand on his shoulder and say, 'I understand
why you feel like that, but can't we be brothers?' Yet
as I walked away, thoughts about what I could have
said and should have said flooded my mind. My
tranquil little river of peace boiled into scalding steam.
Boy, was I mad. (Actually, I told myself I was just hurt.
That's a nice word for angry.)

So I did what you should never do if you want to
get over an offence. (I'll borrow five rhyming words
from Marilyn Hickey to describe the process.) First,
I *cursed* it. I muttered to myself, 'Where does this guy
get off, talking to me like that? Who does he think he

is, anyway? Get him, God!'

I didn't yet know God sometimes allows offences to help us grow and mature, so my next step wasn't any better. I *nursed* it. I let that ugly little offence curl up in my lap and become my bosom buddy. I coddled it, petted it, fed it. And, sure enough, it grew.

Then I *rehearsed* it. I enjoyed full-colour, slow-motion instant replays of the offence in my mind. Oh, yes, I even edited it to make myself look better, magnifying the injury I had suffered.

But when I finally got tired of reruns and was ready to get on with life, I had this full-grown offence following me around. Ignoring it didn't do any good. Trying to push it away from my mind's threshold didn't work. How was I supposed to get rid of this loathsome thing?

Finally, I found the solution. I *dispersed* it. I gave it to God. I confessed it and forsook it. I humbled myself before God and sought his forgiveness, cleansing and strength.

And then, do you know what God did? He *reversed* it! He turned it around, and the thing that could have become my tombstone became instead a stepping-stone to victory and maturity.

Romans 4:25 (KJV) tells us that Jesus 'was delivered [over to death] for our offences' — not just for the offences of others against us, but for all our offences against him. Forgiveness is what Calvary is all about. Therefore, 'Be kind and compassionate to one another, forgiving each other, just as in Christ God forgave you' (Ephesians 4:32).

When you forgive, you release into God's hands the person who has offended you. You drop the offence, let it go, and give up your right to hurt the person who has hurt you. Then you become a candidate for the supernatural. The peace of God that passes all understanding guards your mind, and God himself, in his own time and in his own way, vindicates you.

Years ago I served under a church staff member who seemed 'out to get me'. He kept a critical eye cocked in my direction for over a year and did everything he could to make me look bad.

One morning in the staff meeting he said, 'We don't have cheats on our church staff.' Then he glared at me and barked, 'Larry, stand up.'

Wondering what on earth he was about to do, I slowly stood to my feet.

Turning to our fellow-staff members he announced, 'The other night several of us from the church went out to eat, and Larry left without paying his bill. I'll have you know that we're not gonna have people on this staff who walk out of restaurants without paying for their meals.'

I could feel my heart pounding. I struggled to keep my composure. I hadn't left without paying. A businessman from the church had whispered in my ear, 'I know you're late for your television taping so go on ahead. I want to pay for your meal.' I had thanked him and left.

I was completely innocent of this man's accusations. But I had been praying, praising and flowing in the river of the Spirit that morning, and the Holy Spirit would not let me open my mouth. So I just stood there quietly until the man felt he had made his point and told me to sit down. Then when the meeting was dismissed I went to my office and prayed it through, forgiving and releasing the man to God.

Before long, word of this embarrassing incident got around to the man who had paid my bill. (Ironically, he was twice as big and mean as I was.) He stormed into that staff member's office and let him know in no uncertain terms exactly what had happened at the restaurant.

Five minutes later the staff member, his face as white as a sheet, was in my office apologising. I accepted his apology and had no hard feelings towards him because I had chosen days before to forgive him and release him to God.

When I took that step, I became a candidate for the supernatural, and God came to my defence just as he promised to do: 'Don't be afraid of those who threaten you. For the time is coming when the truth will be revealed: their secret plots will become public information' (Matthew 10:26 Living Bible).

Isaiah 26:3 pledges, 'You will keep in perfect peace him whose mind is steadfast, because he trusts in you.' That word 'steadfast' actually means 'sustained', 'supported by'. Don't fret about the offence. Lean on, rely on and be confident in him, and he will come to your aid, help you to stand and comfort you.

At this very moment the Spirit of God is defying the spirit of anger, revenge and unforgiveness that has ruled in your life. You can continue to curse, nurse and rehearse the offence, or you can disperse the thing right now in prayer and allow God to reverse it. Remember, you must choose to forgive, for forgiveness is not an emotion but an act of the will.

You have a choice to make about this test that God has allowed to come your way. Will your reaction to the offence fashion it into a tombstone or a stepping-stone?

It's your decision. Make it count!

Review questions

1. Below are statements concerning forgiveness. If a statement is true, write 'T' in the blank provided. If it is false, write 'F'

a. _____ God uses those who sin against us to teach us how to forgive

b. _____ Forgiveness is an important key to spiritual victory, freedom and joy

c. _____ An attitude of unforgiveness is a reason for unanswered prayer

d. _____ When John tells us to confess our sin (1 John 1:9), he is saying we must agree with what God says about our sin and be willing to turn away from it

e. _____ Jesus told Peter to forgive a brother who sinned against him, but no more than seven times

f. _____ Your debt of sin against God is greater than any debt an offender will ever owe you

g. _____ When we refuse to forgive a person, we put that individual in bondage

h. _____ If we do not forgive, God will turn us over to tormentors until we choose to forgive

2. Summarise on the lines below what you are to do daily in order to maintain a forgiving attitude

_____

_____

_____

3. What do you think this statement means: 'Forgiveness is not an emotion. It is an act of the will'?

_____

_____

_____

_____

Prayer outline

1. Ask God to forgive you

a. Deal with your sins. Ask the Holy Spirit to reveal areas in your life that are not pleasing to God

b. Confess your sin. Agree with God and say what he says about your sin. Ask him to help you hate your sin with perfect hatred and to deliver you from its dominion. Praise his name, *Jehovah-m'kaddesh*, 'the Lord Who Sanctifies'

c. Do not allow condemnation. Remember: you are the righteousness of God in Christ. You are complete in him

2. Forgive as often as you want to be forgiven

a. Meditate upon your great debt of sin that God has forgiven

b. See your sin actually causing Jesus' suffering on the cross. Get a mental picture of the blood shed for your forgiveness

c. By an act of your will, forgive those who have sinned against you and release them to God. Pray for those who have wronged you

3. Set your will to forgive anyone who sins against you this day

a. Make up your mind to return good for evil by the grace and power of the Holy Spirit within you

b. Make this faith declaration: 'I will love my enemies. I will bless those who curse me and do good to those who hate me. I will pray for those who persecute me (see Matthew 5:44)

c. Pray that you will begin to experience the fruit of the Spirit in your life in greater measure: love, joy, peace, patience, kindness, goodness, faithfulness, gentleness and self-control (Galatians 5:22-23)

Part Six

Power

*'Lead us not into temptation,
but deliver us from the evil one'*

15

Putting on God's armour

What a time to have a heart attack! Unfortunately, Pastor Conatser didn't have any say in the matter.

Although Beverly Hills Baptist Church was exploding with growth, and the only other preaching pastor on his staff was a twenty-two-year-old kid fresh out of Bible college, Pastor Conatser had orders to rest for at least six weeks and let someone else do the preaching. That someone else turned out to be me — the twenty-two-year-old preacher boy.

When the board turned to me and said, 'Larry, it's up to you,' the pressure was awesome. Overnight my responsibilities doubled, and so did my anxieties and frustrations. It wasn't long before a little black cloud of depression followed me around raining gloom and misery on my bedraggled spirit.

But one day a Lutheran pastor visited my study, and he wasn't long in coming to the point. 'Do you put on the whole armour of God every day?' he asked bluntly.

I was a Bible college graduate with three years of Greek recorded on my certificate, so I wanted to impress this pastor and let him know I was no dummy. 'Oh, yes!' I exclaimed, leaning back in my chair and folding my arms across my chest. 'You're referring to that beautiful Pauline metaphor in the sixth chapter of Ephesians. Yes, sir, I'm familiar with its every participle, verb and noun, because I exegeted that entire book from the Greek.'

I knew immediately that he wasn't impressed. 'I'm not asking if you know *about* the armour of God,' he explained patiently. 'I'm asking if you *put on* the whole armour of God every day.'

Somewhat deflated, I shook my head and admitted meekly, 'No sir, I don't.'

The pastor's insightful reply startled me. 'Then maybe that's why you're depressed all the time.'

The whole armour of God

After he left, I took another look at Ephesians 6:10-18, and, phrase by phrase, topic by topic, I studied those nine verses for clues to their relevance for twentieth-century Christians. Would you like to join me in a simplified line-by-line account of what I found?

'Be strong in the Lord, and in his mighty power'
The Christian preparing for conflict needs power. Even if you are fully clad in the armour Paul describes in the verses that follow, you must first have power or the armour is of little benefit. Where do we get that power? Through fellowship with the Lord and in answer to prayer.

'Put on the full armour of God'
As a Christian warrior you are to put on the complete equipment provided, undervaluing nothing, omitting nothing, for how can you know at what unguarded point the enemy may attack?

'So that you can take your stand'
Paul explains that the warrior puts on the whole armour in order to stand. This is a military term that refers to 'the firm and prepared attitude of a good soldier confronting his enemy'.

'Against the devil's schemes'
What is the warrior to stand against? The schemes or stratagems of the devil — the subtle, dangerous ways that evil assails.

'For our struggle is not against flesh and blood, but against the rulers, against the authorities, against the powers of this

dark world and against the spiritual forces of evil in the heavenly realms'

We don't wrestle against visible physical opponents, but against principalities, against the organised forces of evil powers. We wrestle against rulers whose sway over the moral darkness pervading humanity is worldwide. We wrestle against spiritual hosts of wickedness — spiritual cavalry, robber hordes — in all spheres and relations and in the atmosphere around us.

'Therefore put on the full armour of God, so that when the day of evil comes, you may be able to stand your ground'

We are not to rely merely upon human precautions and defences but are to take up the whole armour of God that we may be able to stand against the day of temptation — that special season and circumstance of spiritual or moral testing which may come at any time, and for which it is always necessary to be prepared.

'And after you have done everything, to stand. Stand firm then'

Being in condition for warring a good fight — having done all — we are to stand, intending to conquer.

'With the belt of truth buckled round your waist'

The waist is that part of the body between the ribs and the hip-bones. The digestive system, the reproductive organs and the bowels (which eliminate waste) are contained here.

The leather girdle or apron about the waist of the Roman soldier was the first and most necessary part of his equipment. It not only served to keep the armour in its proper place; it was also used to support the sword.

Paul teaches that our waist is to be buckled around with truth — inward truth, genuineness and determined purpose. The psalmist said, 'Surely you desire truth in the inner parts; you teach me wisdom in the inmost place' (Psalm 51:6).

As a believer, you are to be filled with the truth of God; you are to be a person of total integrity and moral rectitude. You must know who you are in God and who God is in you. You buckle the belt of truth around your waist by reaffirming the truth about yourself and about God and by acting upon that truth instead of upon your emotions.

'With the breastplate of righteousness in place'

The breastplate was a piece of armour worn over the chest. Organs vital to life itself were protected by the breastplate: the oesophagus (the passage for food from the mouth to the stomach), the windpipe, the heart and the lungs.

What is the believer's breastplate of righteousness? It is the righteousness of God through faith. It is justification by the blood of the cross. This righteousness is the result of the renovation of the heart by the Holy Spirit.

The breastplate is an important part of the soldier's defensive armour. The righteous new man within the believer resists, defends against and refuses to entertain evil suggestions. The breastplate of righteousness diligently guards the heart of the believer, for out of the heart are the issues of life.

'And with your feet fitted with the readiness that comes from the gospel of peace'

In hand-to-hand combat, the ability to stand, side-step, walk and run is absolutely essential. Because a Roman soldier's fighting was mostly hand to hand, a firm footing was extremely important. His sandals were not only bound firmly to his feet and ankles, but the soles were thickly studded with hobnails or spikes to prevent the warrior from slipping.

As participants in spiritual warfare, we are to equip

our feet with the the readiness and preparedness, the firm-footed stability, found in the gospel of peace. As we walk daily in the revealed will of God and order our conduct and conversation according to his Word, we will experience a sense of oneness with God and a consciousness of divine aid equal to any problem.

As believers, we are to walk in the will of God and, as my missionary friend Alice Huff says, leave 'footprints of peace' wherever we go.

'In addition to all this, take up the shield of faith'

The shield was a piece of armour carried on the arm or in the hand to protect and cover the entire body in battle. It was a part of the soldier's armament that could be shifted about and lifted up over all parts of the body as needed.

As Christian believers, our faith serves us just as a shield serves the soldier, but how do we get faith? Ephesians 2:8-9 says that faith is a gift. Romans 10:17 says, 'Faith comes from hearing the message, and the message is heard through the word *[rhema]* of Christ.' Galatians 5:22-23 says that faith is part of the fruit of the Holy Spirit. Galatians 2:20 says we live by the faith of the Son of God, who loved us and gave himself for us. That faith is the believer's shield.

'With which you can extinguish all the flaming arrows of the evil one'

'The evil one' does not refer to an impersonal force, but to Satan and the evil foes described in verse 12.

The large shields of ancient soldiers were made of wood (so they would be lightweight) and were covered with hides. The hides were soaked in water to quench flaming arrows, the enemy's most dangerous missiles shot to destroy and wound mortally. Paul assures us that 'the shield of faith' will prevail against Satan's worst forms of attack.

The believer takes the shield of faith and declares,

'I'm trusting in you, Lord, to protect me. Because I'm hiding in you, nothing can touch me today that you do not allow.'

'Take the helmet of salvation'

The helmet, the most expensive piece of the armour, was worn to protect the head. The helmet of salvation protects the believer's mind and thinking.

The word 'take' in this verse literally means 'receive' — to take in hand the helmet of salvation, which is 'the gift of God'. Therefore, the believer is consciously to ask for and receive the mind of Christ and the peace of God that garrisons and mounts guard over his thoughts (see Philippians 4:7 Amp).

'And the sword of the Spirit, which is the word of God'

The sword was an offensive weapon with a sharp blade fixed in a handle or hilt. Used to wound or kill, the sword was a symbol of power or authority, especially to judge and impose sentence.

The Christian's power and authority are the word of God. In speaking of the sword of the Spirit or the word of God, the reference here is not to *logos* or the whole Bible as such, but to *rhema* — the individual scripture, statement, command or instruction which the Spirit speaks to our spirits or brings to our remembrance for use in time of need. Before we are able to wield the sword of the Spirit effectively, we must fill our minds with Scripture.

The Greek indicates that the believer must receive this specific word from God for a specific situation. The special revelation can then be used as a sharp sword against the enemy and his onslaughts.

'And pray in the Spirit on all occasions with all kinds of prayers and requests'

The last powerful piece of the whole armour of God is *praying always in the Spirit*. This means praying in tongues, praying in and with your spirit in your own personal prayer language inspired by the Holy Spirit (Acts 2:4; 1 Corinthians 14:2, 14-15; Jude 20).

Because you are not praying with your mind but with your spirit, it is possible to obey Paul's command to 'pray in the Spirit on all occasions' (Ephesians 6:18). The only way you can pray on all occasions — or continually (1 Thessalonians 5:17) — is to pray with your spirit.

Your mind is limited; it hinders you from praying as you ought. But your spirit, redeemed by the blood and filled with the Holy Spirit of God, is unlimited. As you pray, the Spirit comes to your aid, joins his strong supplication with yours and intercedes before God on your behalf and for the welfare of other believers. As the Holy Spirit enables you to pray according to the perfect will of God, your prayers get through (Romans 8:26-27).

Consider this: your spirit has instant access to your vocal cords just as your mind has. Therefore, by your will, a prayer in your prayer language can come out of your spirit, bypass your mind, go over your tongue and go straight to God. God's response to your prayer can then be registered in your mind, enabling you to pray with understanding (1 Corinthians 14:13-15).

Have you ever groped for words, sensing the weaknesses and limitations of your own mind and understanding as you poured out your heart to God? Have you ever been caught in tense, urgent situations where there was no time to slip away by yourself and pray?

I have. That is why this seventh piece of spiritual armour is so precious to me. I can use it like a laser beam to pierce right through the devil's territory, reach God and receive his immediate response back to my mind. I can live in a constant attitude of prayer, regardless of where I am or what I am doing. I can pray aloud or under my breath; I can pray alone or in the middle of a crowd. God knows. God hears. And God answers. This is how the armour-clad believer can maintain a prayerful frame of mind and pray at all times, on all occasions.

'With this in mind, be alert'
This refers to the care the believer is to take not to neglect the prayer so essential for victory in spiritual conflicts.

'And always keep on praying for all the saints'
No soldier should pray for himself alone, but for all his fellow-soldiers also, for they form one army. The success of one is the success of all.

When Jesus commands believers to pray, 'Lead us not into temptation,' he is instructing us to pray that forces beyond our own control will not lead us into trials. He is commanding us to watch and pray against entering into temptation through our own carelessness or disobedience.

The petition 'Deliver us from the evil one' goes beyond the sense of a test or trial related to our inclination to sin. It introduces the supplication to be saved from the grasping, potent power of evil that seeks to influence, overcome and master us, then lead us astray. This request involves much more than merely asking to overcome a desire to sin; we must also defeat the powerful, evil forces seeking to hinder or destroy God's plan for our lives.

Therefore, in Ephesians 6:11, 13, Paul instructs us to put on the whole armour of God so that we will be able to stand against the schemes of the devil.

What is the obvious reverse of this teaching? If we do not pray, 'Lead us not into temptation, but deliver us from the evil one,' if we do not put on the whole armour of God, we cannot stand against the schemes of the devil. We will not stand!

In Romans Paul again mentions the armour. There

he instructs us to put on 'the armour of light' and to clothe ourselves 'with the Lord Jesus Christ' (Romans 13:12, 14).

The armour Paul describes and commands the believer to put on is really the Lord Jesus Christ. Jesus wants to be our defence and to clothe us with himself.

How to put on the armour

As I learned from the Lutheran pastor, this passage in Ephesians was not written just to be a beautiful metaphor. It was written to be obeyed and applied in everyday life.

But how does a believer put on armour he or she cannot see, touch or feel? By faith, visualising each piece. We put on our armour by believing and confessing God's promises. Each day, the believer should pray Ephesians 6:14-17 and in faith put on the whole armour of God, piece by piece. Take a minute to learn how to put on the armour of light, the Lord Jesus Christ.

Armour	Declaration	Promise
The belt of *truth*	Jesus is my truth.	'I am the way and the truth and the life' (John 14:6). 'You teach me wisdom in the inmost place' (Psalm 51:6)
Breastplate of *righteousness*	Jesus, you are my righteousness	'God made him who had no sin to be sin for us, so that in him we might become the righteousness of God' (2 Corinthians 5:21). 'You have been given fulness in Christ' (Colossians 2:10)
Feet fitted with the *readiness* of the gospel of peace	Jesus, you are my readiness	'I can do everything through him who gives me strength' (Philippians 4:13)

The shield of *faith*	Jesus, you are my faith	'I have been crucified with Christ and I no longer live, but Christ lives in me. The life I live in the body, I live by faith in the Son of God, who loved me and gave himself for me' (Galatians 2:20). 'Faith comes from hearing the message, and the message is heard through the word *[rhema]* of Christ' (Romans 10:17)
The helmet of *salvation*	Jesus, you are my salvation	'Once made perfect, he became the source of eternal salvation for all who obey him' (Hebrews 5:9). 'O Sovereign Lord, my strong deliverer, who shields my head in the day of battle' (Psalm 140:7)
Sword of the *Spirit* which is the word *(rhema)* of God	Jesus, you are my living word	'The words *[rhema]* I have spoken to you are spirit and they are life' (John 6:63)
Praying in the Spirit on all occasions	Jesus, you are my baptiser in the Spirit	'He will baptise you with the Holy Spirit and with fire' (Matthew 3:11). 'He who searches the hearts of men knows what is in the mind of the (Holy) Spirit — what his intent is — because the Spirit intercedes and pleads [before God] on behalf of the saints according to and in harmony with God's will' (Romans 8:27 Amp).

For many years now, I have daily put on the whole armour of God, piece by piece, by believing and declaring God's promises.

How about you? You wouldn't dream of going to work or to church without dressing properly, but day after day are you walking around without your spiritual clothes on? Are you a spiritual 'streaker'? If so, the devil sees you walking around spiritually naked, and he laughs because he knows you are defenceless against his schemes.

Learn to put on the whole armour of God, and do it every day. Refuse to let Satan delay or destroy God's purpose for your life. And pray a hedge of protection around yourself and your loved ones. That's what we learn to do next.

16

Building a hedge of protection

When I was a kid, I never sat in the dust with two puffy eyes and a bloodied nose exclaiming, 'Boy, that was a good fight.'

It wasn't a good fight unless I won!

Then why does Paul call our war with Satan a 'good' fight (1 Timothy 6:12)? It is identified as a good fight because we are supposed to win. We win by praying, 'Lead us not into temptation, but deliver us from the evil one.' We win by putting on the whole armour of God and by building the hedge of protection around ourselves.

Are you tired of eating the devil's dust? Would you like to know how to flatten the dude and plant your hobnail boots on his greedy throat? Then you must prepare yourself to stand in the victory Jesus has already won for you by putting on the whole armour of God and by learning to build a hedge of protection.

Build a hedge of protection

Build a hedge of protection about yourself and your loved ones daily by your faith declaration from Psalm 91:2: 'I will say of the Lord, "He is my refuge and my fortress, my God, in whom I trust."' In the Amplified Bible, the next verse states: 'For [then] he will deliver you from the snare of the fowler.'

Later in the chapter (v9, 14 Amp) are three reasons — or 'becauses' — why you can claim God's protection: 'Because you have made the Lord your refuge, and the Most High your dwelling-place'; 'Because he has set his love upon me'; and 'Because he knows and understands my name'.

Because we have made the Lord our dwelling
As we believers sing praises to the Lord, he sits down
among us, enthroned upon our praises. Psalm 22:3
(RAV) states: 'You are holy, who inhabit [sit down
or dwell among] the praises *[tehillah* — songs, psalms,
the residing song of the Spirit] of Israel.'

Because Paul knew this secret, he instructed: 'Do
not get drunk on wine, which leads to debauchery.
Instead, be filled with the Spirit. Speak to one another
with psalms, hymns and spiritual songs. Sing and
make music in your heart to the Lord' (Ephesians
5:18-19).

In another passage, Paul, an example to believers,
said he sang with the spirit and also with the
understanding (1 Corinthians 14:15). You, too, are to
sing to the Lord in praise and worship. At times, you
will enjoy singing beautiful old hymns or choruses. At
other times, you may feel like making up your own
special songs and singing them to the Lord. And
sometimes, the Holy Spirit may compose a spontaneous song of praise in a language only God's ears
and your own heart understand.

As you sing to God, he inhabits your praises. That
is how you make the Lord your habitation or dwelling.
As you walk with him in the Spirit, he will be your
refuge.

Because we have set our love upon him
We can also claim God's protection if we set our love
upon him. We set our love upon the Lord by focusing
our affections upon him, by seeking him first.

David declared: 'One thing I ask of the Lord, this
is what I seek: that I may dwell in the house of the
Lord all the days of my life, to gaze upon the beauty
of the Lord and to seek him in his temple. *For in the
day of trouble* he will keep me safe in his *dwelling;* he
will hide me in the shelter of his tabernacle and set

me high upon a rock. Then my head will be exalted above the enemies who surround me; at his tabernacle will I sacrifice with shouts of joy; *I will sing and make music to the Lord'* (Psalm 27:4-6).

The word 'dwelling' in verse 5 means 'a temporary, movable tent, or a more permanent building'. During war, the royal dwelling — the king's tent — was erected in the centre of his army, and it was surrounded by a constant guard of mighty men.

David, a king who occupied one of those royal tents in battle, is saying: 'In the time of trouble, God hides me in his royal tent in the very centre of his army, and surrounds me by a constant guard of angels.' In Psalm 91:10-11 we are assured, 'No disaster will come near your tent. For he will command his angels concerning you to guard you in all your ways.' And Psalm 34:7 declares, 'The angel of the Lord encamps around those who fear him, and he delivers them.'

If we want to be surrounded by God's hedge of protection, we must set our love upon him. In Psalm 27:4 David declared, 'One thing I ask . . . .' Have you ever noticed other references to the words 'one thing' in Scripture? To the rich young ruler Jesus said, 'You still lack one thing . . .' (Luke 18:22). To Martha he said, 'You are worried and upset about many things, but only one thing is needed . . .' (Luke 10:41-42). Paul declared, 'One thing I do . . .' (Philippians 3:13).

We, like Martha, are often anxious and troubled about many things, but we lack one important thing. We hurry and scurry about, busy with our own business, but we neglect our Father's business.

Here's an example with which you might identify. When my son was younger and I asked him to mow the lawn, he would sometimes put off the job and play instead. I didn't mind his playing with friends, but his disobedience and his not mowing the lawn disturbed me.

I think it's like that with our heavenly Father. He

says, 'Tarry with me one hour,' but we put our own things first and before we know it, the day is over and we haven't spent time with God. It's time for us to grow up spiritually and learn to give our Father the first hour of our day; then there will be twenty-three more hours to take care of our own things.

We need to allow the Holy Spirit to focus our energies and attentions upon the Lord — to set our love upon him. As we cling to him in absolute trust, he will be our protection.

Because we acknowledge his name
'The name of the Lord is a strong tower; the righteous run to it and are safe' (Proverbs 18:10). The name of the Lord signifies not only who he is, but what he wants to be in your life.

Don't misuse the Lord's name. He is more than saviour. He is your righteousness and sanctifier. He is your peace, and the overflowing one present within you. He is your healer and provider, banner and shepherd. So know his name, for it is a strong tower. Let him be what you need him to be in your life.

Declare God's hedge of protection

Every day, make the Lord your habitation by singing songs of praise. Set your love upon him and seek him first, above all else. Know and submit to his name. Inspect your spirit and make certain you are living in the three 'becauses' of Psalm 91.

Then you can stand in your armour and declare: 'You are my refuge, my fortress, my God. In you do I trust. I know your name. You are my righteousness, sanctifier, peace, healer, provider, banner and shepherd, and your presence dwells within me.'

That is the way to pray a hedge of protection about yourself and your loved ones. When you live in these three 'becauses' and daily declare that he is your refuge and fortress, the Lord's hedge of protection forms around you like a nest around a bird, or a cocoon around a butterfly larva.

I realise that some people laugh at the idea of God's hedge of protection, but the devil doesn't. He knows it's real. Just take a moment to study this complaint Satan made to God about Job: 'Have you not put a hedge about him and his house and all that he has, on every side? You have conferred prosperity and happiness upon him in the work of his hands, and his possessions have increased in the land' (Job 1:10 Amp).

Notice three things God does for his children: he puts a hedge around us, our homes and all that we have on every side; he confers happiness and prosperity (not one or the other) upon us in the work of our hands; he makes our possessions increase, not decrease.

So every day as you pray, 'Lead us not into temptation, but deliver us from the evil one,' declare that hedge of protection around yourself, your friends and loved ones, your home and all that you have. Ask God to confer happiness and prosperity on the work of your hands and to make your possessions — both spiritual and material — increase in the land. Hallelujah!

Clothe yourself in the armour of light — the Lord Jesus Christ — and pray God's encircling hedge of protection around all you hold dear. And having done all, stand . . . . Stand in the victory Jesus Christ has won for you.

Review questions

1. If the following statements are true, write 'T' in the blank; if false, write 'F'.

a. _____ Believers can enter into temptation by their own carelessness and disobedience

b. _____ The armour Paul talks about in Ephesians 6 is actually the armour of light, Jesus Christ

c. _____ If we do not put on the whole armour of God, we will
not stand against the devil

2. Why is our war with Satan called a *good* fight?

3. What are the three reasons — or 'becauses' — in Psalm 91:9, 14
that allow you to claim God's protection?

a. _____

b. _____

c. _____

Prayer outline

1. Put on the whole armour of God

a. Belt of truth

b. Breastplate of righteousness

c. Feet shod with the readiness of the gospel of peace

d. Shield of faith

e. Helmet of salvation

f. Sword of the Spirit which is the word of God

g. Praying always in the Spirit

2. Build a hedge of protection

a. Three 'becauses'
   ☐ Because we have made the Lord our dwelling
   ☐ Because we have set our love upon him
   ☐ Because we acknowledge his name

b. Declare: 'He is my refuge and my fortress, my God, in whom
   I trust'

Part Seven

Praise

'Yours is the kingdom and the power and the glory for ever'

17

Obeying God's most dynamic commandment

As we noted previously, the Lord's Prayer opens and closes with praise.

Praise is the Word's most dynamic commandment. Why do I make that claim? Because regular worship and praise reconstitute God's people — restore us to the spiritual state that God intended — and give believers the dynamic — the supernatural energy and force — so vital to victory, wholeness and harmony. Therefore, we need to learn how to let our hearts go out to God in praise and thanksgiving, magnifying and exalting his perfections and mighty deeds and thanking him for all his benefits.

The Bible states that the unrighteous refuse to offer praise to God (Romans 1:21; Revelation 16:9), but God's people always have been and always will be people of praise. It isn't surprising that the Word of God reveals many ways to express our love, gratitude and worship to the Lord. A survey of the Scriptures shows that we are to praise God with our mouths, through our bodily movements and through the playing and singing of music.

Three Hebrew words in the Old Testament demonstrate how believers are to use their mouths in praising God.

Hallal means 'to be vigorously excited; to laud, boast, rave, to celebrate'. This type of praise is done with a loud voice. *Barak* is 'to bless, to declare God the origin of power for success, prosperity and fertility; to be still'. This praise may be quiet and hushed, while another Hebrew word for praise, *shabach*, means 'to commend, address in a loud tone, to shout'. As we set our hearts to worship God acceptably, the Holy Spirit will teach us how and when to use our mouths in offering praise to God.

Bodily movement is also associated with praise, as we see in two Old Testament words for praise. *Todah* means 'to extend the hands in thanksgiving'. *Yadah* is 'to worship with extended hands — to throw out the hands, enjoying God'.

It is time God's people realised that raising the hands in worship is not a new charismatic fad; rather, it is a scriptural principle. For instance, the psalmist commanded, 'Lift up your hands in the sanctuary and praise the Lord' (Psalm 134:2). Four times Psalm 107 (KJV) urges longingly: 'Oh that men would praise [yadah] the Lord for his goodness, and for his wonderful works to the children of men!'

So as you worship God, obey the leading of his Holy Spirit. Don't be afraid to stand, kneel, bow, dance, clap your hands or lift them to the Lord. Each of these forms of praise is perfectly scriptural when done decently and in order.

We are to use not only our mouths and our bodies in worship; we are also to employ music in praise. *Zamar* means 'to pluck the strings of an instrument, to praise with song', and *tehillah* is the word for singing in the Spirit or the singing of hallals or psalms. We can worship God through singing and playing songs of praise.

We must not be afraid to yield to the leading of the Holy Spirit and to let him teach us how to use our mouths, our bodily movements and our music to worship the Lord.

After we have brought our petitions to God our Father, we should return to praise. The words, 'Yours is the kingdom and the power and the glory for ever,' are idle words to most people. Many believers don't realise that God has lovingly invited us to become participants in his kingdom, his power and his glory.

The kingdom

'The kingdom is the Lord's,' declared the psalmist, and Jesus said, 'Yours is the kingdom' (Psalm 22:28 KJV; Matthew 6:13 margin). But Jesus also said, 'Do not be afraid, little flock, for your Father has been pleased to give you the kingdom' (Luke 12:32).

Paul also teaches that we are partakers in God's kingdom: 'Giving thanks to the Father . . . . For he has rescued us from the dominion of darkness and brought us into the kingdom of the Son he loves' (Colossians 1:12-13). To Timothy Paul declared: 'The Lord will rescue me from every evil attack and will bring me safely to his heavenly kingdom. To him be glory for ever and ever' (2 Timothy 4:18).

Therefore, as you pray, 'For yours is the kingdom,' praise God your Father who delivered you from the power of darkness and brought you into his kingdom of love and light. Make the faith declaration: 'The Lord will deliver me from every evil work and preserve me to his heavenly kingdom.' Give God praise because he has invited you to be a participant in his kingdom.

The power

David wrote, 'In your hands are strength and power' (1 Chronicles 29:12), and he declared, 'Be exalted, O Lord, in your strength; we will sing and praise your might' (Psalm 21:13). God made the earth by his power (Jeremiah 10:12) and will rule by his power for ever (Psalm 66:7).

Yet God our Father has made us participants in his power. He gives strength and power to his people (Psalm 68:35) and gives us power to produce wealth (Deuteronomy 8:17-18). He gives power to the weak (Isaiah 40:29) and shields us by his power (1 Peter 1:5). God our Father, who raised up Jesus, will raise us up by his mighty power (1 Corinthians 6:14).

Jesus declared, 'I have given you authority to trample on snakes and scorpions and to overcome all the power of the enemy; nothing will harm you' (Luke 10:19). Just before his ascension, the Lord instructed the disciples: 'I am going to send you what my Father has promised; but stay in the city until you have been clothed with power from on high' (Luke 24:49). In Acts 1:8 we read again the words of Jesus promising the power of the Holy Spirit: 'You will receive power when the Holy Spirit comes on you; and you will be my witnesses in Jerusalem, and in all Judea and Samaria, and to the ends of the earth.'

Paul instructs us to 'be strong in the Lord and in his mighty power' (Ephesians 6:10). And in 1 Corinthians 4:20 he affirms: 'The kingdom of God is not a matter of talk but of power.'

Give praise to God your Father because he has invited you to be a participant in his power and has made his power available to you.

The glory

'Who is this King of glory?' asked the psalmist. 'The Lord strong and mighty, the Lord mighty in battle' (Psalm 24:8). 'Glory and honour are in his presence' (1 Chronicles 16:27 KJV). God himself declares: 'I am the Lord; that is my name! I will not give my glory to another or my praise to idols' (Isaiah 42:8).

What is God's glory? It is the manifested perfection of his character, especially his righteousness. We know all people fall short of God's glory (Romans 3:23), yet he has invited believers to be participants in his glory. Jesus made this possible, as we see in Hebrews 2:9-10. Jesus, in suffering for the sins of humankind, brought many sons to glory.

Paul assured believers that if we suffer with Jesus, we will also be glorified together (Romans 8:17). Suffering was of little consequence to Paul, for he knew that the present sufferings cannot be compared with the glory which will eventually be revealed in us (Romans 8:18).

As we behold the glory of the Lord — the character and ways of God exhibited through Christ — we are slowly changed into his image by the Spirit of God (2 Corinthians 3:18), and the character and ways of the Father and Son are formed within us. Brought into Christ's likeness, we will enter eternal blessedness, for God our Father has called us to his eternal glory (1 Peter 5:10).

Is it any wonder that Paul charged believers to 'live lives worthy of God, who calls you into his kingdom and glory' (1 Thessalonians 2:11-12)? Give praise to God because he has invited you to be a participant in his glory.

David urges believers to witness to others of God's kingdom, power and glory: 'All you have made will praise you, O Lord; your saints will extol you. They will tell of the glory of your kingdom and speak of your might, so that all men may know of your mighty acts and the glorious splendour of your kingdom. Your kingdom is an everlasting kingdom, and your dominion endures through all generations' (Psalm 145:10-13).

We praise you, Father, for yours is the kingdom and the power and the glory for ever, yet you have invited us to become participants. May we never enter or leave your presence without humbly bowing before you and offering a sacrifice of praise.

May we proclaim with David: 'Praise be to you, O Lord, God of our father Israel, from everlasting to everlasting. Yours, O Lord, is the greatness and the power and the glory and the majesty and the splendour, for everything in heaven and earth is yours. Yours, O Lord, is the kingdom; you are exalted as head over all. Wealth and honour come from you; you are the ruler of all things. In your hands are strength and power to exalt and give strength to all. Now, our

God, we give you thanks, and praise your glorious name' (1 Chronicles 29:10-13).

Review questions

1. _____ is the Word's most dynamic commandment

2. Hebrews 13:15 states: 'Through Jesus . . . let us continually offer to God a sacrifice of _____ — the fruit of lips that confess his name'

3. The Lord's Prayer opens and closes with _____
   _____

4. God has made provision for us to share in his kingdom, power and glory. That provision is _____
   _____

5. Now that you know how and what to pray, will you ask the Holy Spirit to transform you heart into a house of prayer? If so, why not put that desire into words in the space provided below?

   _____
   _____
   _____

Prayer outline

1. The kingdom
a. Praise the Lord because he has transferred you from the kingdom of darkness to the kingdom of love and light
b. Make the faith declaration: 'The Lord will preserve me from every evil work, and preserve me to his heavenly kingdom'
c. Praise God because he has invited you to be a participant in his kingdom

2. The power
a. Praise the Lord because he has invited you to be a participant in his power
b. Meditate on the power of God your Father. Measure your problems against his mighty, miraculous works and his great love for you

c. Make this faith declaration: 'I am strong in the Lord and in the power of his might. I have been endued with power from on high. Greater is he who is in me than he who is in the world. My Father gives me strength and power to obtain wealth. He gives power to the weak. As my day so shall my strength be. He keeps me by his power. He has given me power to tread upon serpents and scorpions, and over all the power of the enemy. Nothing will hurt me'

3. The glory

a. Behold the glory of the Lord — the character and ways of God exhibited through Christ. Ask the Holy Spirit to change you into the same image by forming Christ within you. Ask that you be transformed by the renewing of your mind

b. Ask the Lord to help you walk worthy of him and to help you serve him as he deserves to be served

c. Praise him and give him glory

Part Eight

Prerequisites, patterns, participation

18

Putting first things first

The years 1972 to 1978 were a struggle for Melva and me, as we frantically juggled unbalanced priorities and impossible schedules.

As if the thousand young people in our youth group at Beverly Hills Baptist Church were not enough to keep us busy, Melva drove about forty miles each way to work on her master's degree at North Texas State University in Denton, while I drove almost forty miles to Southwestern Baptist Theological Seminary in Forth Worth to complete my master's.

It was during those years that our three children were born in rapid succession. Our friends probably referred to my wife as 'Melva the saint'. She was amazing. But I wasn't measuring up to the man of God that I wanted to be.

What troubled me? The anointed presence of God seemed to be receding in my life. Why? Because I wasn't rising early day by day, worshipping my Father, praying and receiving from him what I needed.

I wasn't beginning each day by entering God's presence with thanksgiving and his courts with praise. I was carelessly neglecting God's exceedingly great and precious promises by which we are partakers of the divine nature (see 2 Peter 1:4). I wasn't always allowing him to be my righteousness, sanctifier, peace, healer, provider, banner, shepherd and the over-flowing present one within me. Therefore, I often took his names in vain.

Because I didn't set the rudder of my life (my tongue) upon God's priorities for my life by daily declaring,

'Your kingdom come, your will be done in me, my
family, my church and my nation,' my priorities
seemed to be upside down much of the time. Money
was tight, so we barely scraped by every month. We
tithed and gave offerings, but because I wasn't
specifically, tenaciously praying every day, 'Give us
today our daily bread,' we weren't prospering in many
areas.

Furthermore, because of my faults and failures, I
also had a problem from time to time with feeling
'accepted in the Beloved' (Ephesians 1:6 RAV). I
continually asked God to forgive me for things of
which I had repented long before, forgetting that I was
purged from my old sins (2 Peter 1:9). I sometimes had
the notion that I was on probation with God and that
someday, if I became good enough, he would accept
me.

For years I did 'Protestant Penance'. In the Roman
Catholic Church you do penance by repeating a
prescribed act a certain number of times to show
sorrow for sin and to get yourself to the place where
you feel forgiven. But in protestant churches, we don't
do that. (You see, we're more 'spiritual'.) Instead,
when we do something wrong, we spend two weeks,
or two decades, kicking ourselves. Am I right? That's
'Protestant Penance'. But actually God freely forgave
us the moment we confessed our failure to him.

I didn't rise every morning and say: 'I confess every
known sin to you, Lord, even the ones I don't know
I've committed. I accept that you have forgiven me,
and I also set my will to forgive those who sin against
me.' Therefore, it took a long time for the truth to
dawn on me: by begging over and over for God to
forgive a particular sin or failure, I was remembering
what God had forgotten.

I fought battles with fear and depression, but for
most of the time I lost. How could I expect to win
against a wily, well-armed foe when I wore no armour

and didn't know how to wield effectively the sword of the Spirit or skilfully employ the shield of faith to ward off his ruthless attacks?

How could I fight the good fight of faith when I didn't pray in my prayer language daily and live in an attitude of prayer?

Praise didn't continually flow out of my spirit to God. I didn't know that I could put on the garment of praise *(tehillah)* instead of the spirit of heaviness by singing songs of praise to God (Isaiah 61:3).

And the truth hadn't yet registered in my spirit that God my Father has made me a participant in his kingdom, power and glory.

But since 1978, when the Holy Spirit revealed to me that the Lord's Prayer is a prayer outline, I have entered into the presence of Jesus every day. And what have I received in return?

Promises

Each day of my life I thank God that, because of the blood of Jesus, I can call him Father. I praise his glorious names, appropriate his mighty promises and seek to sanctify his name through my manner of living.

Priorities

Although I am busier now than ever before, I enjoy peace inside me, in my home and in my church. Why? Because I pray daily over myself, my family, my church and my nation, declaring that God's priorities in those areas be set in order. I boldly declare that God's righteousness, joy and peace shall come and that his will shall be done.

Provision

No longer am I the anxiety-ridden victim of frustrating circumstances. Instead, I am learning to experience the abundant provision of *Jehovah-jireh,* the one who sees our needs ahead of time and makes provision for them, because I don't take God's blessings for granted.

Every day in prayer, I set my will to make God's kingdom my priority. Then I pray through on my needs, claiming and receiving God's promised provision, and each day he gives me my daily bread. You, too, can experience more and more freedom from frustration by setting your priorities straight.

If daily bread is a constant struggle for you, don't be anxious and fret about it. God gave me a personal promise that you, too, can claim: 'The day you answer the call to pray, I will begin to meet your needs.'

People

If you are plagued by guilt or problems with people, remember, you must forgive. That doesn't just happen automatically. Every day we need to forgive our debtors before we can receive God's washing and cleansing, and then set our wills to forgive those who may wrong us that day. As we learn to forgive and release our offenders and offences to God, we become candidates for the supernatural.

Power

If you want to stop letting the devil push you around, if you want to leave him sitting in the dust for a change, you must learn to put on the whole armour of God each day and to pray a hedge of protection around yourself, your loved ones and all you have. Learn to overcome Satan in the place of prayer by the blood of the Lamb and by the word of your testimony because, if you don't, *you* will be overcome.

These are some of the benefits that have come to me since I learned to give priority to prayer in my daily life. These benefits can be yours as well. The Word of God makes it unmistakably plain. If we are to take our places as participants in God's kingdom, power and glory, we must answer the call to pray.

Think about this: if Jesus needed to pray every day,

how much more must we!

In order to document the importance of prayer in the life of our Lord, I want you to stop for just a moment and meditate with me on one day in his life. Mark, in the first chapter of his gospel, records such a day.

After walking along the shore of the Sea of Galilee and calling Peter, Andrew, James and John to follow him and become fishers of men, Jesus went to the synagogue at Capernaum. There he taught the people, concluding his message by casting an unclean spirit out of a man who had disrupted the service.

Then he went to the home of Peter and Andrew and healed Simon Peter's mother-in-law of a fever. That evening when the sun set, the whole city gathered at the door of Peter's home. They had brought to Jesus everyone who was sick or possessed with demons, and he healed them.

Can you imagine how exhausted Jesus must have been when he finally hit the pillow late that night and drifted off to sleep? But look at the next verse, Mark 1:35: 'Very early in the morning, while it was still dark, Jesus got up, left the house and went off to a solitary place, where he prayed.'

That pattern continued throughout Christ's ministry. Indeed, at the place of prayer Jesus found the power and guidance he needed to fulfil his Father's will each day. He was the Son of God, yet he prayed. Jesus was the busiest, most important man who ever walked the face of this earth, yet prayer was the primary focus of his life.

Isn't it time that you made an agreement with the Lord to meet him every day at the place of prayer?

If you choose an early morning hour, set your clock. When the alarm goes off, don't turn it off, roll over and mumble all the reasons why you need more rest. If you do that, within a few days you won't even hear the alarm. Instead, when it's time to pray, roll out of bed and get dressed. If drinking your morning coffee or having breakfast before you pray will help you wake up and concentrate on what you're doing, then those extra minutes in the kitchen will be well spent.

To develop an effective prayer life, you must overcome these three enemies of prayer: interruptions, drowsiness and wandering thoughts. Let's learn right now how to attack and defeat these enemies.

Interruptions

The telephone and the doorbell can become dire enemies of the believer who seeks to make a discipline of prayer. That is why many busy people choose to pray early in the morning before these distractions begin.

The psalmist David had neither a telephone nor a doorbell, but he did have at least eight wives, ten concubines, twenty-two kids and a kingdom to run. It isn't surprising, then, that one of David's prayer times was early in the morning. David said: 'O Lord, in the morning you hear my voice; in the morning I lay my requests before you and wait in expectation' (Psalm 5:3).

On the other hand, Susannah Wesley, the mother of nineteen children (two of whom were John and Charles who founded the Methodist movement), chose from one to two o'clock each day for her time with the Lord. Every day at one o'clock in the afternoon, Susannah Wesley closed her bedroom door, knelt beside her bed, spread her open Bible before her and talked with God.

Think of it! There were no supermarkets, primary schools, department stores, fast food restaurants, washing-machines and tumble-dryers or modern-day kitchen appliances in Susannah's time. This woman, who was also a preacher's wife, had to make the family's clothes and wash them by hand, clean up after, cook for and home-school all those children, yet she made time every day for an hour with God. How would you like to try to explain to Susannah Wesley why you can't find time to pray?

You may be saying, 'Larry, an early morning prayer time simply won't work for me.'

I understand. Many people, ministers included, don't get to bed before midnight. I'm not trying to induce you to choose an early morning hour to pray, even though that might work best for me. There's nothing 'holy' about four in the morning. What is important is that you choose the time best for you and begin praying an hour every day.

Learn to flow with the Holy Spirit. For instance, your clock may be set for five-thirty in the morning, but the Holy Spirit of God may awaken you at three-thirty and say, 'It's time to pray.' Or your usual prayer time might be eight in the evening. If at six-thirty that evening you sense the Spirit of God stirring your spirit and calling you to prayer, obey his prompting. Don't be bound to a clock; instead, be obedient to the Spirit.

You see, prayer isn't just an hour a day. An hour a day is important only if it develops in us an attitude of prayer for the whole day. Jesus moved and ministered in a spirit of prayer because prayer occupied a much greater place in his life and ministry than just one solitary hour before dawn.

That's what must happen in our lives if we are to become victorious warriors instead of weary worshippers. Paul summed it up for us when he said, 'In him we live and move and have our being' (Acts 17:28). That's it, my friend. That's the secret. God help us not to settle for anything less.

Whether you choose morning, midday or evening as your prayer time, it is important that you have a set *time* and *place* to pray.

Jesus, in teaching his disciples to pray, instructed: 'When you pray, go into your room, close the door and pray to your Father, who is unseen' (Matthew 6:6).

That means that you need to choose a quiet, private place to pray and meet God every day. It doesn't have to be a fancy place; just a chair beside which you can kneel will do. But having a set time and place to pray will help defeat those interruptions.

Drowsiness

How can believers defeat the enemy of drowsiness when they pray? Some of John Wesley's early Methodist leaders who were determined to overcome this problem actually soaked towels in cold water, wrapped them around their heads and went right on praying! That's not the method I would choose, but I certainly admire their tenacity.

If you find yourself dropping off to sleep every time you kneel, cradling your head on your arm and closing your eyes to pray, why not try sitting or standing? Or why not try *walking* as you pray? Move a chair or table out of the way and walk back and forth across a room, or pace up and down a hall. You will quickly grow accustomed to the 'path'. Then you will be able to concentrate solely on prayer and defeat the enemy of drowsiness.

Wandering thoughts

If your thoughts wander and you have difficulty concentrating as you pray, defeat that enemy by praying aloud instead of silently. Putting your thoughts into words and praying them aloud helps you focus your mind on what you're doing. Perhaps that is one of the reasons why Jesus commanded: 'When you pray, *say:* Our Father in heaven' (Luke 11:2 RAV).

Once you learn to defeat interruptions, drowsiness and wandering thoughts, within just a short time the *desire* to pray will have matured into the *discipline* to pray. And as you discipline yourself to pray, that discipline will be transformed into holy *delight*.

Don't worry if some days as you pray you shed no

tears and feel no emotion. Those times when you *feel* the least like praying may be the times you most *need* to pray. Besides, God is moved not so much by your tears and your emotions as he is moved by his Word and by your obedience and tenacity.

Always be sensitive to the Holy Spirit and pray over each request in the manner he directs, for God has sent his Spirit to come to your aid in prayer and plead on your behalf with groanings too deep for words (Romans 8:26). Learn to be sensitive by using your prayer language, praying in the Spirit and listening for the Holy Spirit's promptings.

At times the Spirit will lead you to take verses of Scripture and turn them into petitions or bold declarations of your faith. At other times, you will find yourself weeping and travailing over an urgent need. Sometimes you will break into worshipful singing or laughter as God's peace and joy flood your heart.

Don't try to make any two prayer times identical. Follow the omniscient Holy Spirit's quiet nudges and forceful impressions, for his choices and leadings are never wrong. So be sensitive. Be flexible. Be obedient. Don't grieve the gentle Holy Spirit by demanding your own way.

Pastor B.J. Willhite, our minister of prayer at Church on the Rock who has risen to commune with God early every morning for over thirty years, explains prayer like this: 'Some days you're digging holes. Some days you're planting poles. Some days you're stringing wire. And then one day the circuit is completed, and you make contact!'

God your Father makes this promise: 'When you answer the call to pray, I will begin to meet all your needs.' How about it? Are you ready to make an appointment with God each day to seek his face in prayer? Just name the time and place. He won't be late.

19

Patterns to follow

In Waco, Texas, they did a survey and found there were more Baptists in Waco than people! That's a true story. Most Baptists in Texas — and many others — have probably heard of W.A. Criswell, a patriarch in the Southern Baptist Convention. How I appreciate and love that dear man.

After I had pastored for several years at Church on the Rock, Criswell called and requested that my elders and I come to his office in downtown Dallas. We were surprised and delighted by his invitation to visit First Baptist Church, where he pastors.

We 'small-talked' with this gracious, gentle servant of God for about thirty seconds. Then Criswell turned to me and said, 'I want to ask you a question. Why aren't you a Baptist?'

I was born, raised and educated a Southern Baptist, so I was ready for the greatest rebuke of my life.

Perhaps sensing my apprehension, he phrased the question another way. 'If it were not for the Baptists, son, you couldn't read or write. Why aren't you a Baptist?'

'Dr Criswell,' I began hesitantly, trying to figure out what he was driving at, 'have you got a moment?'

'Yes,' he replied graciously. So I shared my testimony — how Jesus had saved me in the midst of a nervous breakdown in a mental ward, healed me and called me to preach. I told Criswell about reading the red and praying for the power as a student at Dallas Baptist College and how I found myself speaking a language I had never learned after praying, 'Lord, if there's power in this gospel, give it to me!'

I continued sharing with this beloved pastor, telling him of my call to pray and how that call had haunted me until I answered it. I described how I obeyed God and began a church in Rockwall, dedicated to the principle of rising early in the morning, praying and then obeying God's voice.

Not knowing exactly how much Criswell wanted to hear, I hesitated. As I did, he leaned forward and, with tears rolling down his lined cheeks, signalled me to stop. 'That's enough,' he said, not quibbling over our doctrinal differences. Taking my hand in his, he said simply, 'You've done it the Bible way.' Then we wept together for a few moments.

'Dr Criswell,' I asked as I wiped my tears, 'what is *your* secret? You've spent forty successful years in the same church.'

I shouldn't have been surprised at his answer. 'I get up every day and spend the first five hours with God. I spend the first hour in prayer; the next two hours in study; the next hour in meditation; then, in the final hour, I get to thinking about what I ought to do for the rest of the day.'

After the appointment as I walked out of the door, Criswell asked, 'Do you know this man Cho? I've read all his books and heard his tapes, and I'm so intrigued by him.'

I told Criswell that I had met Paul Yonggi Cho and, in fact, was scheduled to preach the very next week in his church in Korea. I promised to tell Cho that Criswell wished to meet him.

That next week I sat beside Cho at a banqueting table. Out of the clear blue he turned to me and asked, 'Do you know this man Criswell? I've read all his books and listened to his tapes.'

Talk about 'holy chemistry'! Then I said, 'Dr Cho, I spoke with Dr Criswell last week, and he said the very same thing about you.'

As soon as I got back to Dallas, I called Criswell and enquired, 'What would you say if I said that Dr Cho would be willing to preach on a Sunday night at First Baptist Church in Dallas?'

Without a moment's hesitation, Criswell replied, 'I'd say, "Praise God, let's do it!"'

So that's how, in the autumn of 1984, I accompanied Cho to First Baptist Church in downtown Dallas on a Sunday night. Cho preached and after the meeting was over, the staff slipped out quickly and put us into a limousine. There I sat with my two pastoral heroes. I wanted to be as quiet as a mouse and take it all in.

Criswell opened the conversation. 'Now, Cho,' he began, 'I've admired you for many years, but I'll be quite frank with you. After reading your books and listening to your tapes, I had concluded that what you've done in Korea was strictly a sociological phenomenon — something that probably couldn't have happened at any other time in history, at any other place in the world. But then I met this lad here.' He gestured towards me.

'So, Lea,' Criswell continued, 'would you tell me how you got it from Seoul, Korea, over here to Texas?'

I cast a knowing glance at Cho, then responded: 'I pray, and I obey!'

Well, I had a glorious time at supper that night because these men of God were so honest, so transparent.

Criswell said, 'Cho, I hear that you pray.'

I should tell you that Cho had preached that morning in our eight o'clock service. Before the service began, my elders and I were in a small prayer room behind the platform interceding when Cho and his assistant, Cha, entered. When I invited them to join us in prayer, Cho replied softly, 'I've prayed. I've already spent three hours in prayer this morning for the service.'

Even so, he and Cha knelt and prayed with us a little

longer. When the service began, Cho ministered under a powerful anointing. I happen to know that Cho also spent two more hours in prayer in the afternoon before going to First Baptist Church that evening to preach for Criswell. So Criswell was correct: Cho prays!

That night at supper Criswell jokingly confided, 'Cho, when I pray for fifteen minutes, I feel as if I've worn God out and worn myself out, too. How can somebody pray as you pray? How do you do it?'

I'm so glad Cho didn't give Criswell a traditional Pentecostal answer such as, 'I speak in tongues and you don't.' Instead, Cho smiled graciously, and said, 'Every morning I get on a "running track" in the Spirit, and I circle that track. I know when I'm one-fifth of the way through, two-fifths, four-fifths and then, finally, I know when I'm done. Then, if I have time, I run it again and again, just as a runner would circle a track.'

The conversation continued for some time that evening. The next morning Cho and I played golf. At least I played golf. Cho was busy communing with the Holy Spirit. He would hit the ball, turn, get back in the cart and not even watch to see where his ball went. It was the funniest game of golf I have ever played.

Finally, I plucked up courage and asked, 'Dr Cho, what is the running track you were telling Dr Criswell about last night?'

I listened in amazement as Cho rapidly described many of the same principles I had learned about prayer from the Holy Spirit. Something leapt inside me in excited confirmation as Cho confided that his 'prayer track' is the Lord's Prayer; the 'laps' he runs around that track are the six timeless topics of the model prayer that Jesus gave his disciples.

Did those early disciples follow the prayer pattern Jesus gave them? Yes, historical literature records that they did. The early Jewish-Christian document *The*

Didache instructed early Christians to pray the Lord's Prayer three times daily. And Christ's desire for his church hasn't changed.

It is to be a house of purity, prayer, power and perfected praise. At what point are you in that divine progression, clay temple of the Most High God? At which stage will your prayer life be this time next year? Desire? Discipline? Delight? It's your choice.

If you don't begin to pray, you will not be any further along with the Lord next year than you are right now. The Spirit of God longs to teach you to walk in the yoke he has fitted for you.

Everyone wants to change, but change demands desire and discipline before it becomes delightful. There is always the agony of choice before the promise of change. Therefore, we must consciously, deliberately choose to go on with God.

If we pray the Lord's Prayer as it should be prayed, we choose to obey the major messages of Christ's life and ministry.

We sanctify the name of God in our worship and in our walk. We repent, place God's priorities before our own and become a part of his kingdom movement. We set our wills to forgive and to live in right relationship with God and others. We tenaciously pray specific prayers for our daily provision.

Clad in the whole armour of God and encircled by his hedge of protection, we resist temptation and defeat the devil and his evil powers. And we give praise to God our Father who has made us partakers in his kingdom, his power and his glory.

You have my word on it. Something supernatural happens when you take your next step with God. He walked me right out of a psychiatric ward. He led a hippy named Jerry Howell into the ministry. My dad took God's hand and walked away from a life of alcoholism and misery. If you are ready for God to do a new thing in your life, you must take your next step with him.

'Could you not tarry one hour?' Someone is asking you that question right now, and his name is not Henry. His name is Jesus.

20

For the sake of ten

Paul Yonggi Cho once lamented to me: 'Americans will give their money, sing songs, build buildings and preach, but they will not pray.' But, thank God, the Lord is changing all that. The Spirit of intercession, the praying Holy Spirit, is overcoming our flesh.

We are in the first stages of the most life-changing, nation-shaping move of God since the beginning of the world. God is bringing to birth a prayer revival — not a doctrine, not a teaching built around the charisma of men, but a spirit of intercession that is invading the lives of his people. Why? Because the word has gone out: mediation or annihilation.

Who among us is not aware of God's gathering storm of judgment? Towering thunderheads of divine wrath loom on the horizon, and prophetic rumblings of impending calamity reverberate throughout the western world.

Centuries ago, Abraham watched such clouds of calamity collect over Sodom and Gomorrah. And one day the Lord delivered a dreaded message to Abraham's doorstep — in person. From that visit and from the events that transpired, we can distil four principles that enlighten our understanding and inspire our intercession. The principles pertain to the prevailing ignorance of the wicked and to the preserving influence, the persevering intercession and the powerful impact of the righteous.

The prevailing ignorance of the unrighteous
The unrighteous are unaware that God holds inquest

on the moral condition of cities, but Genesis 18:20-21 confirms this awesome fact: 'The Lord said, "The outcry against Sodom and Gomorrah is so great and their sin so grievous that I will go down and see if what they have done is as bad as the outcry that has reached me. If not, I will know."'

Then followed Abraham's eloquent, urgent intercession on behalf of the cities: 'What if there are fifty righteous people in the city? Will you really sweep it away and not spare the place for the sake of the fifty righteous people in it?'

And the Lord said, 'If I find fifty righteous people in the city of Sodom, I will spare the whole place for their sake' (Genesis 18:24, 26).

Four more times, Abraham reverently pleaded with God for the city's welfare, each time lowering the number of righteous people required to stay God's hand, turn judgment and avert destruction. Would the Lord destroy the city if there were forty-five righteous? Forty righteous? Thirty? Twenty?

Abraham wasn't merely haggling with God, who has no pleasure in the death of the wicked (Ezekiel 33:11). Abraham knew God's long-suffering, compassionate nature; therefore, he stood before him and pleaded one last time for mercy. 'What if only ten can be found there?'

And God answered, 'For the sake of ten, I will not destroy it' (Genesis 18:32).

The ungrateful, ungodly inhabitants of Sodom would have been amazed to learn the value the Lord sets on the righteous. The entire city could have been spared for the sake of ten righteous people within its walls; indeed, only Lot, the one righteous man in Sodom, and his family were saved (Genesis 19:15-16).

And if Sodom's inhabitants could have overheard the Lord's assurance to Abraham that if fifty, forty, thirty, twenty or even ten righteous people could be found in Sodom he would not destroy the city, they would have been stunned by this staggering truth: it is not the presence of evil which brings the mercy and long-suffering of God to an end; rather, it is the absence of good.

The preserving influence of the righteous

The haughty enemies of God who undervalue and persecute those who live 'self-controlled, upright and godly lives in this present age' are also unaware of the preserving influence of the righteous (Titus 2:12).

According to Sam Shoemaker, the nineteenth-century church historian William Lecky credited John Wesley with saving England from revolution. All across the island Wesley had set up little companies of twelve. Each group had a leader, met once a week and helped hold each other up to Christian standards. [1]

Judge for yourself: Did that small remnant, which lifted the moral and spiritual level of the nation, keep England from going the way of France, where in that same century revolution toppled the government? What would have happened in France if they had had a John Wesley or a spiritual revival to preserve it from decay and destruction?

Remember: God would have spared Sodom for the sake of ten. Some say this would have been approximately one-tenth of one per cent of the city's population — just a sprinkling of salt in the midst of massive decay, a glimmer of light in gross darkness. Yet, in God's eyes, ten righteous people would have been sufficient cause to spare Sodom.

The purposeful intercession of the remnant

Abraham's intercession for Sodom was the result of divine communication: 'The Lord said, "Shall I hide from Abraham what I am about to do?"' (Genesis 18:17). The Spirit sometimes inspires people to pray by showing them things to come. God reveals his intentions to his friends, thus inviting their intercession.

[1] *Extraordinary Living for Ordinary Men*, by Samuel Shoemaker, Zondervan, Grand Rapids, Michigan, 1965

Although God invites our intercession, our prayers must be in line with God's character and his covenant with humankind. Note that when Abraham brought before God the reasons why his request should be granted, the motive behind his intercession was not small, selfish or shortsighted: 'Abraham approached him and said: "Will you sweep away the righteous with the wicked? . . . Will not the Judge of all the earth do right?"' (Genesis 18:23, 25).

God is bound by his nature and by his covenant with humankind; he can do nothing that is not inflexibly righteous. Therefore, Abraham appealed to God to preserve his name and honour before the world. He also pleaded God's perfect justice. God would not destroy the righteous with the wicked, the innocent with the guilty. Was it not better that the wicked be spared mercifully than that the righteous be destroyed unrighteously?

The powerful impact of the righteous

God has given us this unwavering assurance: 'If my people, who are called by my name, will humble themselves and pray and seek my face and turn from their wicked ways, then will I hear from heaven and will forgive their sin and will heal their land' (2 Chronicles 7:14).

But God has also given us this sobering alternative: 'I looked for a man among them who would build up the wall and stand before me in the gap on behalf of the land so that I would not have to destroy it, but I found none. So I will pour out my wrath on them and consume them with my fiery anger, bringing down on their own heads all they have done, declares the Sovereign Lord' (Ezekiel 22:30-31).

The church is sometimes prone to measure influence by numbers of people and money. But we cannot use our arithmetic to estimate the impact of the righteous; God saves by many or by few.

I'm not intimidated to declare to you that God has called me to enlist, instruct, encourage and inspire three hundred thousand believers to pray. On one scale that is a lot more than Sodom's ten, but on another scale it isn't. That is one-tenth of one per cent of the population of the USA. God will not allow a nation to destroy itself if his people will repent over the sins of that nation and seek his face. If we will pray, destruction will be averted and judgment can be turned.

My question is: Will you pledge to pray one hour a day for yourself, your loved ones, the ignorant and the unbelieving? Will you promise to intercede for God's spotted, wrinkled church? That is our only hope. Believe it.

Why not join your prayers with the petitions of thousands of prayer warriors who have already enlisted in this mighty prayer army?

God is setting a mark upon the foreheads of those who sigh and groan for all the abominations of the land (Ezekiel 9:4-6). As in Ezekiel's day, destruction will not come near any person upon whom that mark is set.

May the pledge of God himself echo in our ears and drive us to our knees: 'For the sake of ten, I will not destroy it' (Genesis 18:32).

Prayer guide

1. 'Our Father in heaven, hallowed be your name'

a. Picture Calvary and thank God you can call him Father by virtue of the blood of Jesus

b. Hallow the names of God corresponding with the five benefits in the new covenant, and make your faith declarations:

Benefit	Name	Meaning
Sin	*Jehovah-tsidkenu*	The Lord My Righteousness
	Jehovah-m'kaddesh	The Lord Who Sanctifies
Spirit	*Jehovah-shalom*	The Lord is Peace
	Jehovah-shammah	The Lord is There
Soundness	*Jehovah-rophe*	The Lord Who Heals
Success	*Jehovah-jireh*	The Lord's Provision Shall be Seen
Security	*Jehovah-nissi*	The Lord My Banner
	Jehovah-rohi	The Lord My Shepherd

2. 'Your kingdom come, your will be done'

a. Yourself

b. Your family (partner, children, other family members)

c. Your church (pastor, leadership, faithfulness of the people, harvest)

d. Nation (specific area; local and national political and spiritual leaders; a specific nation)

3. 'Give us today our daily bread'

a. Be in the will of God (prayer life, church, work habits, obedience in giving)

b. Believe that it is God's will to prosper you

c. Be specific

d. Be tenacious

4. **'Forgive us our debts, as we also have forgiven our debtors'**

a. Ask God to forgive you

b. Forgive and release others

c. Set your will to forgive those who sin against you

5. **'Lead us not into temptation, but deliver us from the evil one'**

a. Put on the whole armour of God, the Lord Jesus Christ

☐ Belt of truth

☐ Breastplate of righteousness

☐ Feet equipped with the readiness of the gospel of peace

☐ Shield of faith

☐ Helmet of salvation

☐ Sword of the Spirit which is the word *(rhema)* of God

☐ Praying always in the Spirit

b. Pray a hedge of protection. (The Lord is your refuge, your fortress, your God; in him you will trust)

☐ Because you have made the Lord your dwelling

☐ Because you have set your love upon him

☐ Because you acknowledge his name

6. **'Yours is the kingdom and the power and the glory for ever'**

a. Make your faith declarations

b. Return to praise

PRAY IN THE SPIRIT

The Work of the Holy Spirit
in the Ministry of Prayer

ARTHUR WALLIS

KINGSWAY PUBLICATIONS
EASTBOURNE

CONTENTS

To a true and devoted helpmeet—who has so often behind the scenes held up my drooping hands—with deep gratitude.

PREFACE

A MAN is no bigger than his prayer life, or as Murray M'Cheyne is reputed to have said, 'What a man is on his knees before God, that he is—and nothing more.' In that coming day when the hearts of men are revealed, a day which is now nearer than when we first believed, there will be some 'big men' who will appear very small, and some we had thought small will appear as spiritual giants. How different are spiritual values when God takes them from the balances of human judgment and weighs them on the balances of the sanctuary.

The swift and powerful movement of the Spirit recorded in the Acts was not only initiated by prayer, but fed and sustained by prayer. In a day when God has begun to pour out His Spirit upon His people, even as He promised, we should expect to see among them a new 'spirit of grace and supplication'. However powerful the initial coming upon us of the Spirit may be, if this does not find expression in a life of prayer the blessing will soon become a fading glory. A movement of God will last as long as the Spirit of prayer that inspired it.

The result of the Holy Spirit coming upon a believer should be that he is introduced to *life in the Spirit*. In this new dimension every spiritual activity is energized and controlled by the Spirit of God. Living in the Spirit includes praying in the Spirit. Any claim to a baptism or filling with the Spirit which leaves our prayer life unaffected must be at best a superficial work, for the Holy Spirit of promise is an indwelling intercessor. He comes to each heart open to Him with a deep longing to find there another channel through which to effect this powerful ministry.

This is not intended to be a general book on prayer. It concentrates on the ministry of the Holy Spirit in relation to prayer. It investigates the deeper meaning of that apostolic injunction, 'Pray in the Spirit.' It analyses our many weaknesses in prayer and the spiritual and practical difficulties we encounter, and shows how the Holy Spirit helps us in our weakness and makes up for all our deficiency. It encourages us to yield ourselves to Him and allow Him to pray through us. We need have no fear that this will make us unbalanced or extreme. The more fully we submit to the Holy Spirit the more Christ-centred we become, and the more truly God is glorified in us.

What tremendous possibilities there are when we have plunged into that river of the Spirit which is full of water. Here are 'waters to swim in'. Prayer in the Spirit suggests new avenues waiting to be explored, new resources to be tapped, new power to be released. And when we have begun to enter into all that is opened up in these pages, we shall realize, reader and author alike, how much there is of 'the deep things of God' still waiting to be discovered.

*There the Lord in majesty will be for us a place
of broad rivers and streams, where no galley
with oars can go,* [no room here for human
energy,] *nor stately ship can pass.* [no place for
fleshly show or ostentation] (Isa. 33 : 21).

May God use this book to help us to launch out.

ARTHUR WALLIS

BUT HOW?

SHE was young, she was of lowly birth and, what made it even more perplexing, she was unmarried. Could she be hearing aright? Chosen by heaven to be the mother of the long-awaited Messiah? Doubt, fear, perplexity struggled within her. Turning to the angel Mary asked a simple, practical question, 'How can this be?' Just as simple was Gabriel's answer, 'The Holy Spirit will come upon you.' 'How?' is a question that the believer is for ever asking, even if only deep in the heart. To our every 'How?' heaven gives the same answer as Gabriel gave to Mary—'The Holy Spirit.'

Is it a question of how we may know the will of God in our lives? 'All who are led by the Spirit of God are sons of God.' Are we concerned to know the secret of victory over sin? 'The law of the Spirit of life in Christ Jesus has set me free from the law of sin and death.' Have we difficulty in understanding the Scriptures? 'The Holy Spirit ... will teach you all things.' 'The Spirit of truth ... will guide you into all the truth.' Is it the problem of how to witness effectively for the Lord? 'You shall receive power when the Holy Spirit has come upon you; and you shall be My witnesses.'

Perhaps the fact that we have picked up a book

on the subject of prayer is an indication that we are wanting to know *how to pray* aright, how to prevail in prayer. 'The Spirit helps us in our weakness,' replies the apostle. 'The Spirit Himself intercedes for us.' The gracious ministry of the Holy Spirit is God's complete answer to all our weakness, ignorance and inability in the realm of prayer.

In the Upper Room discourse (John 14–16) our Lord gave His followers their fullest unfolding of the promised Holy Spirit. In five great declarations He revealed what the Holy Spirit was to be to them and to do for them. It is significant that in the same passage we find some five or six great prayer promises. It was through the Holy Spirit that they would find the prayer promises fulfilled. Further, the distinctive title our Lord gave to the Holy Spirit was 'The Comforter' or 'The Advocate', a title that would have suggested to the disciples a ministry of intercession. Our Lord wanted them to know that the Holy Spirit was an intercessor, and that He would accomplish this ministry in them.

The early church was without doubt a praying church, and what tremendous things they accomplished through prayer alone: prison doors were opened, fanatical opponents were struck down and converted to Christ, signs and wonders were done. But the open secret was that the early church knew the presence and power of the Holy Spirit, not theoretically but experientially. Those first believers were mighty in prayer because they were mighty in the Spirit.

We have only to scan the pages of The Acts to discover that the early church met and overcame every great crisis in their early history with the weapon of 'all prayer'. Read, in Acts 4, that account of the first recorded prayer meeting of the young Jerusalem Church for an example of anointed praying. What boldness! What power! What authority! Little wonder the place where they were assembled was shaken and they were all filled anew with the Holy Spirit. So the enduement of the Spirit was both the cause and the consequence of their effectual praying. They prayed because they were filled, and they were filled because they prayed. A victorious circle!

In a day when an increasing number of God's children are recognizing the necessity of a vital encounter with the Holy Spirit, let us always keep before us this prayer aspect of the Spirit-filled life. In Ezekiel's vision (chapter 47) the waters that flowed out of the sanctuary were firstly 'ankle-deep', which suggests walking in the Spirit; and then 'knee-deep', which suggests praying in the Spirit. There is a serious deficiency in the out-working of the Spirit-filled life if it does not issue in a revitalizing experience in the realm of prayer.

When the Lord met with me in this way some years ago, He touched many realms of my spiritual life, but none more deeply and permanently than my prayer life, though I realize there is still a long way to go. If someone should ask, 'How do you know what spirit came upon you?' I would reply, 'By the fruit produced. I soon discovered that the Spirit that had come upon me was an interceding Spirit.'

Praying in the Spirit summarizes in a phrase the New Testament norm for the believer's prayer life. This in turn assumes a definite reception of the Spirit in fullness and power. Our blessed Lord knew this experience, and so did those apostles and believers of the early churches. Everywhere the New Testament writers take it for granted (as they do baptism in water) that their readers have known this rich experience of the Holy Spirit coming upon them (Titus 3 : 5, 6). Today, alas, it cannot be so readily assumed. But without such an experience what follows in this book will be largely theoretical and unreal.

I would invite the reader who is unconvinced of the necessity of such a definite experience, but who is open to the testimony of God's word, to carry out a simple investigation. With the help of a concordance examine all the references in the New Testament to being filled with the Spirit, and see whether there is not overwhelming evidence that this is a distinct and definite encounter with the Holy Spirit, and that those who experienced it in New Testament times knew when and how the Holy Spirit had come. Paul could never have asked the Galatians, 'Did you receive the Spirit by works of the law, or by hearing with faith?' if their experience of receiving the Spirit had not been at least as clearly defined as their experience of receiving Christ.

Let others who, though convinced of the scripturalness and importance of it, are still strangers to the experience, come with purity of heart, cleanness of hands, and simplicity of faith to the risen Lord. He is still calling out, 'If any man thirst let him come to Me and drink.' So come and drink, for the promise is to you.

2

THE TWO ADVOCATES

THERE is only one place in the Bible where we are given any insight into the work of the Holy Spirit as intercessor, and that is Romans 8 : 26, 27 :

Likewise the Spirit helps us in our weakness; for we do not know how to pray as we ought, but the Spirit Himself intercedes for us with sighs too deep for words. And He who searches the hearts of men knows what is the mind of the Spirit, because the Spirit intercedes for the saints according to the will of God.

A few verses farther on we are introduced to Another who also intercedes for us (verse 34) :

Christ Jesus, who died, yes, who was raised from the dead, who is at the right hand of God, who indeed intercedes for us.

So the Holy Spirit intercedes for us, and Christ Jesus intercedes for us. It is important to see that these two intercessions, though related, are quite distinct. There is no duplication in the various activities of the persons of the Godhead. It is certain that we shall never understand how the Holy Spirit intercedes for us unless we distinguish His ministry as intercessor from that of our great High Priest.

When Jesus introduced to His disciples the distinct promise of the Holy Spirit, He said: 'I will pray the Father, and He will give you another Counsellor, to be with you for ever' (John 14 : 16). As for this word 'counsellor', otherwise rendered 'comforter' or 'advocate', there is probably no word in English that fully conveys the original and covers the same breadth of meaning, hence the tendency to anglicize the Greek word by rendering it as 'Paraclete'. Its primitive meaning is 'one called to the side of' another to help him.[1] 'It was used in a court of justice to denote a legal assistant, counsel for the defence, an advocate.'[2] Certainly this connection with the law courts is not now conveyed by 'comforter' (A.V. and R.V.) though that lovely word does cover another aspect of the Holy Spirit's ministry.

When Jesus told the disciples that He would ask the Father to send them 'another Paraclete', He used a word signifying 'another of the same kind.'[3] It was as though He was saying, 'I alone have been your Paraclete up to the present, but the Father will send you another like Me, even the Holy Spirit, whose abiding presence you shall have to the end of the age.' Though Christ was no longer to be with them personally, He would not cease to be their Paraclete, their heavenly barrister, to represent them in the court of heaven. It is the same John who recorded these words who tells us in his first epistle, 'If any one does sin, we have a Paraclete [same word] with the Father, Jesus

Christ the righteous' (2 : 1). So the disciples were not really losing their Paraclete, except in bodily presence; they were gaining another like Him. We now have two heavenly Advocates, both of whom are said to intercede for us.

Suppose a man decides to settle some dispute by litigation. His case may be good, but he knows nothing of court procedure, or how to carry his case by debate and argument. He is incapable of presenting the facts so as to convince the judge, so he calls to his aid a barrister who accepts the man as his client, and conducts the case on his behalf. So do these two divine Advocates, though in different ways.

Notice that there is a difference in the location of these two intercessors. Christ intercedes 'at the right hand of God' (Rom. 8 : 34). He is our 'advocate with the Father' (1 John 2 : 1). The Holy Spirit on the other hand intercedes in the hearts of men (Rom. 8 : 27). Christ's intercession is apart from us, the Holy Spirit's is within us. We cannot help, nor can we hinder the intercession of Christ Jesus, our great High Priest. Whether we follow hard after Him or follow afar off; whether we are hot or cold, spiritual or carnal, His intercession continues unceasingly. 'I am praying . . . for those whom Thou hast given Me' (John 17 : 9). Nothing we do can touch that intercession, for it proceeds on the ground of what He has done for us. His death and resurrection, not what we have done or are doing for Him. It is therefore not affected by our ups and downs. What an encouragement to know that He has inscribed our names on His 'prayer list' for all time.

When we turn to the intercession of the Spirit the position is very different. It is a solemn fact that we may facilitate or frustrate the Spirit's intercession in us, by our co-operation or the lack of it. Though Christ does not require us for His intercession, the Holy Spirit most assuredly does for His. Here we can no longer be spectators, we must be participators. Christ prays for us in the sense that He makes us the *object* of His praying. The Holy Spirit prays for us in the sense that He makes us the *vehicle* of His praying. He prays on our behalf by enabling us to pray, helping us in our weakness, who do not know how to pray as we ought.

The life truly possessed by the Holy Spirit is the indispensable channel of the Spirit's intercession. There appears to be no suggestion in Scripture that the Holy Spirit ever intercedes except through the believer. This is emphasized in Romans 8 : 15, 16 in the R.S.V. by an interesting variation in punctuation: 'When we cry "Abba! Father!" it is the Spirit Himself bearing witness with our spirit that we are children of God.' Notice what Paul is saying, 'When we cry . . . it is the Spirit.' We do the crying, but the Holy Spirit does the inspiring of the cry. Compare this with the day of Pentecost when 'they began to speak . . . as the Spirit gave them utterance' (Acts 2 : 4). Notice that Romans 8 : 16 does *not* say that the Spirit bears witness *to* our spirit, but *with* our spirit. The divine Spirit and the human spirit become joint witnesses by the cry that comes from within us.

All this is borne out by other aspects of the Spirit's ministry. He is a witnessing Spirit, but this witnessing He effects through the believer (John 15:26, 27; Acts 5:32). He is a convicting Spirit, but this is 'when He comes' 'unto you' (John 16:7, 8). He is a wooing Spirit, but not apart from the Bride (Rev. 22:17).

The Holy Spirit needs us to accomplish His intercessory ministry, and we certainly need Him to accomplish ours. What a privilege to be invited to join in this heavenly partnership. He wants to be free to think through our minds, feel through our hearts, speak through our lips, and even weep through our eyes and groan through our spirits. When a believer is thus at the disposal of the Holy Spirit, praying in the Spirit will be a reality.

[1] *Parakletos* from *para*, beside, and *kaleo*, to call.
[2] Vine's Expository Dictionary of N.T. Words.
[3] Greek *allos*.

IN THE SPIRIT

To understand rightly the expression 'Pray in the Spirit' we must first understand what Scripture means by 'in the Spirit', for it is used not only in connection with prayer. It is necessary to define our terms carefully as there has been a tendency in some quarters to assume too readily that *praying in the Spirit* and *praying with the spirit* are identical terms. This latter expression, found only in 1 Corinthians 14:15, denotes praying in tongues, as the context clearly shows. Failing to distinguish the two terms, some have concluded that praying in the Spirit is limited to praying in tongues. In fact praying in tongues is but one of three distinct kinds of praying in the Spirit mentioned in Scripture.

Examination of the above reference in Corinthians with the two references to praying 'in the Spirit' or 'in the Holy Spirit' (Eph. 6:18 and Jude 20) indicate that they are not synonymous. There is a difference in the Greek which our translators have been careful to convey by not only using different prepositions, 'with' and 'in', but by using a capital 'S' for 'in the Spirit' and a small 's' for 'with the spirit', and that is true of all the main versions.

Take the expression, 'Pray with the spirit.' If we

follow Paul's argument we shall see that 'spirit' here refers to the human spirit. He says:

> If I pray in a tongue, my spirit prays but my mind is unfruitful. What am I to do? I will pray with the [my] spirit and I will pray with the [my] mind also.

It is in the realm of the human spirit that the spiritual gift operates. In fact so closely is the human spirit identified with the spiritual gift in the minds of the New Testament writers that they seem to use the one where we would have expected the other. For example, Paul commends the Corinthians that they were 'eager for manifestations of the Spirit' (1 Cor. 14:12. 'spiritual gifts' A.V., R.V.), but the original says that they were 'eager for spirits'. Similarly, John says 'Test the spirits to see whether they are of God ... every spirit which confesses that Jesus Christ has come in the flesh is of God' (1 John 4:1, 2). What could be meant by 'every spirit which ... is of God'? It surely refers to the human spirit manifesting a spiritual gift, such as prophecy. Again, 'the seven spirits who are before His throne' (Rev. 1:14) must mean seven manifestations of the one divine Spirit, as in Isaiah 11:12.

It is clear, then, that in 1 Corinthians 14 praying with the spirit is equivalent to praying with the spiritual gift. This involves the human spirit as distinct from the human mind. The emphasis here is not on the Holy Spirit, as with the expression 'in the Spirit', though of course His presence and activity are implied, for we cannot pray rightly with the spirit, or even with the mind for that matter, apart from the Holy Spirit. But it is important to see where the emphasis lies.

Let us take this comparison further. Paul says, 'I will pray with the spirit and I will pray with the mind also.' The repetition, 'I will pray . . . and I will pray . . .' proves that Paul envisages two kinds of praying, not as some have supposed, the human spirit and the human mind praying together. He means that he will pray with his new tongue (Mk. 16 : 17) and he will pray with his native tongue. But in Ephesians 6 : 18 he exhorts us 'Pray *at all times* in the Spirit.' So praying is only sometimes 'with the spirit' (i.e. in tongues) but 'at all times in the Spirit'.

Paul contrasts 'in the Spirit' with 'in the flesh' (Rom. 8 : 9). So the alternative to 'praying in the Spirit' is praying in the flesh. No wonder he says, 'Pray *at all times* in the Spirit.' But in 1 Corinthians 14 the contrast is between praying 'with the spirit' and praying 'with the mind', both of which may be 'in the Spirit' and pleasing to God. 'In the Spirit' is therefore a much broader concept than 'with the spirit.' To identify the one with the other is to imply that all the great intercessors of the Old Testament and even our blessed Lord Himself did not pray in the Spirit because, to our knowledge, they did not pray in tongues.

Now prayer is not the only activity 'in the Spirit' required of us. The New Testament speaks of living in the Spirit, walking in the Spirit, worshipping in the Spirit, joying in the Spirit, etc. All that is meant is that each activity is performed by the power and enabling of the Holy Spirit. This is in exact agreement with what we have already learned is meant by praying in the Spirit. Expressed in the most practical terms it means that the Holy Spirit inspires, guides, energizes and sustains the praying.

The contexts of the only two references to praying in the Spirit in the New Testament are instructive. The first reference concludes that great passage in Ephesians 6 on the armour of God in the believer's warfare. The other, in Jude, follows the exhortation to build ourselves up on our most holy faith. So it is in the context of battling and building that we are exhorted to 'pray in the Spirit'. These two figures in fact sum up what the Christian life is all about. We are reminded of Nehemiah and his compatriots engaged in their God-given task of restoring Jerusalem, sword in one hand and trowel in the other. Our Lord emphasized these two aspects when He spoke of the necessity of first counting the cost before committing ourselves to the path of discipleship. He used the twin parable of the man intending to build a tower and the king going out to battle against another king (Luke 14:28–32). So discipleship too is a matter of building and battling. If we are to build to a successful conclusion and to wage a victorious warfare against our implacable foe we must learn to pray in the Spirit.

4

HELPING OUR WEAKNESS

I don't seem to have any real desire for prayer. I do it more out of a sense of duty than anything else.

When I pray I feel as though God is a million miles away. I don't seem to have any real assurance that He hears me, and that I am truly talking to Him.

I pray but nothing ever seems to happen. I get so discouraged and feel, What's the use?

I suffer from wandering thoughts in prayer and cannot seem to concentrate.

SUCH remarks are commonly expressed by believers both young and old, and provide a living commentary on what the apostle says concerning 'our weakness' in prayer, and the fact that 'we do not know how to pray as we ought' (Rom. 8:26). Most of us are very ready to acknowledge the truth of this. We strive to pray more often, more fervently, more believingly. Challenging ministry on the subject stimulates us to fresh resolve. The biography of a man of prayer stirs us up. Some pressing need in our lives drives us to our knees, and for a while we pray with greater feeling and fervour, only to slide back sooner or later to the drudgery and even monotony of our old prayer life.

It may come as a word of hope to some child of God, discouraged by the hardness of the way, that the great apostle was not merely referring to weaker Christians, to those young in the faith, or to the spiritually immature when he said, 'We do not know how to pray.' He used the word 'we' and so included himself. He is making a statement which must in the very nature of the case, be universally true of every believer. We are inherently, inevitably and incorrigibly weak when it comes to prayer, and we never can be otherwise.

Paul had come to see this in his own experience, not by reasoning but by revelation. But many Christians who are ever bemoaning their inadequate prayer life have never had this revelation. That is why they strive and struggle to demonstrate to themselves and to God that they are not really so weak after all. Setting themselves to disprove divine facts, the battle is lost before it has begun. The way through is not to be found along these lines.

Of course Paul's discovery of his own weakness was not only related to prayer but to the whole business of living a life that was pleasing to God. Some account of how he arrived there is given in the very context of the verse we are now considering, the latter part of Romans 7 and the beginning of chapter 8. Elsewhere he speaks of other experiences that brought home the same great principle, as when he prayed unsuccessfully for the removal of his 'thorn in the flesh', and God said, 'My power is made perfect in weakness' (2 Cor. 12:9). When the Holy Spirit brings home to us this truth of our insufficiency, we shall bow and accept it, and prove with Paul that it is not *out of* weakness (that is, the thorn removed), but *in* weakness that God's power is made perfect. Even so in prayer, 'the Spirit helps us *in* our weakness'.

Some know 'the rest of utter weakness' and others only know the striving of utter weakness. The one is a thing of faith, the other a thing of works; the one a thing of the Spirit, the other a thing of the flesh. It is, after all, only the pride of our own hearts that causes us to rebel against this innate weakness, to strive to escape from its clutches and attain a place of strength, of independence, of self-sufficiency. It seems to cut right across our efforts to achieve self-significance. How wonderful it is when we discover, often through the discipline of repeated failure, that this weakness with which we seem to be permanently saddled is not 'the end', but a new and wonderful beginning—the gateway to heaven's resources. 'The Spirit helps us in our weakness.' The weakness is perpetual only that we might be perpetually dependent on the Holy Spirit.

The word 'help' used here is the translation of one of those fascinating compound verbs so difficult to convey adequately in the English. It is found in only one other passage, Luke 10:40, where Martha complains to the Lord about her sister leaving her to do all the work: 'Tell her then to *help* me.' Primarily the word means 'to take hold of', but it has a double prefix, meaning 'together with' and 'instead of'. This may at first seem to be a contradiction in terms, to say that the Spirit 'takes hold of [our weakness], together with, instead of'. We have in fact a marvellous truth, not merely that the Spirit intervenes in our weakness, but that He does so 'together with' us—for He requires our willing co-operation—and 'instead of' us, for He does for us what we could never do for ourselves.

In the following chapters we shall be examining some of the weaknesses we experience in prayer, and seeing how the Holy Spirit helps us in each one, as we trust Him and obey Him.

5

THAT APATHETIC SPIRIT

AN obvious reason why many of us do not pray when we should and as we should is lack of desire. A spiritual lethargy and inertia seem to settle upon us with paralysing effect. The excuse may be that we are too busy to pray; the fact is, as we well know, we always find time for what we want to do, and are only too busy for what we don't want to do and don't have to do. Apathy is perhaps the major reason why the prayer life of so many professed believers is minimal—just enough to maintain, at least in their own eyes, their Christian respectability (horrible phrase!) and clear themselves of the charge of backsliding. Lack of desire means that prayer is perfunctory and legalistic, a duty instead of a delight.

Now this state of heart may be caused by sin. If we have a controversy with our Lord, if we are rebelling against the Holy Spirit, if we have not performed our vows, or if we have allowed envy, bitterness or anger to mar our feelings towards our fellows—such things as these are enough to bring a pall of death over our times of fellowship with God. The remedy is in our own hands: 'If we confess our sins, He is faithful and just, and will forgive our sins and cleanse us from all unrighteousness.' The proof that the sin was the cause

of our barren prayer life is that when it is confessed we find ourselves out of the shadows, and
once again in the sunlight of God's presence.

But what of those who tell us that they have
confessed and dealt with all that God has shown
them, and still there is no real desire? This is a
chronic spiritual state with many, and it must be
recognized as part of our weakness in the realm
of prayer. But let us not be discouraged. God knows
all about this kind of weakness in the heart of one
who has a real longing for a vital prayer experience. The Spirit has been given to help us in our
weakness.

It is obvious that we cannot be possessed by a
spirit of fervent intercession, and at the same time
by a spirit of lethargy in prayer. The Spirit that
God has given us is an interceding Spirit. It is He
who inspired every prayer that ever reached God's
throne and brought down heaven's blessing. He is
the great Advocate who produces within us a spirit
of intercession, if we will but trust Him to do so.
'Because you are sons, God has sent the Spirit of
His Son into our hearts, crying "Abba! Father!"'
(Gal. 4:6).

Let us confess to the sin of indifference and neglect in relation to this ministry of the Holy Spirit.
Let us confess to the sin of unbelief in that we have
so often acted as though there were no Holy Spirit.
If He has not filled and possessed us, we must begin right here, and ask Him to do so now. If He
has, let us believe that as we yield ourselves afresh
to Him He takes full possession as an interceding
Spirit, to do His work in us and through us. Re-

member the lesson of Romans 8:26. 'The Spirit helps *with us* and *instead of us*.'

The verse from Galatians, quoted above, tells us that the Spirit that God sent forth into our hearts, crying "Abba! Father!" is *the Spirit of His Son*. This is the Spirit that came upon our Lord at the Jordan in the form of a dove. This is the Spirit that rested upon Him as He continued all night in prayer on the lonely mountain side. This is the same Spirit that moved Him to rise a great while before it was day and go out into a solitary place to pray. This was no ritual, no legal duty that He was performing. There was a great hunger in the heart of the Son of Man for fellowship with His God and Father. The Spirit of His Son in you will create a like hunger, if you will but give Him liberty to do so.

If before you felt as though a team of horses could scarcely drag you to the place of prayer, now you will feel as though a team of horses could scarce drag you away. What a difference it is when we come to the place of prayer as a lover to the meeting place, or when, like Hannah, we pray with the burden of prayer upon us, and pour out our soul before the Lord.

6

GETTING THROUGH TO GOD

PERHAPS it is our experience that when we pray God seems very far away. We feel that our praying is like speaking into the air or talking down a dead telephone line. In that case our weakness focuses on this problem of 'getting through to God', or, to use the biblical word, the problem of 'access'. The Bible has a lot to say about this, for the truths about access to God and fellowship with God lie at the heart of our salvation. There are two aspects to this matter that we must consider. The first is generally known and understood by believers, but it needs to be restated as it provides the basis of the second aspect which is often completely overlooked. Let us call the first aspect—

THE RIGHT OF ACCESS

God made man for His own pleasure, that He might enjoy fellowship with His creatures. But sin came, and with it separation from God. An iron curtain, more terrible than that which separates East from West, fell between the holy God and His sinning creatures. The message of the Bible reveals how God dealt with that dread curtain through Jesus Christ to bring man back to His original purpose. 'For there is one God, and there is one mediator between God and men, the man Christ Jesus' (1 Tim. 2:5).

What hope could there be of man ever approaching that throne of God's holiness without the presence and work of the mediator Christ Jesus? He said Himself, 'No one comes to the Father, but by Me' (John 14:6). What does this mean? Simply that Christ's death, resurrection and ascension have torn the curtain apart and opened a way for man into the otherwise inaccessible presence of God. Peter the apostle puts it this way:

> For Christ also died for sins once for all, the righteous for the unrighteous, that He might bring us to God (1 Pet. 3:18).

This picture of a curtain of separation is in fact the very one that the Bible uses. In Old Testament times there was a curtain (or veil) that separated the Holy Place where the priests ministered from the inner sanctuary or Holy of Holies where dwelt the concentrated glory of God's presence in both the tabernacle and the temple. This was to show that the way was not yet open for man to have direct personal access to God (Heb. 9:8). No man could pass beyond that curtain on pain of death, the only exception being the High Priest; he was permitted to do so once a year, but not without the blood of sacrifice.

The gospel record tells us that when Jesus died a strange portent took place within the temple. The curtain separating the Holy Place from the

Holy of Holies was torn in two, and the record is careful to add, 'from top to bottom', to emphasize that it was no act of man that performed this, but an act of God (Mat. 27:51). The way into the presence of God had been opened at last. How beautifully this is expressed in the epistle to the Hebrews (10:19–22):

> Therefore, brethren, since we have confidence to enter the sanctuary by the blood of Jesus, by the new and living way which He opened for us through the curtain, that is, through His flesh . . . let us draw near . . .

The curtain (or veil) represented the invisible barrier separating God and man on account of sin. When Jesus died on the cross He took that sin barrier on Himself, bearing our sins in His own body (1 Pet. 2:24), and so fully was He identified with our sin that God was said to have 'made Him to be sin who knew no sin' (2 Cor. 5:21). Thus the crucifying of that sinless body was looked upon as a tearing of the curtain of separation, and the opening of a way into the presence of God for us.

This work of Christ as mediator is a truth that became obscured in the medieval era of the church, but was brought fully into the light by the Reformation, and is dear to the heart of all true believers. We need no human priest or inter-mediary, for we have one great High Priest in the presence of God for us. Through Him every believer has the right of direct access to God.

It is good to be reminded that we can never approach God, whether in prayer or praise, supplication or intercession, except through Christ.

If then we have this *right of access* as believers, how can there be any problem in getting through to God in prayer? Why is it that we find those who, knowing and believing that they have this right to enter into God's presence through Christ, find themselves faced with a practical problem in the outworking of it? The right to draw near with boldness does not seem to ensure a living audience with the King. Despite all that people say, despite all that they themselves believe, their prayer life remains dull and lifeless, and the God whom they address is a God afar off.

Of course the simple explanation may be a matter that we have touched on already. Even though we have the right of access we are still required to come with clean hands and a pure heart into God's presence. Only by the confession of known sin, and the thorough renunciation of it does the death of Christ and the power of His blood avail for us as we draw near to God. Otherwise, by countenancing sin in our hearts, we stop God's ears (Isa. 59:2; Psa. 66:18). Any form of disobedience may easily produce an impenetrable barrier to our prayers, and keep us out of touch with God. Where we are conscious of 'something between' but do not know what it is, the Holy Spirit is ready and waiting to reveal it, if we will only seek the Lord. Where we do know, the remedy is simple; we must tread the humbling pathway of confession, renunciation and maybe restitution, and so be restored to God's fellowship.

But what of those who have genuinely examined themselves before God without being convicted of any specific sin that could account for their inability to get through to God? The solution is found, I believe, in the second aspect of this truth. This we will call:

THE POWER OF ACCESS

We may say that *the right of access* is the result of the work of Christ, and *the power of access* is the result of the work of the Holy Spirit. Both are included by Paul when he says:

For through Him [Christ] we both [Jew and Gentile] have *access in one Spirit* to the Father (Eph. 2:18).

This phrase, 'access in one Spirit', teaches us that the Holy Spirit has a vital part to play in our getting through to God. What Christ has accomplished *for us* by providing us with the right of access, the Spirit must now work *in us* by providing us with the power of access. Paul is teaching us here that our access to God through Christ is in the power of, or through the working of, one Spirit, even the Spirit of God. In other words, the same Spirit that proceeds from God is available to conduct us to God. In fact all our fellowship with God is dependent upon the gracious activity of this one Spirit. We should be reminded of this every time we hear the benediction pronounced, concluding with the words, 'the fellowship of the Holy Spirit be with you all' (2 Cor. 13:14). It is a fellowship with the Father and with His Son Jesus Christ effected and maintained by the Holy Spirit.

If a man is summoned to the king's palace to receive some decoration, the royal summons is his right to enter the king's presence. It takes him past the sentries and officers of the guard who would otherwise debar him from the palace. But having gained entry he would be at a loss to find his way into the sovereign's presence if left to himself in that labyrinth of corridors. He needs a palace attendant to conduct him personally to the audience chamber. The work of Christ provides us with the royal summons and constitutes our right of entry, but the indwelling Spirit is also needed to conduct us into God's presence. It is His work to make access to God a reality; to bring to us the deep conviction that we are not talking into the air when we pray, but communing face to face with a loving heavenly Father.

The Holy Spirit thus provides the answer to our weakness in this matter of getting through to God, for He makes our praying a conscious experience of fellowship with God. What a wonderful thing is 'the fellowship of the Holy Spirit'. Let us draw near to God and pray with the full assurance of faith that the Holy Spirit will indeed help us in our weakness. 'The Lord God is a sun' (Psa. 84:11), and when we commune with Him in the Spirit we shall be conscious of a spiritual

warmth pervading our beings, and when we go
our way, like Moses descending the mount, we
shall be unconsciously reflecting something of the
glory.

7

KNOWING GOD'S WILL

ANOTHER obvious and serious weakness from which we all suffer in the realm of prayer is that in so many situations we have to admit that we do not know the will of God. The Authorized (or King James') Version puts it this way: 'We know not what we should pray for' (Rom. 8:26). Later versions: 'We do not know how to pray.' We may apply this to the subject matter of our praying. When we get beyond the well-worn paths, having prayed for our families and friends, our churches and fellow-Christians, servants of God at home and overseas, there are still endless needs and possibilities for intercession. If we try to cover every need and respond to every call our prayer life becomes a river without a river bed, that flows here, there, and everywhere, until its energy is swallowed up in a marsh. Here is a basic rule: if intercession is to be effective it must be selective. But here lies our problem, 'We know not what we should pray for . . .'

Even on those occasions when we do know what we should pray for, there is a real problem as to how we should pray for it. For example, an elderly believer, who has been in failing health for some time, is taken seriously ill and is not expected to live. How should we pray for him? We have to face the possibility that his time on earth is done. In that case, for us to pray with all the faith and zeal we can muster for his restoration to health would be to pray contrary to the mind of God, and our hope would certainly be disappointed. This kind of thing often happens.

Let us take another case. There is the problem of the church member who it seems is bent on making trouble and causing division. Should we pray for him to be restored or removed? During her time at missionary training college my wife, together with one or two other students, used to help in a mission situated in a rather notorious district of London. In the childrens' meetings there was a disruptive element, and she wrote me of her quandary as to how to pray for these little hooligans—'for grace to keep them in, or for strength to chuck them out'! How true it is of so many situations, 'We do not know how to pray.'

Of course many find an easy way of escape from this kind of dilemma. They pray for whatever they think best, and then qualify it with—'if it be Thy will'. This is particularly the case when it comes to prayer for the sick, and it is generally looked upon as signifying commendable submission to the unknown will of God, or perhaps by others as the best that is possible under the circumstances. Among the many examples of Bible prayers, this kind is conspicuous by its absence. How can a hit-or-miss prayer of this sort be in faith? And if not in faith how can it be pleasing to God? The New Testament does not encourage us to wander on in our ignorance, it emphasizes the need of

being 'filled with the knowledge of His will' (Col.
1 : 9); it commands us to 'understand what the will
of the Lord is' (Eph. 5 : 17); it exhorts us to 'prove
what is the will of God' (Rom. 12 : 2).

The apostle John writes:

And this is the confidence which we have in
Him, that if we ask anything according to His
will He hears us. And if we know that He hears
us in whatever we ask, we know that we have
obtained the requests made of Him (1 John
5 : 14, 15).

Now if we are always falling back on to the
safety of these 'if-it-be-Thy-will prayers' we are
debasing this most well-known prayer promise of
the apostle John, and making it a prayer 'let-out',
a useful carpet under which we can sweep all our
unanswered prayers. We imply that what he is
really saying is this: 'And this is the lack of confidence which we have in Him, that unless we
happen to ask according to His will, He will *not*
hear us, and we shall not have our petition.' So the
promise that was intended to confirm our faith
serves only to cover our unbelief and to confirm
us in our state of weakness, in seeking to prevail
with God.

How then are we to reconcile these two facts
—we are ignorant of the will of God, and yet, in
order to receive, are required to pray according
to it? Here is a weakness serious enough to render
all our praying ineffectual. But the apostle points
us to this wonderful fact that Someone has been

sent to help us who has a perfect knowledge of the will of God. 'The Spirit helps us in our weakness . . . the Spirit Himself intercedes for us . . . the Spirit intercedes for the saints according to the will of God.'

We have already seen that this same Spirit creates desire within us for such fellowship with God; that He not only proceeds from God but is available to conduct us to God. Now we see that He is able to make up for all our deficiencies in understanding God's will. There must of necessity be perfect harmony between the mind of God and the mind of the Spirit. How wonderful that He has sent forth His Spirit into our hearts, to help our weakness, to supply our lack, to do for us what we cannot do for ourselves. How vital that we depend on Him to do this work.

All this is but another aspect of that promise of our Lord concerning the Holy Spirit, 'He shall teach you all things'—all things that you need to know to fulfil your ministry. When the disciples said to Jesus, 'Lord teach us to pray,' He gave them their first lesson by teaching them the Lord's prayer. When we now ask Him to teach us to pray He points us to the Holy Spirit, and says, 'He will teach you.'

But we may well ask, 'How *does* the Holy Spirit teach us to pray according to God's will?' Not by imparting facts and then leaving us to get on with the job, but by interceding for us, with us and in us. Once I wanted a small adjustment done on the engine of my car. I phoned my friend who not only knows all about cars but also of my ignorance about them! He could have given me instructions over the phone which might, or might not, have proved successful. Instead he graciously came and did the job for me. 'The Spirit Himself intercedes for us ... the Spirit intercedes for the saints according to the will of God.'

This interceding Spirit dwelling within us is also 'the Spirit of wisdom and understanding, the Spirit of counsel and might, the Spirit of knowledge and of the fear of the Lord' (Isa. 11:2). As we pray He is waiting to be to us our fountain of wisdom, understanding, counsel, might, knowledge and fear of the Lord. Later we shall discuss the practical ways in which He guides and inspires us to pray according to God's will, and how in practice we are to co-operate with Him.

8

WHEN FAITH WOULD FAIL

LACK of faith is one of the most obvious and prevalent weaknesses in the realms of prayer. Of course this is closely related to what has just been said about knowing the will of God, for one Scripture assures us that we must pray according to God's will, if we are to receive, another that we must pray in faith. But even in the well-known verse that we have been considering about praying in the will of God there is a clear reference to faith :

> And this is the confidence [and what is that but faith] which we have in Him, that if we ask anything according to His will He hears us. And if we know that He hears us [this too must be faith] in whatever we ask, we know that we have obtained the requests made of Him (1 John 5 : 14, 15).

Earlier in this same epistle John had cleared the ground over this question of faith by showing the importance of having a clear conscience if we are to approach God with assurance.

> Beloved, if our hearts do not condemn us, we have confidence before God; and we receive

from Him whatever we ask, because we keep His commandments and do what pleases Him (1 John 3:21, 22).

There is nothing more destructive of faith than a guilt complex or a heart that condemns us, as John calls it. The blood of Christ, applied by confession, is the complete answer to this condition. Then we can draw near to God 'with our hearts sprinkled clean from an evil conscience' (Heb. 10:22).

If our prayers are to avail faith is not simply desirable, it is essential.

Without faith it is impossible to please Him. For whoever would draw near to God must believe that He exists and that He rewards those who seek Him (Heb. 11:6).

So faith is a 'must' if our prayers are to be pleasing to God. James stresses the same point in connection with asking God for wisdom. If we ask for this He will give liberally provided we 'ask in faith', but the doubter or the double-minded man need not expect to receive anything from the Lord (James 1:5–8). His wavering faith disqualifies him from receiving the answer to a petition which would otherwise have been acceptable to God.

Sometimes our unbelief is revealed by the timid, half-hearted, almost apologetic way in which we approach God. We are like the man who almost puts a 'No' in his friend's mouth when he asks

him, 'I suppose you wouldn't be willing by any
chance to let me have so and so?' Certainly when
we come to God in such a spirit we are inviting
His refusal, for our attitude is a denial of our
standing in Christ as sons of God and of our access
through Him to God. 'In whom we have boldness
and confidence of access through our faith in
Him' (Eph. 3 : 12 cp. Heb. 4 : 16, 10 : 19).

Sometimes our lack of faith is uncovered by a
delayed answer. God keeps us waiting, and our
faith which ought to be strengthened by this testing begins to fade and wither. Either we give up
praying altogether or we pray on without any
real confidence. At other times we continue steadfastly in prayer, despite the waiting time, until
something happens which seems to knock the
bottom out of our hopes. Casting away our confidence we conclude too readily that we must have
been mistaken, and so the debris of another unanswered prayer is swept into the rubbish bin of
'Couldn't have been the will of God'. This is not
God's way.

> Therefore do not throw away your confidence,
> which has a great reward. For you have need of
> endurance, so that you may do the will of God
> and receive what is promised (Heb. 10 : 35, 36).

So many of these exhortations of Scripture
sound so simple, and yet in practice we find them
so difficult. We readily acknowledge that we must
have this boldness in approaching God, this confidence that He hears us, and this faith to hold on

for the answer. But how? Once again heaven
answers, 'the Holy Spirit'. Just as certainly as we
recognize and confess that this lack of faith is a
weakness in prayer, so we stand on the promise,
'The Spirit helps us in our weakness; for we do
not know how to pray [in faith] as we ought, but
the Spirit Himself intercedes for us [in faith].'

Think for a moment of that time before you
knew Christ. Whether you were thoroughly god-
less, or whether you had a form of godliness which
denied the power, you were in a state of unbelief.
Then, by a gradual process or a sudden crisis, a
change took place. Christ was revealed to you in a
new way, and you came to see your need of Him.
In some mysterious way faith was born in your
heart and you became a child of God. What happened? You were born of the Spirit, for regenera-
tion is His special work (John 3 : 5–8; Titus 3 : 5).
He convicts of sin; He reveals Christ; and He
creates faith in what was until then an unbelieving heart.

We may not know how the Spirit creates faith,
it is enough to know that He does. Faith is one of
His gifts, even as faithfulness is part of His fruit.
Stephen and Barnabas were men 'full of faith and
the Holy Spirit.' I take this to mean that they had
a special manifestation of faith as a result of the
Spirit's fullness.

We find that Scripture and experience confirm
that revelation and faith are closely connected.
'Who has *believed* . . .? And to whom has the arm
of the Lord been *revealed*?' (Isa. 53 : 1). These two
questions are really one. Those who believed the

report concerning Christ are those to whom Christ (the arm of the Lord) has been revealed. There is no faith without revelation. As at conversion, so throughout the Christian life, impartation of faith, strengthening of faith, increase of faith involve a continuing work of revelation.

The Holy Spirit is the great Revealer. His task is to teach us all things, as Jesus promised, but He does this by revelation, illumination and enlightenment. So Paul prayed for the Ephesians, 'that the God of our Lord Jesus Christ ... may give you a spirit of wisdom and of revelation in the knowledge of Him, having the eyes of your hearts enlightened' (1 : 17, 18). Just as it is man's heart that is enlightened, so it is man's heart that believes (Rom. 10 : 10).

Often the Holy Spirit will give us revelation on the word of God. We may have read a certain promise in the Bible time and again, but one day it lights up. The Spirit of God has given us revelation or enlightenment, and simultaneously faith is born in our hearts for the fulfilment of that promise. 'So faith comes from what is heard' (Rom. 10 : 17), but only through the operation of the Holy Spirit.

All this is deeply relevant to praying in faith. As we seek the Lord we may count on the Holy Spirit giving us revelation, and so imparting faith. He may make Bible promises to come alive, relating them to the situations for which we are interceding. Or apart from any Scripture He may simply give us revelation about those situations, so that we see them from the divine rather than the human standpoint. A conviction is born within us that God will work in that matter, though the prospect of His doing so may appear to our natural minds remote, if not impossible. That is how the possibility of the Flood must have seemed to those to whom Noah preached. That is how the birth of a baby boy promised to the aged and barren couple, Abraham and Sarah, must have appeared to their contemporaries. But these Old Testament saints believed God with a faith inspired by the Holy Spirit, and the impossible was fulfilled. Let us trust ourselves to this faith-creating Spirit. He is waiting to help us in our weakness by praying through us in living faith.

9

CONTENDING WITH CIRCUMSTANCES

IN a book mainly concerned with the spiritual principles of intercession there is a tendency to overlook some of the practical problems. It all sounds so easy until we come to put the thing into practice; then we meet a hundred and one difficulties and discouragements which the textbooks don't seem to mention, and soon our new enthusiasm has evaporated and we find ourselves back to 'square one'.

In these three chapters we want to anticipate some of these, for it is certain that we have all been affected by some of them at least. The point we want to emphasize is that the same Holy Spirit, whom we have seen is able to take care of the spiritual problems, can be counted on to do the same for the practical problems. He not only works positively to give us the guidance and strength we need in this ministry but also in enabling us to combat the many hindrances and discouragements we shall certainly meet. When we consider that He comes to work in us all that Christ has done for us, it is not surprising to discover that He is essentially a practical Holy Spirit.

The fact that we are so susceptible to these discouragements constitutes another aspect of our weakness in prayer, so that the same promise that

He helps us in our weakness applies here. The difficulties we have in mind proceed mainly from three sources. In this chapter we shall think of those produced by our circumstances. In the next those that are bound up with our physical weakness. And finally those that are satanic in origin.

Now there are circumstances over which we have no control which may combine to hamper our prayer life, if not to render it largely ineffective. There are the interruptions, the unexpected visitors, the telephone calls, the demands of the family. There may be a general lack of quiet, or the pressure of work that either keeps us out of the secret place or haunts us while we are there. All these and many more can be most distracting and frustrating to the would-be intercessor.

'May not these be the work of Satan?' someone is sure to ask. It is true that Satan may be responsible for a good deal of the vexing and harassing of the saints. But this is not the important question. What we need to know is, 'Is this thing the will of God for me?' It is unsound reasoning that says: 'This thing is hindering my prayer life, therefore it is of Satan and it is not the will of God for me to put up with it.' This fails to take account of the fact that many things that are the work of Satan are also equally the will of God. We only need to mention the greatest example of all—the cross. It was both the work of wicked men inspired by Satan and also the will of God. This was why Jesus did not fight against the cross but bowed His head in submission to it, though He knew that Satan was behind it (John 14:30).

Already Jesus had taught His disciples, 'Do not resist one who is evil. But if any one strikes you on the right cheek, turn to him the other also.' (Matt. 5:39). The slap on the cheek may well be inspired by Satan, but that is not a reason for resisting. God has willed this, therefore we submit to it in the confidence that it will be for His glory and for our good. There can be serious misunderstanding here due to believers having an unhealthy over-emphasis on the power and working of Satan. We ask the wrong questions and therefore arrive at the wrong conclusions. There are so many situations in which we need to see, not the working of Satan, even though he may be actively involved, but the hand of God. We should not be asking, 'What is Satan doing here?' but, 'What is God saying here?'

I find it difficult to determine which are in the more dangerous position, the majority who seem to be blind to the activity of Satan and almost completely ignorant of his devices, or that small minority of 'experts' who have become much too devil-conscious and demon-conscious, and discern satanic overtones in almost every untoward event. This is not the New Testament emphasis any more than the other. Because there are certain occasions when we may rightly resist the devil's attacks, whether through our circumstances or some other way, and experience the Lord's deliverance, we are not to assume that this is so with every case. This can mean resisting things which are the ordering of our Heavenly Father, permitted for our good, and in so doing we only succeed in frustrating both ourselves and God's purpose in that trial.

In the book of Job we are given in the first two chapters a peep behind the scenes, so we know who was responsible for the sufferings he endured. Yet it never occurred to Job or his friends to ask, 'Are these calamities the work of Satan?' Nor is there any further mention of him in the debate that followed, not even by the Almighty when He intervened. Both Job and his friends were agreed on this, if on nothing else, that these things were from the hand of God. God was speaking through these afflictions, and the moment Job got the message he was 'through', and God turned his captivity.

If we have some clear revelation or conviction that the circumstances are purely the product of Satan's malice, and therefore to be resisted, we shall of course follow this leading, and the confirmation will be the subsequent removal of the difficulty. More about this in the chapter, 'When Satan attacks'. In the absence of any such conviction we are right to take our circumstances as the providential ordering of our Heavenly Father, proving that 'in acceptance lieth peace', as Amy Carmichael expressed it.

Immediately following the remarkable scripture which is the main theme of this book, Romans 8:26 and 27, Paul reminds us that all things work together for good to those who love God (verse 28). This is a verse that we find easier to quote than to believe. Too many of us have it by rote, but not by revelation. We rebel against the providences of God. We resist the hand that afflicts us in love. Vexation and frustration are the inevitable result.

Once again the Holy Spirit is available to help us in our weakness, and that along two lines. Firstly He gives us a revelation of a sovereign God who is working all things after the counsel of His will, overruling the schemings and workings of Satan to accomplish His purpose, making the wrath of man to praise Him, and causing all things to work together for our good. The revelation that there is a divine purpose in those very things that have hindered and discouraged us in prayer, will transfigure them before our eyes.

Then He works in us a spirit of submission, so that we accept these divine orderings instead of kicking against the goad. But this is not a passive, fatalistic attitude, the 'kismet' of the Moslem— 'God wills it, therefore I accept it.' It is that acquiescence which is the product of an active faith that my very problems will be made the stepping-stones to success. It is not simply that God works all things together—the Moslem and the Hindu believe that—but that He works them together *for good*. Through facing and conquering these very difficulties we had thought were insurmountable, the Holy Spirit will work in us grace and grit, faith and fortitude, patience and perseverance—in fact the very qualities that are needed to make us real intercessors. Glory to God!

10

IN WEAKNESS AND WEARINESS

WE must now deal with some practical difficulties in the physical realm. If we are suffering from physical or mental fatigue we may find ourselves battling with drowsiness, wandering thoughts, heaviness of spirit and even depression. Here it is necessary to exercise a little discrimination. There is a tiredness that is quite legitimate in the Christian life. Even our Lord Himself was on one occasion wearied with His journey, and on another He fell asleep in the boat. When we know the Lord wants us to fight and overcome this tiredness we have that wonderful promise of Romans 8 : 11, 'He who raised Christ Jesus from the dead will give life to your mortal bodies also through His Spirit which dwells in you.' Though this refers primarily to the resurrection of our bodies, it certainly has a present application as many have proved. The Holy Spirit is able now to renew our weak or tired bodies so that we may do the will of God.

When Jesus sat down by the well He was 'wearied ... with His journey', and no doubt hungry too. But when the disciples returned with food and found Him busy telling the Samaritan woman of the water of life, He appeared to have forgotten all about His weariness, nor was He interested in food. 'I have food to eat of which you

do not know' (John 4:32). His body had been renewed by the Spirit of God dwelling in Him.

I well remember the first mission I conducted
after God blessed me in the Holy Spirit. A week
had passed with some measure of blessing. God
was beginning to stir the hearts of His people and
there was a widespread desire for a prolonged
time of prayer following the Sunday evening service. Tired after a full day, and with a slight headache, I wondered just how much more I could take.
By 11 p.m. there were seven of us left, almost all
young men. The time that followed till we reluctantly ended at 3.30 a.m. was probably the most
remarkable season of corporate intercession I have
ever experienced. It proceeded with barely a
moment's intermission for more than four hours.
When we rose from our knees my headache had
gone, and I felt as fresh as the proverbial daisy.
The others appeared to be the same. The Holy
Spirit had given life to our mortal bodies.

There is also a state of perpetual weariness
which is unjustified, in fact dangerous, for it puts
a weapon into our enemy's hand with which to
attack us. It is a sure indication that we have got
our priorities wrong, and sooner or later the most
important things will be neglected. This situation
usually indicates that we are being ruled, even in
spiritual matters, by personal preferences, by
carnal desires, by a concern to please men—even
fellow-believers—rather than God, by an enthusiasm which results in taking on what God has
not appointed for us.

The solution is to seek the Lord with real determination until the matter is sorted out. In this we may count upon the Spirit's guidance and help. In fact we shall need all the help that He can give, for this readjustment of our priorities is neither easy to effect, nor easy to maintain, but His grace is sufficient. Unless we do this the enemy will not find it difficult to neutralize our prayer life.

Sickness of body may have much the same effect on our times with God as weariness of body. There is, of course, sickness which is a direct attack of Satan to put us out of commission if possible, and this is no more to be taken lying down than is a temptation to evil. Again, we must reserve this till the next chapter. Not all sickness, however, is in this category. Even though Satan may have a finger in it, we need to know whether or not God has a purpose in it. We have already seen that the important thing about Job's sufferings, including his physical affliction, was not that it was perpetrated by Satan but that it was permitted by God, and was for the purifying of Job's character. Very often sickness, whatever may be its direct cause, is God trying to get our ear. In that case we need to be quiet and listen to what He is trying to say to us.

On earth they say : 'Laid aside by illness';
In heaven they say : 'Called aside for stillness.'

A book on prayer is not the place to enter into discussion on the many problems that cluster around this ministry of healing, and in particular the mystery of why sickness seems to have dogged the steps of some of the Lord's choicest saints. That such cases are exceptional I do not doubt, and it is generally the will of God for His saints, as it was the prayer of the apostle John for his friend Gaius, that health of body should go hand in hand with prosperity of soul (3 John 2).

Though I have known the Lord's healing touch on more than one occasion, and believe that this ministry is for today, I cannot assert or imply, as some do, that these suffering saints were culpable in their lack of faith for healing, that they missed God's best, etc. The ready answers that are so often produced do not seem to me to be answers; they leave the mystery unravelled. Most of these great saints triumphed over their sicknesses. They did not lie down under them in defeat and self-pity. It is surely significant that Hebrews 11 not only records the faith of those who 'escaped the edge of the sword' (verse 34) but also the faith of those who were 'killed with the sword' (verse 37). Which glorified God the more—the faith of those who escaped or the faith of those who endured?

One fact is clear. Many of these saints who suffered in this way were mighty intercessors. Rightly or wrongly they accepted their afflictions as the providential ordering of the Lord. They counted on the help of the indwelling Spirit in their bodily weakness. One could make mention of Frances Ridley Havergal, Praying Hyde of India, David Brainerd of the American Indians or Robert Murray M'Cheyne of Dundee. All of these died prematurely, humanly speaking, suffering most of their lives from indifferent health, brought on by their labours for the kingdom of God. The lesson that we can surely learn from their lives is in the way they were so marvellously sustained and strengthened to prevail with God. In the midst of weakness or weariness we too may count upon the Holy Spirit coming to our aid.

11

WHEN SATAN ATTACKS

THE deeper one is led into this ministry of intercession the more conscious one becomes that it is essentially a warfare in the Spirit. Before exhorting the Ephesians to pray at all times in the Spirit Paul reminds them of the true nature of this conflict, that it is not 'against flesh and blood, but against the principalities, against the powers, against the world rulers of this present darkness, against the spiritual hosts of wickedness in the heavenly places', and so he exhorts them to put on the whole armour of God.

Our Lord pictures the intercessor as a widow with a lawsuit, wearying the judge with her incessant plea, 'Vindicate me against my adversary' (Luke 18:3). Yes, our adversary the devil is ever present, and no one is more conscious of this than the intercessor who stands in the front line. In this chapter we are to consider those attacks of Satan which are designed to hinder or even nullify the believer's intercession. We are concerned here with those situations which are not the will of God for us in the sense of demanding our willing submission, but which we are to resist. Such attacks may be made on our spirits, our minds or our bodies.

Sometimes we may be oppressed by Satan with

a strange heaviness of spirit, which is not caused by any weariness of mind or body, nor is it the usual type of depression. With others I was once engaged in a fierce battle to free someone who was demon possessed. We decided to break off that night and resume in the morning. When I awoke I felt as though a dark cloud was enveloping me. I am not, thank God, normally subject to bouts of depression, and for a moment I was at a loss to account for my state of mind. As soon as I recalled the battle of the previous day and remembered that it was about to be resumed I realized from where the depression came. It was Satan's counter-attack to try to put me out of commission. I jumped out of bed and fell on my knees resisting and rebuking in the name of the Lord. I did not at this point address the Lord or ask for His help. I addressed Satan, using the authority the Lord had given me, and in the power of the Spirit told him to quit. Immediately the cloud lifted, and later that morning the Lord gave us the victory in prayer for the one in need. It was the Spirit who came to the rescue, giving revelation first as to the real situation, and then authority in resisting the enemy.

Sometimes we are attacked by uncertainty or perplexity. This may be especially the case when we are called by the Lord to walk with Him in the dark, not knowing quite where we are going in the path of intercession, and wondering what, if anything, is being accomplished by it all. As we do look to Jesus the Holy Spirit is free to minister to us His consolation, comfort and strength.

The prophet Zechariah was shown Joshua the high priest standing before the angel of the Lord, and Satan standing at his right hand to accuse him (Zech. 3 : 1). Now Joshua's ministry was to represent the people of God in the sanctuary which of course involved intercession. In this he was a type of our great High Priest who ever lives to make intercession for us. Because of the devastating effect upon his kingdom of such a ministry Satan is obliged to resist it with might and main. One way he does this is by accusing the brethren before God, hence his place at the right hand of Joshua.

Job was another who exercised a priestly and intercessory ministry (Job 1 : 5) and was similarly accused (Job 1 : 9–11; 2 : 4, 5). We learn from Revelation 12 : 10 that these accusations go on day and night. Often the devil makes the intercessor aware of his accusations, to bring on him a spirit of self-condemnation. We cannot approach the throne with boldness, as we are exhorted to do, if we are heeding a little voice that whispers, 'You know very well you are not fit to be interceding. What about this, that and the other?' Here is a direct attack by Satan which must be resisted.

In the case of Joshua the high priest we see that the Lord rebuked Satan, and we may rebuke him too in the Lord's name. Has he not given us authority to tread on serpents and scorpions, and over all the power of the enemy (Luke 10 : 19)? Those filthy garments—the ground of Satan's accusations—were removed from Joshua, and the Lord said, 'I have taken your iniquity away from you, and I will clothe you with rich apparel' (Zech.

3:4). The answer to Satan's accusations is the blood of Christ, that cleanses us from all sin, and the clothing with His righteousness.

All this is borne out by Revelation 12:11 to which we have already referred. There we see the saints overcoming the accuser 'by the blood of the Lamb and by the word of their testimony'. In other words, they bore witness to the blood. In this the Holy Spirit has a vital part to play, for the believer never witnesses apart from the Spirit (John 15:26, 27; Acts 5:32), and the Spirit answers to the blood. We could have no sense of a cleansed conscience or of acceptance with God apart from the witness of the Spirit. Speaking of the water and the blood John says. 'And the Spirit is the witness, because the Spirit is the truth' (1 John 5:6, 7). Weak and failing as we are, and so susceptible to these attacks of Satan, we can praise God that the Spirit helps us in our weakness.

Finally, as we have already indicated, Satan may be permitted to attack our bodies with sickness, and so render any concentrated intercession difficult, if not impossible. We have to recognize that such an attack is permitted by God—Satan cannot raise his little finger without first God permits it— but equally that it is the will of God that we resist it. As soon as we take up a position of faith and use our spiritual weapons in the power of the Spirit the attack will quickly pass. We have examples of this in the ministry of our Lord when He rebuked the fever that had laid low Simon's mother-in-law. and when He rebuked the storm on the lake that threatened the lives of Himself and His disciples.

The fact that He 'rebuked' suggests that there were satanic forces operating in both cases.

In these situations it is the Holy Spirit who gives us revelation and conviction as to the true nature of the attack. It is He who also gives us faith and authority to obey the scriptural injunction, 'Resist the devil and he will flee from you' (James 4:7).

12

HOLDING ON

'STAYING power' in prayer is a rare quality. Our Lord realized this, and so gave at least two parables to encourage us to persevere (Luke 11:5–8; 18:1–8). There is no realm of the Christian life in which we weary so quickly as in prayer. Like Moses on the mount, our hands hang down and our knees become feeble. The reason is that persevering prayer requires a pure faith, and so often our faith is the sort that too easily rests on the visible and the outward. If there are encouraging signs to the natural eye our faith seems strong; but when, as with the story of the shipwreck in the book of Acts, neither sun nor stars appear for many days, we tend to abandon hope. It is not so much that a trial like this weakens our faith, it simply uncovers the true state of our hearts and shows us how weak our faith really is; that we are not truly walking by faith at all, but walking by sight.

The problem of holding on is chiefly the problem of learning to walk in the dark. It is hard to persevere day after day in the path of intercession, when you don't know whether anything is being accomplished by it, or whether you are any nearer your goal. If only we could see into 'the unseen'. If only we could be sure that something is happening. It is just here that the Spirit comes to our aid.

We are weak because we are in the dark, but 'the Spirit helps us in our weakness'. Are we getting tired of the refrain? It ought to be music to our souls. The spirit comes to lighten our darkness, causing us to see where we would not otherwise see and to know what we could not otherwise know.

It is not that the Spirit necessarily gives us at such times visible or tangible tokens of the Lord's working, although these will be granted from time to time. He lightens our darkness in the unseem realm. It is here we begin to see. We still have to walk by faith, but we learn that, contrary to the popular saying, 'believing is seeing'. This is of the very essence of faith. It was the secret of Moses' staying power in a day of darkness and disappointment. 'He endured as seeing Him who is invisible' (Heb. 11:27). Every intercessor has to learn to endure because he is dealing with what is invisible to the natural eye. The Holy Spirit will not tell us everything that is happening or give us the answer to all our questions, but He will show us all that we need to see and tell us all that we need to know for the strengthening of our faith and to enable us to hold on.

To the weary traveller the sight of another milestone is an encouragement. The Spirit of God may show us, as we pray, that we have reached another milestone on the way. At times He may shed light on the situation, so that we get a glimpse of what God is doing. Or He may permit us to see in advance the end of the road, so that we view the situation as it will be when our prayers are fully answered. By such tokens the Spirit strengthens us to persevere.

We see all this in the case of Abraham. After he had received the promise of a son, during the waiting years that followed, God from time to time revealed Himself to the patriarch. Each time He showed him a little more of His plan, and gave him glimpses of the goal that lay ahead. These more than offset the physical facts that stared him in the face—that, as far as reproductive powers were concerned, at a hundred years old he was 'as good as dead', and that 'it had ceased to be with Sarah after the manner of women'.

In hope he believed against hope . . . He did not weaken in faith when he considered his own body . . . or the barrenness of Sarah's womb. No distrust made him waver concerning the promise of God, but he grew strong in his faith as he gave glory to God, fully convinced that God was able to do what He had promised (Rom. 4 : 18–21).

With the eye of faith Abraham could see himself holding that baby in his arms, so real had God made that promise to him. This is the work of the Spirit, and we may confidently expect Him to sustain us in the same way.

The Holy Spirit will often give an intercessor a great burden, in relation to some need, from which he can only obtain relief in intercession. It is not uncommon for this to be the case in times preceding a visitation of the Holy Spirit. With the burden the Spirit also gives the supernatural strength to sustain it. In this way the problem of 'holding on' is solved.

A Christian mother needs no fervent exhortation to pray without ceasing for her only child who is dangerously ill. However fitful her prayer life normally is, now she sighs her heart out in prayer all day long. There is no problem of perseverance here; the burden resting on her has solved that. Of course we can explain this in terms of natural affection and maternal instinct. But the Spirit of God is able to give the intercessor a burden of prayer for needs that would not naturally or normally concern him greater than that mother is capable of bearing, even in relation to her sick child.

The same Holy Spirit, who is able to keep us at it until the work is done, may also at times bring our praying to an abrupt halt. There was a time when the sins of Israel reached 'the point of no return', and God had to say to Jeremiah, 'Do not pray for this people' (Jer. 7:16, etc.). God would not permit His servant to waste his breath or expend his energy in vain. Just as Paul and his company were 'forbidden by the Holy Spirit' to labour any further in Asia, and so a door was opened into Europe (Acts 16:6–10), so there are times when the Spirit shuts one door in prayer so that He may open another.

The knowledge that the Holy Spirit is ready to do this kind of thing is in itself a source of great encouragement to the intercessor. He is made aware that even when he is treading the darkest path there is with him an unseen guiding hand.

Similarly, the Holy Spirit will cause him to know that his prayer is heard, that he has prevailed with God, even when there is no outward token of it, only the lifting of the burden and the welling up within him of praise. He needs no outward confirmation—that will come later—he knows by the Spirit that heaven has added its 'Amen'.

In Psalm 6 we find David labouring in prayer, with a heavy troubled spirit, as he prays for deliverance from his enemies. Then the tone of the Psalm alters abruptly (verse 8): 'Depart from me, all you workers of evil; for the Lord has heard the sound of my weeping. The Lord has heard my supplication; the Lord accepts my prayer.' He is confident that he has prevailed with God, although the outward fulfilment as far as his enemies are concerned is still future, for he concludes, 'All my enemies *shall* be ashamed and sore troubled; they *shall* turn back, and be put to shame in a moment.'

Another fine example of 'praying through' is the case of Hannah. In her great longing for a child we find her in the temple fasting, weeping, praying and making her vows to God. When Eli said to her, 'Go in peace, and the God of Israel grant your petition' (1 Sam. 1:17) the Spirit registered within her that her cry was heard; her burden of sorrow was lifted, and she went away with a deep peace and assurance in her heart. I am sure that she never asked God again. She knew that she had prevailed.

So much for the various ways in which the Holy Spirit helps us in our weakness. We must now return to Ephesians 6:18 where we are exhorted to pray in the Spirit 'with all prayer and supplication', that is, with *all kinds of prayer* and supplication. In the next chapters we are to deal with the three kinds of praying in the Spirit referred to earlier: praying with the mind, praying with the spirit and praying without words, all of which are taught in the New Testament.

13

WITH WORDS UNDERSTOOD

WHEN we 'pray with the mind', as Paul expresses
it, we must of necessity use words that we understand, even though the prayer may be inaudible.
In the next chapter we shall speak of the second
kind of praying in the Spirit, with words that are
unknown. For the moment we are concerned to
know how the Holy Spirit girds our minds and
guides our thinking as we pray with our understanding.

We have no right to expect a special leading of
the Spirit here, if we are not submitting to His
leading in other realms. In Romans 8, where we
find the theme verse of this book, Paul reminds us
that the leading of the Spirit is a mark of sonship
(verse 14). The leading of the Spirit in the realm
of prayer is nothing more than a development of
this general principle.

Paul speaks at the commencement of that same
chapter of what God has done to free us from the
domination of the flesh (verse 3). Walking according to the Spirit is contrasted with walking according to the flesh. Walking according to the Spirit is
basic to praying in the Spirit. We must have the
waters to the ankles before we can know waters
to the knees (Ezek. 47:3, 4). Can we really conceive of someone who walks after the flesh and yet

prays in the Spirit? Can carnal living and spiritual praying go together? Whatever spiritual praying this is, it is not the New Testament variety, the product of an ungrieved Holy Spirit. It is foolish to expect to be led into these deeper realms of Spirit-led intercession, if we are not submissive to our Guide in the practical issues of daily life. An uncondemned heart is essential (1 John 3:21, 22). As we move on in the path of intercession we shall find that the Holy Spirit will require more implicit obedience, and greater sensitivity to His will.

The matter of the Holy Spirit directing our thoughts in prayer takes us to the basic fact that all prayer begins in the heart of God. Matthew Henry said: 'When God intends great mercy for His people he sets them apraying.' Indeed, when God wants anything accomplished in His Kingdom He moves men to pray. God is always the initiator. All effectual prayer was moving in the heart of God before ever it began to move in the heart of man. What Kepler said as he unlocked the secrets of the starry heavens, could well be said by the man who prays in the Spirit: 'O God, I am thinking Thy thoughts after Thee.'

Some have used the electric circuit as a helpful illustration of this truth. If there is to be a flow of electricity, then there must be a source of power. In the circuit of prayer, the power supply proceeds from God, but the power itself is the Spirit who is ever proceeding from the Father (John 15:26). The intercessor is like an electric lamp wired into the circuit. God wishes to work in a certain situation, and so He moves upon a believer by His Spirit. It is God that burdens him to pray. As he yields himself his whole being becomes a willing instrument for the Spirit's activity. The spiritual current flows through him as electricity through a lamp, and his prayer returns by the Spirit back to the heart of God.

All illustrations have their limitations, and this is no exception. It helps us to see the truth about prayer originating in God and returning to God, but when it comes to such practical matters as how we can be wired into the circuit, and how our minds and wills are to be blended with the mind and will of the Spirit, it cannot help us. How may our minds be so controlled by the Spirit as we pray that we do in fact think God's thoughts after Him?

Often this will be spontaneous, almost instinctive. The mind and will of the believer is yielded to the Spirit, and the Spirit is expressing Himself through him, without his being necessarily conscious of this. When Paul speaks of being led by the Spirit (Rom. 8 : 14) the thought is not so much of a conscious apprehension of the mind of the Spirit, followed by a conscious act of obedience, but rather an instinctive action by the believer who is now animated, not by an evil spirit, not even merely by the human spirit, but by the Spirit of God. Family traits are instinctive; so that what Paul is saying is that God's family traits are apparent in the behaviour of God's sons, because they are led by God's Spirit. They are naturally spiritual, and spiritually natural (using 'natural' in its general, not its theological sense). This applies to the prayer life as much as to any other realm.

Not far from the home of a small boy lived a famous artist. The youngster heard all about this great man, and dreamed of the day when he too would paint great pictures. When the artist died the boy thought to himself, 'If only I could have one of his brushes I would paint great pictures.' He knocked at the door of the great house where the artist had lived. The lady dressed in black smiled sadly at the flushed and eager face. She brought him one of the artist's brushes, and he took it home with great excitement. It was a crestfallen little boy that later returned the brush to the lady saying that he couldn't paint any better with it than he did with his own. 'To become a great painter,' explained the lady, 'you need more than the artist's brush, you need the spirit of the artist.'

As the Spirit of our great Intercessor inspires us, we shall often pray instinctively, just as the artist is inspired by the artistic spirit within him. As far as we are concerned they are our thoughts, our petitions, our pleadings, but since we are led by the Spirit God will know that they are really those of the One who dwells within us.

There may be, however, a conscious apprehension of the Spirit's burden followed by a conscious response to it. In this case the intercessor is not so much like a lamp in the electric circuit as a radio which is both a receiver and transmitter. The receiving aspect is often quite overlooked in the ministry of intercession. Communion with God should surely be a two-way traffic. We speak of prayer as our 'coming to the mercy seat', but when God first spoke about this to Moses He said nothing about it as a place where Moses would speak with Him, but rather as a place where He would speak with Moses (Exod. 25:22). In other words, the mercy seat was to be first a place of revelation, and then a place of intercession.

This revelation may indeed be given to the intercessor as he prays, but it will often be necessary to tune in and hear what heaven is saying that he may know how to pray. To learn how to talk to God we must first learn how to listen to God. 'Let every man be quick to hear, slow to speak' (James 1:19) was said about our converse with one another, but we would do well to apply it also to converse with God. How often we rush thoughtlessly into God's presence and blurt out our requests. No human subject would behave like this in audience with his sovereign or head of state. How fitting are Solomon's words here:

> Guard your steps when you go to the house of God; to draw near to listen is better than to offer the sacrifice of fools; for they do not know that they are doing evil. Be not rash with your mouth, nor let your heart be hasty to utter a word before God, for God is in heaven, and you upon earth; therefore let your words be few (Eccl. 5:1, 2).

Many believers today when they read, 'The word of the Lord came to Elijah', or 'The Lord said to Samuel', assume that this was some audible voice, and that God does not speak to men nowadays, since He has spoken once for all in His Son and in

His written word. Although God did occasionally
speak to men in an audible voice, I am sure that in
most cases it was the inner voice that God used. It
is certain that He still most often uses this means,
though one has heard of rare cases of an audible
voice being heard today. It is essential that we seek
God's face and train ourselves to listen.

In my early days as a soldier in the Armoured
Corps we were trained in wireless telegraphy. We
were sent out in army trucks over Salisbury Plain,
each having its own transmitter, and we had to
maintain a radio link with the control station at
base. From time to time control would send out a
tuning call, and we had to check our receiver. If
the receiver was tuned in, then the transmitter was
automatically tuned in. So often our spiritual receiving sets have never been tuned, and so our
transmissions are 'way out', and 'Control' never
hears us.

This tuning in to heaven involves the lost art of
waiting on God. David had learned how to do this,
for he says in Psalm 62 : 1 (R.V.), 'My soul waiteth
only upon God' (Heb. 'is silent unto God'; cp. verse
5). There is a waiting on God that involves being
silent in God's presence; in other words, listening.
God will speak to us by His Spirit, and when He
has spoken we shall know how to pray.

The ways in which the Holy Spirit speaks will
vary with different individuals, and may even vary
with the same individual on different occasions. It
may be an impression or a burden in one's spirit.
He may stimulate our memories and bring back to
us some incident or some need. He may speak in

the quietness of our hearts or illumine some Scripture to us. He may enlighten our minds concerning some matter for which He would have us intercede. Let us expect Him to do it. Let us give Him opportunity to do it. Let us yield our minds to the Spirit that our praying may be the expression of His mind. But remember, we shall need to exercise faith. Having yielded our minds we must resist that whisper, 'It's just you making it up.' We must trust ourselves to the Spirit of truth, believing that we are indeed receiving His message, His burden, His impression, and the confirmation will follow.

14

WITH WORDS UNKNOWN

WE come now to another kind of praying in the Spirit, which Paul distinguishes from that just considered in which the mind or understanding is the vehicle of the Spirit's activity. As there has been much misunderstanding here we must read what the apostle says carefully, and then examine it in its context.

Therefore, he who speaks in a tongue should pray for the power to interpret. For if I pray in a tongue, my spirit prays but my mind is unfruitful. What am I to do? I will pray with the spirit and I will pray with the mind also (1 Cor. 14: 13-15).

The apostle's argument in the preceding verses (6-12) is clear. Speaking in tongues in the church does not profit the hearers if they do not understand what is being said. Thus, in seeking for gifts, let your main object be the building up of the church. 'Therefore'—to return to the opening verse of our passage—'he who speaks in a tongue should pray for the power to interpret' (verse 13). So Paul is here making a plea for the exercise of interpretation of tongues, which the Corinthians were evidently neglecting. It is the public use of tongues that Paul is dealing with here. Unless we are clear on this point we shall misunderstand what immediately follows.

Paul goes on to explain that when he prays in tongues he is praying with his spirit, but not with his mind (verse 14). His mind is unfruitful since he does not understand the language. This, of course, is true for the minds of his hearers; since they do not understand either, they are not edified. Now he is in a quandary, for if God has given him this gift then surely it is to be used. 'What am I to do?' he asks himself. The answer is in this gift of interpretation which he is here emphasizing. So he continues:

> I will pray with the spirit [that is, in a tongue] and I will pray with the mind also [that is, giving the interpretation of the tongue].

Paul had said earlier (verse 2) that speaking in tongues (whether in public or in private) was primarily a speaking unto God and not to man; that is, it took the form of prayer rather than exhortation. Now we learn that the interpretation of a tongue may also be in the form of inspired prayer or thanksgiving, rather than a prophetic utterance to the people.

Having spoken of praying with the spirit followed by praying with the understanding, of singing with the spirit followed by singing with the understanding, he adds, by way of explanation:

> Otherwise, if you bless with the spirit [that is,

give thanks in a tongue—without also blessing
with the understanding] how can anyone in the
position of an outsider say the 'Amen' to your
thanksgiving when he does not know what you
are saying?

Clearly, then, it is *in church* that Paul is contemplating this praying with the spirit, singing
with the spirit and blessing with the spirit. Otherwise there would be no question of the outsider being able, or unable to add his 'Amen'. Until we
reach verse 18 it is not clear whether Paul personally prayed in tongues. 'If I pray in tongues' and 'I
will pray with the spirit', etc., could be hypo-
thetical. But now he goes on to say:

I thank God that I speak in tongues more than
you all; nevertheless, in church I would rather
speak five words with my mind, in order to instruct others, than ten thousand words in a
tongue (verses 18 and 19).

It is important to take these two verses together.
In one breath he says that he spoke in tongues more
than any of the Corinthians—and that was certainly saying something!—and in the next breath
that *in church* he would prefer to speak five words
with his mind, in order to instruct others, than ten
thousand words in a tongue. We cannot escape
from the clear statement of verse 18, that Paul used
the gift of tongues extensively, but hastening to
add, 'nevertheless, in church I would rather ...'
implies that his extensive use of the gift was *not*

in church. This is not to say that he never used it in church, or that it was wrong to use it in church, provided there was interpretation (verses 13–17). Presumably it was because God had equipped him with other and greater gifts 'in order to instruct others' (verse 19) which he generally preferred to use.

If then Paul spoke so much in tongues, but did not do so in church, where did he exercise this gift? The answer can only be, in his private devotions. Without a doubt praying and giving thanks with the spirit (i.e. in tongues) played a very important part in the devotional life of this great apostle. Far from disparaging it, as some do, Paul gave thanks to God for the extensive use he was able to make of it. We too must be careful not to disparage it if only for this reason that it is a precious gift of God.

As we have already said Paul was discussing the use of this gift in church, for that was where things had gone wrong at Corinth, but he himself testifies to the use of it out of church. It was an invaluable tool in his devotional kit, a powerful weapon in his spiritual armoury, and it is this aspect that concerns us here. If he could refer to praying with the spirit, singing with the spirit, and blessing with the spirit *in church*, then it is certain that these were rightful uses of the gift in the privacy of one's own devotions. Some have been quick to point out how limited was the use of this gift in public, according to Paul; but from this very teaching we can learn how unlimited was its use in private.

The devotional use of this gift, and particularly
its use in the ministry of intercession, takes us
right back to the commencement of this chapter of
1 Corinthians where the apostle says, 'For one who
speaks in a tongue speaks not to men but to God'
(14:2). This was even true at Pentecost. The
tongues then was not a preaching of the gospel in
other languages—this Peter did later and was
understood in his mother tongue—but was a declaration of the mighty works of God (Acts 2:11),
presumably an ascription of praise to God in
similar vein to what we have in Psalms 135 and
136. The manifestation in the house of Cornelius
was similarly described as 'extolling God' (Acts
10:46) which Peter later referred to as 'the same
gift . . . as He gave to us' on the day of Pentecost
(Acts 11:17). It is clear, then, that the primary use
of tongues is Godward, not manward.

Though our main emphasis is intercession, a word
may not be out of place here on the use of tongues
in praise and thanksgiving. 'If you bless with the
spirit . . . you may give thanks well enough' (verses
16, 17). Paul's restricting of the gift here is because
of the presence of 'the other man' who is not
helped by an utterance he does not understand. In
the solitude of one's own devotions these restric-
tions no longer apply. Only God is present, and
'one who speaks in tongues speaks not to men but
to God' (verse 2).

But is it not better to do it in your mother
tongue and understand what you are saying? Not
necessarily, or God would never have given this
gift, nor would Paul have used it so much. Have

we not known times when, in adoration of the Lord, we feel the inadequacy of our own language to express all that we feel in our hearts? The very language which is usually an indispensable channel of communication seems to become a barrier to communication. It is then that this gift comes to our aid, and the human spirit is released in an utterance of praise or thanksgiving that would not have been possible in our native tongue. We are not necessarily speaking of ecstasy but simply of liberty in the Spirit. The use of the expression 'ecstatic gift' in referring to tongues is a misnomer. One is not required to be in an ecstatic state to exercise this gift.

There is also an experience of personal edification in the exercise of this gift, as Paul explains in verse 4. This is not difficult to understand when we remember that edification is not primarily a thing of the human mind but of the human spirit. The Holy Spirit can bypass our minds and minister direct to our spirits. Have we never had an uplift by simply a sense of the Lord's presence? To those who find all this somewhat mystifying we would say, the experience is not nearly so difficult as the explanation!

In the realm of intercession we should look on tongues as another weapon in our armoury. We may pray more generally with our understanding, yet this gift has a value and importance all its own. Sometimes it is manifestly an advantage to pray in a language that you do not understand, provided of course the Holy Spirit is inspiring the language, and that is always so if one is praying in the Spirit.

We have already seen that the Holy Spirit is able to illuminate our minds when we are praying over some matter with inadequate knowledge. But there are times when we do not need to know the facts— perhaps important that we do *not* know. It is here that praying with the spirit may take over from praying with the mind, enabling us to pray beyond our knowledge of the situation, because the Holy Spirit who inspires the language knows all the facts.

We usually know at such times that our words are intercession, rather than praise or thanksgiving, and although we do not know what we are saying, it is enough to know that the Holy Spirit is inspiring it, and that the prayer will therefore be right 'on target'. What does it matter that we do not understand the words when we know that God does?

As we have pointed out earlier, praying in the Spirit is not necessarily praying in tongues, but praying in tongues should always be praying in the Spirit. It is possible for a gift that is truly of God to be operated in a fleshly way. As Paul shows in Chapter 13, if I have divine gifts without divine love, 'I am a noisy gong', 'I am nothing', 'I have nothing'—no reflection on the gift, only on me. There was nothing wrong with the gifts at Corinth, but there was a lot wrong with the Corinthians. How could they be 'carnal' or 'of the flesh' (3 : 1–3) and at the same time expect to operate their gifts in the Spirit?

To return to the matter of praying in tongues, it is not that tongues is a superior kind of prayer, just that it is another very valuable kind. Paul says 'Pray at all times in the Spirit with all [kinds of] prayer and supplication'—and this, with words unknown, is one of them. It has this added advantage over praying with the mind that the mind can relax, which is a great help when the mind is too tired for prolonged concentration. There is no suggestion here of making the mind a blank, for that can be dangerous.

An experience, some years ago, brought home to me the authority we may wield by this form of prayer, and how Satan fears it. I had assumed that James' words about the demons trembling or shuddering (James 2 : 19) referred to the abyss or some other unseen realm. I never thought that I would witness it. It was a case of demon possession. I had prayed in English, and also rebuked the enemy in the name of the Lord. This only served to stir him up, and the manifestations were fearful to behold. I was suddenly moved to rebuke the demon in tongues, a thing I had never done before. I was conscious of the authority with which the words came forth. The effect was electric. The person, by now in a kind of coma and completely under the control of the spirit, trembled from head to foot. When a little later I repeated this action the effect was the same, which assured me that this was no coincidence.

The devil knows that there is authority in the right use of this gift, but I believe he fears it, not so much because of what it is in itself, but because, manifested as it was on the day of Pentecost, it is a symbol of the power and gifts of the Spirit in this age, the weapons that God has given us to plunder the strong man's house. If demons realize this, how much more Satan and those higher orders, the principalities and powers in the heavenly realm. Perhaps this is why Satan has attacked this gift so vehemently and relentlessly, seeking to corrupt and spoil it on the one hand, and to despise and vilify it on the other.

How may this gift be received? Generally it is given through the experience of the baptism in the Spirit. Seek the Lord for the promised enduement and if there is in your heart desire and faith for this gift He will surely give it. If you have truly received the Holy Spirit in power but without tongues, then ask Him for the gift. Someone may be quick to warn us, 'Seek the Giver, not the gifts —the Person, not the power.' This may sound very spiritual, but it is not in accord with Scripture. We are to 'seek the Lord *and His strength*' (Psa. 105:4). We are to seek the Giver *and* His gifts. It is certainly wrong to seek gifts for themselves, but right to seek them because we want more of Him, and He comes to us in His gift—they are manifestations of Him. Like everything else gifts are received simply on the basis of faith. Rest your faith on God's promises. The references given at the conclusion of this chapter will be a help here.

Let us, then, use this gift as a weapon of intercession. We are exhorted to 'pray in the Spirit . . . with all [kinds of] prayer' including praying in tongues. Let us not be ashamed of being imitators of the great apostle who thanked God that he used this gift more than the Corinthians abused it. Remember, the answer to misuse is not non-use but right use.

Psa. 37:4, 84:11; Mat. 7:11 with Luke 11:13; Mark 11:24; 1 Cor. 14:1.

15

WITHOUT WORDS

WE have seen that praying in the Spirit may mean praying with the native tongue, that is, 'with the mind'; or praying with the new tongue (promised in Mark 16:17), that is, 'with the spirit'. But it may also mean praying with no tongue at all, that is, 'with sighs too deep for words' (R.S.V.) or 'groanings which cannot be uttered' (A.V., R.V.). This is a very important aspect of the teaching of Romans 8:26, 27 that we must now consider.

If some have found the idea of praying in an unknown tongue perplexing, they may find this idea of inarticulate praying even more so, for here there is no language at all—the only speech is sighs and the only grammar groans, and even these are silent because inexpressible. It should be emphasized here that this type of praying is not generally for the public gathering but for the secret place.

Let us not shut our minds to what at first may appear to be incomprehensible, even irrational. Of course it is not irrational; like so much else in the realm of the Spirit it is super-rational. Faith can lead us into this realm, but not reason. Let us come, then, to this teaching of God's word with a reverent and humble spirit, and the prayer: 'Teach me what I do not see' (Job 34:32).

Notice that in this passage Paul speaks of the groaning of the whole creation (verse 22), the groaning of the believer (verse 23) and finally the 'groanings which cannot be uttered' (A.V., R.V.) of the Spirit Himself (verse 26). Since the same root word is used in this last verse (26) as in the other two verses (22 and 23)[1] we shall follow the A.V. and R.V. rendering and refer to the 'groanings' of the Spirit, rather than the 'sighs too deep for words' of the R.S.V. However, the important point is that, whichever rendering we prefer, this refers to a form of praying without words.

To many this reference to the groaning of the Spirit presents no problem. They assume that this intercession of the Holy Spirit is, like the intercession of Christ at the Father's right hand, performed quite apart from us. It has not registered with them that it has anything to do with the believer, except that it is performed on his behalf. Once we grasp the fact that the Holy Spirit never intercedes for us except He intercedes in us and through us, we begin to see the significance of the Spirit's groaning.

In an earlier chapter we referred to the change of punctuation adopted by the R.S.V. in verses 15–16: 'When we cry, "Abba! Father!" it is the Spirit Himself bearing witness with our spirit . . .' When *we* cry, it is *the Spirit* crying. The action of the divine Spirit merges with that of the human spirit to produce a joint-witness. In the same way this groaning is a joint-groaning of the believer (verse 23) and the Spirit (verse 26).

Notice that we who groan are said to have 'the

first fruits of the Spirit'. Ours is therefore of a different order to the groaning of the whole creation; it is wholly spiritual because it is the product of the Spirit. We may think of the groaning as part of the first fruits—the produce of His working in us.

Note that it is the Spirit who groans, and that God has sent Him forth into our hearts. So it is *in our hearts* where His groaning takes place. 'And He who searches the hearts of men,' continues the apostle, 'knows what is the mind of the Spirit' (verse 27). In speaking of the One who searches the hearts of men he is obviously referring to God (1 Sam. 16:7; Jer. 17:10). Why, then, does he not say 'God'? Surely to impress upon us that it is the great *Searcher of human hearts* who knows what the Spirit's groaning means, for it is in human hearts that the groaning takes place. Notice also how the reference to the believer groaning 'inwardly' (verse 23) corresponds to the Spirit's 'groanings which cannot be uttered' (verse 26 R.V.).

Can we groan inwardly and not be aware of it? Can the Spirit groan within us and we not know it? Surely not, if these two groanings are one. What has been said of the other two kinds of praying in the Spirit is equally true of this. It is our praying inspired and energized by the Spirit within us. The believer is praying without words simply because that is the manner in which the Spirit is moving within him.

In the earlier chapters much truth has been drawn from these two verses in Romans 8 without any mention of this particular kind of wordless praying. That is because the basic facts of our weakness and the Spirit's help are true, whatever the kind of praying. There are principles here that can have wider application than that which Paul gives to them. This should not obscure the fact that the reference here is specifically to inarticulate praying. Since this is the only passage in the Bible which teaches us what praying in the Spirit really is, it should at least impress us with the importance of this aspect, even if it does not actually lead us to conclude that this is the highest and most powerful form of prayer available to man.

On the face of it the idea of prayer being conveyed in the form of groans or sighs rather than words is difficult. How can such convey anything to God?—we may ask. The apostle seems to anticipate this question, for he continues:

> And He who searches the hearts of men knows what is the mind of the Spirit, because the Spirit intercedes for the saints according to the will of God.

Though the prayer be but an inaudible sigh or groan deep in the heart of the intercessor, God the searcher of hearts knows what the Spirit is conveying. Here surely is what may be rightly called 'the language of the Spirit'—that which is peculiarly His own, while 'tongues' is but the language of men, or possibly angels.

Now the original does not actually say that the

Spirit intercedes 'according to the will of God', but simply 'according to God'. This is even stronger, for it suggests that the Spirit's activity is not merely in harmony with God's will but actually regulated by God. So we are back to the picture of the electric circuit—the impulse that comes from God by the Spirit returns to God.

Groaning is the expression of physical or mental suffering, and here, in the context of Romans 8, the figure that Paul uses is the pain of childbirth. In verse 22 he speaks of 'groaning in travail'. A woman in labour not only groans because of her labour pains but also with desire to bring forth. It is not just pain, but pain transfigured by longing, by hope, by expectation.

In this realm of prayer-travail described by Paul in verses 26 and 27, there is inevitably suffering, but its nature is spiritual, though it may have physical accompaniments. Naturally we shrink from this, but let the following considerations strengthen us for whatever the Spirit may demand. Firstly, this is one aspect of the 'fellowship of Christ's sufferings'. It is said of Him in the garden, 'being in an agony He prayed more earnestly; and His sweat became like great drops of blood falling down upon the ground' (Luke 22:44). He invited three disciples to share that lonely prayer vigil, but they failed Him. Shall we fail Him now in His great unfinished work of intercession?

Then there is the glorious fact which we have emphasized throughout this book, 'the Spirit helps us in our weakness'—even in this weakness we feel in the face of suffering. He comes in His capacity as the Comforter, to solace our griefs, to ease our pains, to strengthen our wills that we may not faint, nor even flinch, but endure to the end. Finally, there is the glorious hope which is the subject of the whole passage to spur us on. We are travailing to bring forth. A new age is about to be born—and how much nearer we are to it than when Paul penned these words to the Roman believers. The sons of God are to be manifested. A new 'man' is to appear before the universe in the perfection of his manhood, having come to the measure of the stature of the fullness of Christ.

We may have read the lives of great intercessors like 'Praying Hyde' of India, and perhaps we have associated this kind of praying with such. No doubt, we argue, these had a special call and a special ministry in this realm, but it is altogether beyond people like ourselves. This may provide us with an easy escape, but let us first ask ourselves whether it may not be a cover for our unwillingness or our unbelief. And before we settle for the 'specialist' theory let us read the passage again with hearts truly open to the Lord, and ask ourselves if there is any hint in Paul's words that this is a special ministry involving a special call. He says:

We ourselves, who have the first fruits of the Spirit [are you included here?], groan inwardly as we wait for adoption as sons, the redemption of our bodies. For in this hope we were saved ... But if we hope for what we do not see, we wait for it with patience. Likewise the Spirit helps us in our weakness; for we do not know how to pray as we ought, but the Spirit Himself intercedes for us with sighs too deep for words.

It would seem that Paul is speaking in very general terms, and that if we have ears to hear, hearts to receive, and wills to obey, we may trust ourselves to our Heavenly Teacher to lead us into this deep mystery of prayer. I believe that in these closing days of this age the Lord will raise up an army of intercessors who pray at all times in the Spirit, with all kinds of prayer, including this.

¹ In verses 22 and 23 the verb forms, *sunstenazo* (to groan together), and *stenazo* (to groan) are used. In verse 26 it is the noun form, *stenagmos* (a groaning).

16

TRAVAIL AND TEARS

To illustrate and amplify what has been said I want, in this chapter and the one following, to call a few intercessors into the witness box. I know them each personally, and I am grateful to them for being willing to lay bare their hearts in order to share with us, anonymously of course, some of those deep and intimate things that they have experienced in the secret place—things which would not normally or generally be shared. To those who have not yet begun to move in this wonderful realm of the Spirit there may be some things here that will perplex or even offend. But we must take this risk for the sake of others in quest of a life of power with God, who will find here that 'deep calls to deep'.

Please remember that we are dealing with experiences which belong to the solitude of the prayer room. Here are words of those who have gone farther in than most, just as the Saviour in Gethsemane left His foremost apostles and went 'a little farther', where He prayed in a way that would certainly shock most Christians if it happened in the church prayer meeting—with strong crying and tears, His sweat like drops of blood, as He lay prostrate on the ground.

One thing that must surely impress the reader is

that there is both similarity and diversity in the experiences recorded here. This is one of the hallmarks of God's workmanship which we find in the physical as well as the spiritual realm. The similarity teaches us that there are principles operating here which hold good for all those who would pray in the Spirit. The diversity is a warning not to pattern our prayer life after this one or that. The Spirit will express Himself through us in His own way.

This testimony comes from a married woman with a family, whose husband is a business executive. In addition to both husband and wife being involved in evangelistic and church work, they have a very busy household to which many come for counsel and help. It has proved to be for many a meeting place with God. In the personal letter which accompanied her testimony she wrote:

I am very conscious that in disclosing these intimate spiritual experiences, even though under God's definite direction and with the knowledge that my testimony is to be anonymous, I must be meticulously careful to remind myself and you that I am nothing, have nothing and never will be anything outside of His amazing grace; and that 'of Him and through Him and to Him are all things'.

I asked this sister to share particularly her experiences of inarticulate praying, and so she has concentrated on this particular aspect.

'During times of prayer when the burden has

intensified to the point where words ceased, the Holy Spirit has used two main methods to express the burden of the Father's heart for the object of prayer. Firstly, loud involuntary regular groanings, exactly the same as when I was in labour before giving birth to my children, except that instead of the pain there were intensity of desire and deep longing in the Spirit. The mind is centred on God in an attitude of faith that He is doing something deep and permanent to bring about the requests for which I have prayed.

'I have no sudden or dramatic results to report from this form of intercession as it has only come upon me when praying for people and projects that take a long process to accomplish. It happened when praying for a vital Christian couple to go further in discipleship. Christ prayed for this in John 17, and what followed showed that the results were not immediate in the case of the disciples. I have experienced this too when praying individually for men of God to become greater men of God—more holy, more humble, more Christlike, and more effective for God. Scripture teaches that the development of the man of God takes many years to accomplish, and I am confident that, on the occasions that the Holy Spirit has travailed through me in this way, something very real has been accomplished which may not be immediately apparent. I have also known this travail when praying for an outpouring of God's Spirit upon my own nation (Isa. 66:8).

'Secondly, there have been times when a deep desire begins with words, and then goes on into intense, uncontrollable weeping as though the heart would break. This has happened when praying for lost souls over many years. On one occasion I was praying at home for prisoners in a jail at the time an evangelist was preaching the gospel to them. It lasted for about ten minutes during which time I felt within my whole being something of what it was like to be bound by their sin, their guilt, their helplessness, their despair, especially those on long term sentences. It was awful. The intense desire of the Spirit expressed through the weeping was for them to have hope and freedom through receiving Christ.

'I believe this experience in prayer prepared me as nothing else could have for the years that followed when I regularly visited these men and had the great joy of leading some of them to the Lord while they were still in the prison. One of these was on a long sentence, having committed one of the worst offences, and was greatly despised by the other prisoners. Another, on release, commenced to worship regularly with other Christians, married a fine Christian girl, and established a Christian home. I cannot describe the joy I felt at his wedding.

'When, over the years, I have been burdened to pray for those bound by the chains of sin and Satan, especially those in the grip of drug addiction, alcoholism, prostitution and sex perversion, I have known the same intense weeping and feeling of utter despair. Years later God led me into a work which reached out to such, and I have seen some of them find deliverance in Christ.

'After a day of prayer and fasting, for souls to be saved prior to an evangelistic crusade, this intense weeping came upon me as I prayed for a Jew, very influential in both religious and business circles. I had already prayed for him for two years. He came with us to the Crusade and was deeply stirred by the Holy Spirit. This was followed by a further year of intercession, after which he died suddenly, without our knowing whether or not he had found Christ. God alone knows the destiny of this man's soul. I learned much through this experience of God's pursuing love.

'Perhaps the greatest agony I have experienced for a lost soul was in circumstances which made it inexpedient for any groanings to be expressed at all. One Sunday morning the preacher announced that he would be preaching that night on the subject of hell from the story of the rich man and Lazarus, and that there might be someone in the evening service for whom it would be the last opportunity to receive Christ. He asked for special prayer. I knew at once that this referred to an unconverted friend, a business executive, to whom my husband had faithfully given the gospel on several occasions, and for whom much prayer had been made. We phoned him and he consented to come. In the afternoon as I prayed the burden of his desperate need came upon me, and words gave way to intense weeping, with a great longing that he would repent before it was too late. That evening he sat beside me throughout the service as the Holy Spirit agonized through me for his salvation. In utter silence and perfect stillness of body I experienced a travail of spirit as intense as anything I have ever known. It seemed I could see his soul spiralling down to a lost eternity, and, as I prayed without ceasing, I sensed the force of the Holy Spirit's work was gradually but surely drawing the man back. The only outward indication that anything was happening to me was the silent falling of tears. He responded to the appeal, and after the service he knelt with the preacher and myself, repented of his sin and committed his life to Christ.

'I had been praying regularly for some years for a very fine minister's only son who had professed Christ as a boy, but who had for years been right away from God. He had made a mess of his life, and had been the heartbreak of his parents. One night as I prayed for him, words ceased and prolonged uncontrollable weeping came upon me. This greatly encouraged me to believe that God was still striving with this young man, though so many had been praying for him for so long with no apparent result. Subsequent events have confirmed that God is working in him.

'When in prayer for the nation to be saved from the judgment we so obviously deserve, pleading God's character of long-suffering and mercy, intense and heart-breaking weeping has come upon me, that we might be spared all that He has planned in judgment. Only one oft-repeated word has come from my lips with the weeping—the word "mercy". Following the weeping has been a feeling of physical exhaustion.

'One other experience I would record concerns a deep purging work in my own life. God had been dealing with me for some days over the sin of pride in several specific matters. I became concerned that there must be a considerable root of this sin in my heart for all these little branches to be showing up. So one day I shut myself in a room and asked God to show me my heart as He saw it —especially the sin of pride. Nothing happened. I prayed more earnestly, looking to Him in faith, believing that I was asking according to His will, for His glory and my good. Still nothing.

'I began to wrestle with God, told Him repeatedly that I would not let Him go, that I meant what I was saying with all my heart, and wept before Him with deep desire. Then it came, just as I had asked. I could do nothing but weep and weep as though my heart would break as I saw the awfulness of this sin in the sight of a holy God. With such a revelation, repentance was instantaneous. I knew I had to acknowledge the conviction of pride to a servant of God before whom much of it had been committed. I did, and the wonderful peace that followed more than compensated for the humbling experience of having to make confession in this way.

'In the preceding testimony I have concentrated on one particular aspect of prayer, as I was requested to do. I hope that the reader will not be left with the impression that this ministry of intercession is all tears and travail. I find that God also gives me times of great joy and exhilaration. Words cannot convey what a wonderfully varied and thrilling ministry it is.'

17

THE UNPREDICTABLE HOLY SPIRIT

THERE is nothing routine about the path of the Spirit-led intercessor, and consequently he is never liable to be troubled by monotony. Labour and self-discipline there certainly is, but to this is added the spice of mystery and even excitement. The intercessor never knows what lies 'just around the corner'. He can never assume that because the Spirit led this way yesterday He will do so again today. He comes almost to expect the unexpected and to look upon the unpredictable as usual, as indeed a characteristic of the Spirit's working.

Our Lord alluded to this in speaking to Nicodemus of the regenerating work of the Holy Spirit. He said, 'The wind blows where it wills, and you hear the sound of it, but you do not know whence it comes or whither it goes' (John 3:8). 'Wind' here is the usual word for 'spirit' (or 'breath'), and elsewhere in Scripture, as we know, wind is used as a symbol for the Spirit's activity (e.g. Ezek. 37 and Acts 2). But the interesting thing about our Lord's reference to the wind is that He does not apply it directly to the Spirit—'so it is with the Spirit', but to the believer—'so it is with everyone who is born of the Spirit'. In other words, just as the wind is to us incomprehensible and unpredictable in its movements, so is the activity of one born of the Spirit.

This fact may be applied to praying in the Spirit. This unpredictable feature of the Spirit's working is reflected in the prayer life of the believer who is led of the Spirit. Of course we must never entertain the thought that the Holy Spirit is unpredictable in the sense of being unreliable—as many humans are. If His ways are incomprehensible they are certainly not irrational. There is nothing freakish or capricious about the Holy Spirit's activity. He is not subject to whim and fancy. His working will often transcend reason, but will never contradict it. That we do not know the 'whence' and the 'whither' of the Spirit's movings is simply due to our limited vision and understanding of the unseen realm.

Before that confrontation with the prophets of Baal on Mount Carmel, Elijah told Obadiah, the steward of Ahab's household, to tell his master Ahab, 'Behold, Elijah is here.' Obadiah was terrified at this suggestion :

As soon as I have gone from you, the Spirit of the Lord will carry you whither I know not; and so, when I come and tell Ahab and he cannot find you, he will kill me.

Of course, Obadiah's fear was groundless, for the Spirit does not move a man to say one thing and then immediately act contrary to it. But behind the fear was the knowledge of the unpredictable element that marked the man of God, because he was led by the Spirit. It appears that Paul too was accused by some of being fickle because he did not carry through his original plans (2 Cor. 1 : 15–18).

This unpredictable element may serve to reassure the intercessor. The mysterious union of the Spirit and the believer in the activity of prayer subjects him to a subtle temptation. He begins to wonder whether what he had assumed was the activity of the Holy Spirit might not after all be merely psychological. What you have learned to expect, by a kind of auto-suggestion is brought to pass. 'Is this the Holy Spirit, or is it just me?' It is here that he is helped by this unpredictable element. He soon finds that these operations are not always according to his own preconceptions but often quite contrary to them. The conviction that this is indeed the Holy Spirit is further strengthened when, in retrospect, the reasonableness and rightness of the Spirit's leadings are confirmed.

We shall notice this unpredictable element appearing in these further testimonies. The first is from one who had been praying for some time for his own locality, and in particular about a certain property that the Lord had shown him was needed for the work of God.

'The Lord has told me that the time has now come to wage a spiritual war for the possession of——. I was impressed that there was Satanic opposition to its release, and that there was a need for sustained prayer in the Spirit. I had never received such a prayer commission before and I asked the Lord to show me how I was to fulfil it. Was I to undertake this alone? Was I to set aside a certain time each day? If not, what priority was I to give to this intercession? The Lord's answer was clear and simple. I was to walk this path alone, and He would burden me when He wanted me to give myself to prayer in this way, and then everything else was to be laid aside.

'Next morning I woke at 5 a.m. with slight stomach discomfort. My first thought was that I should have been up at 4.00 for special intercession that I have once a week at that time. I jumped up, thinking, "Better late than never." Not until I was on my knees did I realize that this prayer vigil was not due till the following morning! I knew at once why the Lord had got me up at that early hour, and could not but smile at the way He had done it. A time of praise was followed by fervent intercession in tongues. This in turn gave way to a convulsion of dry rapid sobbing, all inward and almost silent. I was conscious of battling with the powers of darkness. I saw that specific intercession was also needed for the release of the finance—a considerable sum—for the obtaining of the property. I then had a repeat of the intercession, first praise, then tongues, and finally wordless praying, only this time I knew that this was for the necessary finance. This second time the wordless praying was quite different; instead of dry sobbing there was an inner groaning or yearning, a kind of travail to bring forth.

'The pattern has continued much the same from day to day, first for the release of the property and then for the finances involved. Almost every day the Spirit has moved upon me to pray in this way, and sometimes I have had the burden more than once in the day. The constraint to lay aside what I am doing is not usually strong, and I have to be very sensitive to the Spirit. Once or twice I have been gently reproved because I missed hearing His voice—too preoccupied! Occasionally I have got down before the Lord expecting the intercession to come upon me, and nothing has happened, but the Lord has given it later. This assures me it is not of me, and is also a salutary reminder that the Spirit does not work to order.

'Looking back over this first month there has been no noticeable lengthening in the periods of intercession, but a definite intensifying of the Spirit's activity. This has been very gradual and like watching the waves when the tide is coming in, one can only see the advance over a period. Sometimes the wordless praying is marked by a holy violence that shakes my whole body and leaves me for the moment breathless and exhausted. I begin to understand what Jesus meant when He said of His kingdom, "The violent take it by force."

'One day at the end of the first week when the Spirit's moving was becoming more powerful, I was surprised when His sobbing within me was as gentle as the summer rain. I waited for "Part Two" (for the finance) and it didn't come, and what a comfort and confirmation to find I couldn't produce it! Instead I received a gentle anointing, more a kind of "presence" pervading my being, as though the Spirit was saying, "I want to get fuller possession of you." With this, several things from

the Scriptures were opened to my mind in a new
and wonderful way. Then, without the usual preliminaries of praise and tongues, I went straight
into deep silent prayer for the release of the
finance.

'I have sensed in the Spirit that the sobbing in
the first part of my intercession indicates an initial
phase in the Spirit's work, while the groaning of
the second part indicates that His work is more
advanced. The Spirit has warned me of the necessity of a pure heart and right motives in praying
for this money. Now the sobbing usually ends up
with groaning and travail, with occasional wailing
or deep sighing in the Spirit. The amazing thing is
that all this is inward and virtually silent—very
necessary in view of my domestic circumstances.
I don't think that anyone outside my door would
hear anything.

'One morning I found myself in an agony of
prayer pressing down on the floor with my hands
and virtually lifting myself off my knees. This happened three times, and each time I found myself
saying, "I break it in the name of the Lord." Then
a sense of relief, of finality, as though something
really had been broken, though I do not know
what. I am encouraged to believe that a definite
milestone has been passed. Whatever is happening
in the unseen realm, the Lord is certainly working
in the outward situation. We see so many changes,
none big in itself, but together adding up to something quite impressive. In addition the Lord is certainly working in me. There is a renewing of faith,
a new sensitivity to the Spirit, and a deepening of

my whole prayer life. No doubt there is a good way to go yet, but I am waxing strong in faith for the ultimate fulfilment. All this is the Lord's doing, and marvellous in my eyes.'

Finally, there is an account by one who has been for many years engaged in a ministry of intercession. She writes first of the way the Lord prepared her over the years:

. 'Though I had known intercession before, I had no knowledge of the type of intercession into which God desired to take me. God had to take me like a little child and teach me right from the beginning. First I was taught to know the Holy Spirit in such a deep, deep fellowship, not only to know how to yield to His moving, but much more to know Him personally, with a great love and appreciation.

'Then I was brought into a wonderful relationship with the Father, to know Him with a very deep personal knowledge until I understood something of His great love and compassion, His holiness, His justice and His glory. Since then God has begun to bring me into a much deeper relationship with His Son.

'It was about four and a half years ago, the Father again started to bring me in to a deeper place of intercession, after some very difficult years. Though He took me a long way at that time —I was praying alone—He told me He could only take me so far, as the way was too difficult without prayer support. Now He has given me two partners. J. is a university student, K. is a mother with a young daughter and I am middle-aged. God has bound us like a threefold cord, that we might not be broken, as we pray together for His people in these last days. We would rather do this work of intercession than anything else on earth.

'Let me tell you what God did for us one night recently. We started as we always do by being led of the Spirit of God into deep worship and praise. As we worshipped and sought God we became aware that we were again in the secret, hidden place into which God had brought us. This place we had been brought into after months of consistent praying, two, three or more hours a night, four nights a week. It is a special place of hiding and safety from which we can do battle against the powers of darkness for God's people. It is not an end in itself, but a stopping place along the way for a special purpose. This night a brother was with us. B. is a friend who has a similar ministry and knows how to do battle against the enemy.

'At the beginning we did not understand what God was doing, but as we followed the Spirit of God in deeper we became aware of two things. Firstly, there was deep sorrow of spirit with weeping and crying for some of His people who were suffering and in very great need. Who they were we had not yet been shown. Secondly, and running parallel with the sorrow and travail, was an acute awareness that we were up against very strong powers of darkness in this matter. As we continued in the Spirit, K. was shown in the mid-heavens a throne set, with a being enthroned on it. Before this throne stood a group of demons, armed and set in battle array. Then we knew we were up against a "principality". We continued to seek God, standing on His word with strong praise and dependance on the redemption of the Lord Jesus Christ and the triumph of His cross.

'Gradually God showed us for whom we were praying. Looking down from the heavenly place we were in, K. could see a number of little grass huts hidden in a swamp. With deep sorrow and weeping she told us what God was showing her, Christians tortured, sick, suffering, hungry, and hiding in a swamp. To us this bore the witness of the Spirit upon it. With outstretched hands we pleaded their cause before the Father and stayed pleading until He had filled our hands with supplies for their need. But we were in heavenly places and they were in a swamp. We could not take these supplies ourselves. We sought God until He reminded us of His angel messengers and permitted us to ask Him to send them in our stead. Then we could hand over, as it were, to the appointed angels the succour God had given us for our brethren and wait until the angel contingent was on its way to meet their need.

'As we waited God was showing us a further need requiring urgent attention. K. saw a Christian who had been tortured, mercilessly beaten and kicked into insensibility, being dragged along the ground. His head hung in unconsciousness and he had a mortal wound in his left side. Much of the pain of his suffering she felt in her own body so that she cried out in pain. With this before us we cried to God for this brother. God showed us that this was His "key man" and He needed him alive, but he was so badly injured that apart from a miracle of God he could not survive. With many tears and groanings that were too deep for words, we sought God for our beloved brother.

'After we had prayed in this way for some time we became aware that J. was speaking, almost in a whisper. Then our weeping hushed; we waited before God while the Holy Spirit took of the heart's cry of one who, in his unconsciousness could not speak for himself, and poured it out to the Father through J. as she lay, not on a filthy prison floor, but on the carpet thousands of miles away. As we listened and marvelled at the beauty of this man's spirit, tears streamed down our faces. We heard, whispered and halting, as from the lips of one whose physical life was ebbing fast, "I'm so tired. I'm ... so ... tired. Oh, Father ... I'm so tired I just want to die. I just want to die. Please take me home, Father. I don't think I can stand any more. Take me home, Father ... nevertheless ... not ... my will ... but yours be done." Then the soul seemed to struggle for a little while before words came again, "I shall ... not ... die. I shall not die but I shall live. I shall not die but I shall live to declare Thy works, O Lord." Then there followed such an outpouring of that dear man's soul in long passages of Scripture that we knew it was not J. who was speaking.

'Suddenly, breaking into the flow of Scripture came a cry of fear—"Oh, God, I'm so cold. What is happening to me? Is this death? Oh, my God, save me! Now I know you want me to live—but this coldness, it's creeping up over me. Oh, God, save me." Realizing what was happening to our brother, the three of us who were watching took this matter up with the Father, urgently, desperately, until the Holy Spirit poured faith into our hearts and gave us the authority to rebuke the angel of death and turn him back. When the Holy Spirit had finished, and the words which poured from J.'s lips were psalms of praise in the midst of suffering, it was given to others of us to join in and lift the heart's cry of our unconscious brother to God, "Father, I believe you. Father, I believe you."

'At last we knew the Holy Spirit had gained from the Father that which He desired and we were freed from our task. We rested in the presence of the Lord and could now speak to each other again. K. said, "One thing I don't understand is the way he was dressed. He was clothed in a golden garment which covered his head and his whole body right down to his feet like a space suit." B. replied, "Yes, Sister, he was clothed in a garment of faith. Remember 1 Peter 1:7, 'The trial of your faith, being much more precious than of gold that perisheth, though it be tried by fire . . .' That's how God saw him, clothed with faith." '

In concluding this chapter it must be stressed that such remarkable experiences as we have just recorded are comparatively rare, even among those who are constantly praying in the Spirit. Nevertheless it should stimulate our faith to know that God can and does work in such ways today. Though it may never be given to us to experience such visions and revelations, it *is* given to us to intercede in the Spirit—to yield ourselves and trust ourselves to His gracious control—to expect that He will pray through us. Then, whether or not we have dramatic experiences, we shall know with deep joy and thanksgiving that we have prayed in the Spirit, and God who sees in secret will reward us openly.

18

TILL BREAK OF DAY

LIKE the theme of some musical composition the wonderful truth that 'the Spirit helps us in our weakness' in prayer has recurred again and again throughout this book. Nowhere else in the Bible are we given such an insight into the way the Holy Spirit works in the heart of the believer who prays in the Spirit as we have in Romans 8 : 26, 27. We must now set the whole matter in perspective by pointing out that Spirit-inspired praying is not really the theme of Romans 8, and what Paul tells us about it is only incidental to his grand objective. To this great apostle praying in the Spirit is not the end—and we must not make it that—it is simply the means to the end. What then is the end?

The theme of Romans is 'the gospel of God' (1 : 1). But what length and breadth, depth and height we find here as the epistle unfolds. It could hardly be summarized by 'Come to Jesus and be forgiven'! After a thorough unfolding of man's condemnation, Paul moves on to the ground of his justification, his sanctification, and his glorification. It is in this very Chapter 8 that the emphasis changes from the believer's present sanctification to his future glorification. The transition in the apostle's development of his theme is not sudden but gradual, as one colour in the rainbow merges into the next. The goal, then, is the glory of the age to come.

Let us now read carefully verses 1–25 of Romans 8 and try to grasp the trend of Paul's argument. Having spoken of life in the Spirit, he declares (verse 11) that the Spirit who now dwells in us will (future tense) give life to our mortal bodies. Though there is a present application of this in a physical strengthening and quickening, the apostle has future resurrection primarily in view. This truth, that the present blessing of the Spirit is both a preparation for and a guarantee of the resurrection or redemption of our bodies and the title to our future inheritance, occurs in several epistles:

We ourselves, who have the first fruits of the Spirit, groan inwardly as we wait for adoption as sons, the redemption of our bodies (Rom. 8:23).
Here indeed we groan, and long to put on our heavenly dwelling (resurrection body) ... He who has prepared us for this very thing is God, who has given us the Spirit as a guarantee (2 Cor. 5:2, 5).
You ... were sealed with the promised Holy Spirit, which is the guarantee of our inheritance until we acquire possession of it (Eph. 1:13, 14). And do not grieve the Holy Spirit of God, in whom you were sealed for the day of redemption (Eph. 4:30).

What Paul is saying in verse 11 of Romans 8, is that the Holy Spirit within us—the very same

Spirit that raised Jesus from the dead—will also raise us up. Just as the lunar module speeding towards its historic first landing on the moon had residing within it the power to bring it back from the moon at the touch of a button, so we have within us, in the person of the life-giving Spirit, the power that will one day effect our resurrection.

The Holy Spirit, continues Paul (verses 15-17), has delivered us from a slavish spirit of fear and given us instead a spirit of sonship. He inspires within us the cry, 'Abba! Father!' He brings to us the consciousness of being God's children, and that implies heirship—'heirs of God and fellow-heirs with Christ'. As a young heir to some important title is specially trained for his future responsibilities, so the Holy Spirit is teaching and training us for the day when we shall enter upon our inheritance.

Now the apostle warms to his subject. In thrilling terms he describes (verses 18-23) what this inheritance will mean for us and for the whole universe. Suffering he has certainly known in full measure (and for him there was more to come), but in his opinion it is 'not worth comparing with the glory that is to be revealed to us' (verse 18). Notice how he relates the sufferings to 'this present time' (cp. Acts 14:22; 2 Cor. 4:17), and the glory (in its full manifestation, of course) 'to be revealed to us' in the coming age. This is the trail blazed by the Pioneer of our salvation. He trod the pathway of suffering, that through death and resurrection He might enter into His glory. (Luke 24:46; 1 Pet. 1:11).

What then is the glory? It is the revealing of the sons of God. Paul paints the picture of the creation groaning with desire, breathless with expectation, for this moment for which all the past ages were but a preparation, when God will display to the wondering eyes of the whole universe His masterpiece. Poets and hymnists have used their art to try to describe the glory of that scene when Christ returns, but so often they have missed the point Paul is emphasizing here. He is not to be revealed *without us*. When that day dawns and that hour strikes—and only God knows when that will be—when the heir of the universe steps on to the dais, He will not be alone, His fellow heirs will be with Him. Certainly He is coming to be glorified, but it is, 'in His saints ... in all who have believed' (2 Thes. 1 : 10). The world will indeed see a glorified Man, but that Man will comprise not only Christ the Head but also the church, His body; not only the Bridegroom but also the Bride, invested with the beauty, dignity and glory of her Lord. As Paul puts it in verse 17, if we 'suffer with Him' now, we shall 'be glorified with Him' then.

As man's sin brought futility and bondage to the whole creation, so man's final redemption will effect its release. This will be when the sons of God are revealed. It is for this that the creation waits with eager longing (verses 19–21). It is for this that it groans as a woman in travail (verse 22). This then is the goal towards which we press. This is the glorious hope in which we were saved; a hope that is not yet seen, not yet realized, but for which we patiently wait.

This waiting, however, is not for us a waiting of inactivity, for we are sharing the travail of the rest of creation for the birth of the new age. 'We ourselves, who have the first fruits of the Spirit, groan inwardly as we wait for adoption as sons, the redemption of our bodies' (verse 23). As we wait we groan. This groaning, as has already been pointed out, is intimately connected with the first fruits of the Spirit, and so to be distinguished from the groaning of the rest of creation. It is a groaning of the Spirit in us. Thus praying in the Spirit, especially this inarticulate praying, has an indispensable part to play in the birth of the new age.

We commonly think of this present age as 'the age of the Spirit', or 'the age of service', and the coming age as 'the age of rest'. This may be misleading. The expressions which the New Testament uses in relation to the blessing of the Spirit are deeply suggestive, for they imply that a much richer age of the Spirit is yet to come. Here in verse 23 we are said to have 'the first fruits of the Spirit'. Now first fruits are but the foretaste of the harvest that is to follow. How disappointed the Israelite would be if having gathered the first fruits there was no main crop to follow. His barns would be well nigh empty. Have we realized that the power of the Spirit displayed at Pentecost, and demonstrated in the ministries of Peter, Paul, Stephen and others, is after all, only first fruits? What then will the harvest be like when the new age is born?

Elsewhere Paul speaks of the same blessing of the Spirit as 'the guarantee' (R.S.V.) or 'earnest of the Spirit' (A.V. and R.V.) (see 2 Cor. 1:22, 5:5;

Eph. 1 : 13, 14). The basic meaning of the word is 'earnest money', just like the 10% downpayment or deposit that is nowadays paid when a house is purchased. It is the guarantee of the full sum. What vendor would be satisfied if the 10% deposit was all he received? If the pentecostal outpouring was but a downpayment, what will the full payment be like?

Those who have received the baptism in the Holy Spirit and the wonderful gifts that accompany or follow it, are said to have merely 'tasted the heavenly gift . . . and the powers of the age to come' (Heb. 6 : 4, 5). If what we now have is but a foretaste, glorious as it is, of that which in its fullness is reserved for the coming age, what will the banquet be like? No wonder the great apostle thrilled at the prospect of 'the glory that is to be revealed to us'. We shall certainly need redeemed bodies, resurrected and transformed, to be fit vessels for such an inflow of divine power and glory. One wonders how believers who now recoil in fear from any supernatural manifestations of the Spirit will fare in that coming day? If the downpayment is too much for them, how will they handle the full payment? If they are put off by the taste, how will they stomach the feast?

All this accords with the other teaching in the New Testament, that this age is only a probationary period for the believer, in preparation for the true age of service to come (Mat. 25 : 14–30; Luke 19 : 11–27). In the parable of the pounds the master on his return told the first servant, whose one pound had gained ten pounds, 'You have been faithful in a very little, you shall have authority over ten cities' (Luke 19:17). Had he said to his servant, 'Have authority over ten *houses*' that would have implied a greatly increased responsibility, but he said 'ten cities'. From stewarding a modest sum of a few pounds which his master describes as 'a very little', he finds himself ruler of a sizeable province of his master's kingdom. The principle on which the Lord will determine His appointments in that day is now operating. 'He who is faithful in a very little is faithful also in much.' The day of reckoning must soon come. Let us look to the talent and to the pound entrusted to us.

Is not the ministry of intercession an important part of our stewardship? As we pray in the Spirit are we not trading in the spiritual realm and producing eternal profits? Our Lord Jesus has become the first fruits of those that sleep. He is the guarantee that we shall one day have glorified bodies like His. Has His glorification terminated His intercession? No, indeed, one would think that it had enlarged it. For now, as our great High Priest 'He always lives to make intercession' for us (Heb. 7:25). May not our glorification also open up far greater possibilities in the ministry of intercession when the kingdom of our God and His Christ has fully come? If we are unfaithful in the 'very little' now, how can He entrust us with 'much' then?

It is essential that we rid our minds of any idea that intercession is a special ministry to which God calls a favoured few. It was not to any select class, but to disciples in general, that Jesus told the parable 'to the effect that they ought always to pray and not lose heart' (Luke 18 : 1–8). Whatever else our ministry may involve the Lord would remind us that we 'ought always to pray'. Similarly the apostle Paul was not addressing a particular class in the church at Thessalonica, but believers in general, when he said, 'Pray constantly' (1 Thes. 5 : 17). And those thus addressed were not seasoned warriors of many years standing, but new converts who were little more than babes in Christ. Whether young or old in the faith, intercession is not an optional extra.

The message of this book, however, is that we are not only commanded to pray, not only commanded to pray without ceasing but also to 'pray in the Holy Spirit'. The apostle Jude sandwiches this between two other commands—'build yourselves up on your most holy faith' and 'keep yourselves in the love of God' (verses 20, 21). The importance of these two we all recognize, but the middle one is seldom understood and therefore neglected. Paul goes even farther than Jude, for he says that we are to pray in the Spirit 'always' (A.V.) or 'at all seasons' (R.V., R.S.V.). This disposes for ever of the idea that this is a special kind of praying reserved for the favoured few, or one that we exercise on special occasions. It is of course the only standard of praying the New Testament recognizes. Anything less is subnormal.

Is there within you a real desire to be led into a ministry of praying in the Spirit, even to know that groaning in travail of which the apostle speaks? In that case we cannot leave Romans 8 without mentioning the three keys that Paul gives us in this chapter which are essential to the opening up of this ministry.

In verses 12 and 13 he speaks of the mortification of the body:

> So then, brethren, we are debtors, not to the flesh, to live according to the flesh—for if you live according to the flesh you will die, but if by the Spirit you put to death the deeds of the body you will live.

Prayer in the Spirit spells death to the flesh. Being almost entirely a secret ministry there is nothing here in which the flesh can glory. How true it is that the desires of the flesh are against the Spirit, and the desires of the Spirit are against the flesh '. . . to prevent you from doing what you would' (Gal. 5:17). This is the primary reason why many never enter this realm. The flesh strongly objects and they weakly give in. But Paul says, 'You don't owe the flesh anything! Don't give in to it, put it to death, mortify the deeds of the body!' That is key number one.

In verses 17 and 18 he speaks about *suffering*:

> And if children, then heirs, heirs of God and fellow heirs with Christ, provided we suffer with Him in order that we may also be glorified with Him. I consider that the sufferings of this present time are not worth comparing with the glory that is to be revealed to us.

Travail and bringing forth inevitably involve a measure of suffering. People may talk nowadays about painless childbirth, but there is no such thing in the spiritual realm. I am not suggesting that we are called to suffer as Paul did. It is a question of recognizing that we are called to suffer (Phil. 1 : 29; 1 Thes. 3 : 3) and so of arming ourselves with such a mind (1 Pet. 4 : 1). If we do not cultivate the mind to suffer we shall never be a vehicle through whom the Spirit can travail. Naturally we recoil from this, but that merely emphasizes the need of the third key.

In verses 24 and 25 he speaks of our *future hope* :

> For in this hope we were saved. Now hope that is seen is not hope. For who hopes for what he sees? But if we hope for what we do not see, we wait for it with patience.

It was the vision of the coming glory that sustained our Saviour in His night of travail, 'who for the joy that was set before Him endured the cross, despising the shame'. Similarly Paul tells us that he did not consider that his sufferings were worth comparing with the glory that was to come. This is our hope, and 'in this hope we were saved'. Let the Holy Spirit once set that hope on fire in our souls, and we too will ever after call our sufferings 'our light affliction', and declare that it is not worth comparing with the glory. This hope has yet to fire the hearts of God's people. When it does it will become the major incentive in the final proclamation of the gospel of the kingdom to all the nations of the earth, as well as in the producing of that prayer travail which will give birth to the coming age.

As the darkness deepens and the dawn of Christ's appearing draws steadily nearer, let us give ourselves to this vital ministry. If our priorities need adjusting let us adjust them. If some good and desirable things have to go, let them go. Has not the good ever been the enemy of the best? 'The night is far gone, the day is at hand. Let us then cast off the works of darkness and put on the armour of light.' Let us believe that the great interceding Spirit will pray through us, until the day dawn. The world has yet to see such a manifestation of the glory of God that can only come through a church, cleansed and purified, praying in the power of the Holy Spirit.

Praying Together

Mike & Katey Morris

KINGSWAY PUBLICATIONS
EASTBOURNE

To our parents
who suffer so much of the criticism
and receive so little
of the credit.
Thanks.

Contents

Foreword

People who write books on prayer are often thought to
be predictable, set in their ways and 'well stricken in
years'. However, there is nothing stuffy or formal about
Mike and Katey Morris. Their obvious joy in the Lord—
and in each other—bubbles over, making a deep and
lasting impression on the reader. Behind Mike's puckish
appearance is a very fine mind (honoured by Oxford
University) and a spiritual maturity which those who
know him best deeply respect and honour. Katey's ebul-
lience could easily mask a gentle caring heart and an
ability to cope with disappointment and turn it into creative testimony.

In this book they show how prayer touches three
worlds at the same time. It touches heaven since prayer
affects God more than anything else. It touches earth
since prayer affects man at a depth and a reality beyond
anything else. And it touches hell since prayer disturbs
the devil more than any other human enterprise. The
whole emphasis of Mike and Katey's writing is on the
limitless power of prayer and how this can be experienced in practical ways in our day-to-day living.

They would not underestimate the value of praying alone. Indeed, they show we are never really alone when we pray, for God the Father is listening, God the Son is involved and God the Holy Spirit draws alongside to help. The angels also come into the picture, as do the demons of darkness. But the aim of this book is to highlight the joy and effectiveness of praying together. This they do with great honesty.

I am privileged to commend this book to you. I know the authors, and love and trust them. I also know the realities of which they speak and believe the truth of what they write.

JIM GRAHAM

Introduction

'Surely not another book on prayer! And what's more, praying with one's partner! This is too much. I've been told to pray ever since I stumbled into the kingdom of God, and I still haven't got it together. What's more, if I pray with my partner it's even worse—so we don't. I can certainly do without a lecture on what I ought to be doing.'

If this is your immediate reaction hold on just one more minute before you throw this book down in frustration. This book is not really a book—it's a manual. Quite simply, a practical guide to help us all to learn how to pray together. We promise you at the outset it is not a lecture nor the confessions of a mystic's successful encounters with God to make you feel more miserable.

Throughout the book you will find that some of the headings appear in **_bold italic_** type, with a symbol (▶). This means that there is something to pause and think about, commit to memory, or put into immediate action by 'having a go'.

Suddenly you feel a wave of panic sweeping through you. A book that actually demands action? Well, yes. As we've said, we have designed it as a manual, with a very practical approach to prayer, providing everything you need to lay the foundations for an effective prayer life together. As with any manual, it will teach you and enable you to become proficient at putting the contents into practice.

The book actually took shape following a series of seminars entitled 'How to pray with your partner', which we ran at Spring Harvest in 1984. These seminars took the form of practical workshops, and we were amazed at the number of people who crowded in. In the months and years following we have had letters from and met a good number of couples who came to those seminars with a poverty of prayer experience together, and yet from that point on have discovered an effective and, I'm glad to say, enjoyable prayer life together.

We believe that if worked through, this book will produce some fruit in your life together. It is intended, in current jargon, for 'hands on' experience—not simply being talked at, but responding by doing. Each chapter is self-contained and can be read on its own. Ideally you read the book in tandem—i.e. you both read together—and hence two copies would not go amiss. When we say, 'Get together with your partner,' that's what we mean. Don't go through the 'Action Stations' on your own—that rather defeats the object of the book.

The book is intended for couples at whatever stage they are, whether married, engaged or just going out together. We know you will have a lot of fun putting the content into practice. So go for it and let us know how you get on.

I
Prayer Is a Problem

What a negative title for a chapter! However, read on because I believe that phrase is the one on more Christians' lips than any other. From the moment we make our entrance into God's kingdom as 'soundly saved' individuals, we are assaulted from every quarter with exhortations to pray. Very quickly we take on board the assumption that every real Christian prays and our salvation is in doubt if we find we don't, so to admit to such a failure becomes an impossibility—we would probably be stoned or some twentieth-century equivalent!

In a recent survey individuals were asked how much time they spent praying in a day. Honesty was demanded and to some degree guaranteed through anonymity. The results were hailed as shocking and surprising: Mr & Mrs Average prayed approximately five minutes every day. And yet does that figure really shock you? When I heard the results I found them an affront to my Christian 'outer garment', but that which lurked within, i.e. the real me, was not at all surprised because the results reflected my experience.

Just to check it through further, the same questionnaire was circulated to a random number of clergy. The result was exactly the same, which if it proves nothing else demonstrates a dog-collar does not remove one's humanity!

Now the purpose of this book, as stated, is praying together. So why not, right now, pause and jot down how long you as an individual spend in prayer on average every day. And then how long you spend in prayer on average as a couple together.

Before you feel utterly condemned (years of exhortation about prayer leaves us brimful with condemnation because we haven't ever got it sorted), just remember you are no different from Mr & Mrs Average as revealed in the survey, and maybe better. What's more, you are as competent as your spiritual leader so that should encourage you.

At the Spring Harvest seminars, when Katey and I asked, 'How many of you have a regular and effective prayer life together?' only half a dozen hands out of about 400 would go up. We all start in the same boat. You are not alone but share the same experience as countless thousands of people. The good news is that prayer does not have to remain a problem, and if you work through this manual consistently we can assure you that your prayer life stands every chance of being dramatically improved.

Getting to grips with the task

Imagine a Sunday morning—one of those long slow wake-up days when nothing is going to be demanded of you. As consciousness dawns you remember it's Sunday, a day off, so you luxuriate with a stretch and drift back into unconsciousness. This process can continue for a long time if, like ours, your church has no morning service.

It was one such Sunday when, with great gallantry, I had tumbled out of bed and made my way downstairs to make the tea and pick up the paper. (Ours being a house of distinction we take the *Sunday Times;* the one problem is that having paid out for it, the whole day can be marred by the pressure to read it all to get one's money's worth.) I returned, tray in hand, and climbed back into bed where Katey and I began to survey the paper. As usual I ploughed into the news and Katey wandered through the supplement.

All was well until Katey interrupted my attempts to grasp the Middle Eastern situation with a sharp nudge indicating that I look at the magazine. My eyes took in the title 'The ABC Diet Plan' and my heart sank. 'Just what we need!' exclaimed Katey. It was at that moment in time I considered revoking my TV licence because just two weeks before, as the screen projected scores of eager runners jogging round the streets of London, I had made the rash statement that I fancied getting fit and having a go. Now, as if to mock my athletic ambition, the *Sunday Times* in all its wisdom was providing a step-by-step approach to fitness. Katey, with her normal rash enthusiasm, declared this was for us. We would follow the schedule week by week and within a year compete in the London Marathon.

Well, the weeks passed. We collected, read, appreciated and filed the supplements, and yet neither of us improved in stamina, strength or suppleness. The problem, as you may have guessed, was that although we had clear intentions to get fit and lose some fat, and even though we had a well produced, step-by-step guide for achieving it, we never actually put it into practice. And there's the rub! Belief is only valuable when it is accom-

15

panied by the will to act. God has always recognized that 'faith without works is dead'. We did not have the will to turn our good intentions to practical effect.

Some years later we are not measurably fitter. Similarly with our prayer life, we can have all the Scripture, all the teaching, all the tapes, videos and books we like— but if we won't decide to *do* something positive our prayer life will continue at the low level we currently experience. However, if we will agree to do something positive—like read this book and work through the exercises—our prayer life can and will improve. Ask each other now what you are going to do about it. Are you prepared to get 'stuck in' in concrete ways? Read on.

What does Jesus think?

The great news is that not only do we appreciate we have a problem, but Jesus knows we have one too. Interestingly enough, when Jesus was asked by the disciples about prayer he did not deliver a lecture but taught them the 'how to' of prayer. In fact it was the practical 'how to' that the disciples were keen to learn, as Luke 11:1-4 reveals.

I can imagine the disciples observing Jesus drawing aside to spend time discussing issues with his Father. There was a tremendous amount of pressure upon Jesus, and he always consulted his Father about what he should do; he never did anything that his Father did not want him to do. The disciples who travelled with Jesus also ate with him, slept by him and generally observed him at close hand. Thus they could see the benefit in Jesus' life of drawing aside and just taking time with the Father— and they wanted to get in on the action for themselves. Just imagine them observing Jesus praying, and asking one another, 'What's he doing?', 'Why don't we go and ask him?', and eventually summoning up the courage to go to him and put their request before him, 'Teach us how to pray like you pray.'

Yet having shared intimately with Jesus for three years, as well as having the 'how to' of prayer, the disciples still 'blew it' when Jesus asked them to pray in Gethsemane (Lk 22:39-46). They demonstrated that simply knowing is not sufficient in itself, but that we develop and learn as much, if not more, by the mistakes we make as well as the things we get right. Falling asleep did not mean the disciples couldn't care a fig about Jesus, they were simply exhausted and quite naturally fell asleep. Often the principle is not the problem, it's the practice.

Katey and I have been married for nearly nine years. Ours is a good marriage. I love Katey very much and cannot imagine life without her. I want to please her and ensure her happiness. However, in spite of these noble desires there are times, and not that infrequent, when we will have a conversation, usually while I am reading a book or watching the television, in which I promise to fetch something, purchase something or phone someone. I then instantly forget these promises and fail to perform the task. Although this occasionally produces a fair measure of exasperation on Katey's part, it is not evidence of lack of love on my part—it is one of the realities of life and marriage.

So also with God. He fully appreciates the problems we humans have with prayer. He does not expect you to pledge yourself to a three hour vigil every night. He understands when having promised faithfully to pray for sick Aunt Mathilda you forget to do so until reminded by a phone call thanking you for your prayers. God created us human, he therefore fully appreciates the nature of our humanity. He is intimately interested in our praying, he is fully committed to guiding us in the 'how to' of prayer, and he totally appreciates the problems we have and the mistakes we make and the failures we experience. But, as you'd expect, he urges us to keep going and discover the development we can make. God is on our side rooting for us so let's get on with it.

Returning to the illustration of good old Aunt Mathilda, why not make it a practice that when someone asks you for your prayers that you pray for them right there and then. It's a practice that was suggested to us by Doug Barnett and one that we've made our own. If nothing else we have at least honoured our word in praying for the particular situation that the person has asked us to remember. It's a great practice to get into together. Often when I return home from being away on a ministry weekend or from the Evangelical Alliance the first thing we'll do when I come through the door, after a heart-warming kiss, is to hug one another and pray, thanking God for his goodness in keeping us and bringing us back together and for the good things that we've enjoyed.

Learning from personal experience

It was among the dreaming spires of Oxford while studying at the University that I became a Christian. While sitting in St Aldate's listening to the then Bishop of Coventry, the Rt Rev. Cuthbert Bardsley, describing the person of Jesus, I decided that if Jesus was all that he was claimed to be by the Bishop, I'd better go and find out more. I did, Jesus was and I was placed in a 'beginners' group' to learn the basis of being a Christian.

I remember early on in my Christian life that the need to read the Bible and pray was a daily imperative for every proper Christian. When you've got no Christian background you follow everything you're told to the letter, and so I would sit in my room and read my Bible and pray every day. I remember the first vacation from university following my conversion. Every day I read the Bible and prayed—I think my parents were a bit overwhelmed by this strange new behaviour—but it was so boring and apparently meaningless. Hard though I tried, it was about as exciting as a test-match interrupted by rain! However, being a great perseverer I steadfastly continued and was glad to get back to Oxford to ask some questions about this activity.

The questions were soon answered. Every sermon I heard about prayer was that God said one of two things: either he said, 'No,' in answer to our prayers or he said, 'Wait' (this was only so that he could say, 'No,' later!). It seemed that God called us to pray, only to turn down our many intercessions. Indeed, the fact of answered prayer was totally beyond my experience, apart from the very odd occasion, such as when I led Katey to Christ following half an hour of private intercession to that end, as much to build up my courage as to see God's kingdom extended.

It was at some point at this stage that, having faithfully read my Bible daily, I discovered that God was not one who only said, 'Wait,' or, 'No,' in response to our prayers. Indeed, he had a very positive attitude to prayer. Take, for example, the words of Jesus in Mark 11:24, 'When you pray and ask for something, believe that you have received it, and you will be given whatever you ask for.' That sounded pretty positive to me and a very clear statement from the lips of the Son of God. With the stipulation of verse 25 it became even clearer. I avidly looked up other references to prayer in the gospels. In Luke 11:9-10 Jesus says,

Ask, and you will receive; seek, and you will find; knock, and the door will be opened to you. For everyone who asks will receive, and he who seeks will find, and the door will be opened to anyone who knocks.

Here Jesus clearly supported the view that God was in the business of answering prayer. The word 'everyone' in verse 10 meant this was true even for wallies like me. I lapped this up. This was good news indeed. In fact it was what I'd expected of God when I became a Christian, but had since lost sight of in seeking to take on board the 'Christian converts'' package and conform to it as a new disciple wanting to do the decent and expected thing.

Words such as those in John 14:13—'And I will do whatever you ask for in my name, so that the Father's glory will be shown through the Son'—continued to develop a picture of a God who was committed to me and who expected me to be committed to him. My love was such that I wanted him to be pleased with me and I wanted extravagantly to give all that I knew of myself to all that I knew of him. I began to realize that the people, situations and personal needs that I had prayed about were all as important to God as they were to me and he wanted to get involved in a way that would highlight who he was and what he was about.

It was John 16:23-24 that finally clinched it for me—

I am telling you the truth: the Father will give you whatever you ask for in my name. Until now you have not asked for anything in my name; ask and you will receive, so that your happiness may be complete.

I had not asked anything in Jesus' name in any other sense than fulfilling the Christian's responsibility to pray —not expecting God would acknowledge the request with an answer. Indeed, I was grateful that I had been taught that the Bible was a true and trustworthy manual for the life of the Christian disciple, because I could practically accept all the above promises and if that wasn't enough have them all underlined with 2 Corinthians 1:20, 'It is he who is the "Yes" to all God's promises. This is why through Jesus Christ our "Amen" is said to the glory of God.'

I emerged from this journey through the Scriptures enthused and informed, and it acted as a turning point in my Christian life and indeed ultimately in our prayer life together.

Word and experience

One of the consequences of growing up, apart from grey hair, is that one's perspective on life and indeed one's expectations from life are directly affected by one's experiences. In spite of a fine 'macho' image, Mike is petrified of going to the dentist. Indelibly imprinted on his mind are the memories of bleak days of childhood amidst the normally joyous school holidays. These were the six-monthly trips to the dentist. He can still recall the churning stomach and blind fear which gripped him on the morning of such trips as he ferociously brushed his teeth for twenty minutes hoping this would assure him of a clean bill of health. On the trip to the surgery everything else paled into insignificance as his mind concentrated upon the forthcoming encounter with the masked driller!

The waiting-room, comfortably set out and with a plethora of colourful magazines, was filled with equally nervous-looking people, all apparently reading or holding conversations in hushed tones but everyone with an ear to the whine of the dentist's drill. Once in the chair, somehow immortalized for Mike on TV through *Mastermind,* it was a case of gripping the arms of the chair till the knuckles turned white, opening one's mouth and locking it in an extremely uncomfortable position, screwing up the eyes as tightly as possible, and grunting incomprehensibly in response to the dentist's barked commands of, 'Relax!', 'Open wider!' and, 'I'm not going to hurt you,' which he promptly did!

Experiences like this at the hands of a man, who became affectionately known in the Morris household as 'Mac the Hack', shaped Mike's whole view of dentistry in Britain. As soon as he was old enough he ceased visiting the dentist and for the past ten years his teeth have remained unexposed. His total expectation is that of fear, anxiety and pain. However, as I frequently remind him, he is being small-minded and bigotted to which he agrees—but it has got him no nearer to the dentist. Fortunately, since moving to Chichester there is a fine lady dentist in the fellowship whom Mike respects and likes. It is possible in the not-too-distant future that he will put his trust in her assurances that dental care need not be a painful and negative experience and once again risk everything and place himself in 'the chair', submitting his molars for examination.

Amusing though such an account may appear, there is a very real principle of truth enshrined within it. We are all to one degree or another a product of our experiences. These have helped form our opinions and determine our expectations. Unfortunately in the area of the spiritual life, when we read the promises about answered prayer in the Bible we discover we are on the wrong side of a credibility gap because we have a long experience of unanswered prayer.

For years we have prayed: a good exam result for Tom (he failed), a successful visit to the doctor for Audrey (she's diagnosed as having cancer), sufficient finance for a holiday (nothing is forthcoming), a friend to be saved (they show no interest in the gospel) and so the list could go on. When our prayers appear unanswered we employ a mental conjuring trick, rapidly forgetting what we had been so earnestly praying for and beginning on something else for no other reason than the strict Christian injunction we were brought up on that we must pray. Is it really any wonder that calls to corporate prayer in our churches meet with such little enthusiasm? 95% of the congregation are living the experience of unanswered prayer and the fear that their poverty-stricken prayer life will one day in some way be revealed before the whole fellowship. Horrendous!

Obviously, none of us could continue with any integrity as disciples if we constantly lived with the tension of this credibility gap. So what we do is read the Bible on the one hand and subtly interpret it at the level of our experience. In essence we reduce what God has declared to fit our own experience of life and wear it as a coat that fits rather than keep it as a garment which is several sizes too large and apparently not for us. We may read a passage like 1 John 5:13-15—

> I am writing this to you so that you may know that you have eternal life—you that believe in the Son of God. We have courage in God's presence, because we are sure that he hears us if we ask him for anything that is according to his will. He hears us whenever we ask him; and since we know this is true, we know also that he gives us what we ask from him.

We then spend our time rationalizing the whole thing so that it no longer says what it appears to say at first reading, but something quite different which fits with our experience. Otherwise we concentrate on the phrase 'according to his will', and conclude we have nothing we pray for because it isn't in accord with his will. Quite frankly, if as Christians we are incapable of discovering God's will we have little understanding of being born again of the Spirit of God. Furthermore, Scripture is a general revelation of God's will, part of which reveals that prayers are for the answering. It is interesting to note that no one would take a second glance at the phrase 'you may know that you have eternal life' because we are happy to accept it although we cannot prove it but only receive it by faith. Since eternity begins the day we meet Jesus, and one of the consequences of eternal life is God's will being done, how can we stumble over prayer in accordance with God's will and practical prayers receiving practical answers?

If that appears rather complicated do read it over again because it is essential to developing an effective prayer life. Consider the moment when you became a Christian. I don't know when that was, where that was or how that was. I had heard about Jesus and I went and discovered all the facts I could about this man and the claims that he had made. I learned about these things by reading the Bible and listening to Christian friends, and all that I heard confirmed to me that what Jesus claimed was true and could be effective for me. However, having said that, I could not discover if Jesus would meet with me until I risked everything and invited him to take over my life, till I said, 'I'm out of order and I need to get right with you, God.'

The illustration that most graphically depicts this for me is one where a child is standing at the top of a flight of stairs that lead down into a cellar. There is no light in the cellar and the child sees blackness. While the child is standing at the top of the stairs and looking down he hears a familiar voice. It is his father's voice and that voice says very simply, 'Jump.' Now the child's mind can reason that if the voice is that of his father, and he recognizes it to be so, then he can jump with confidence because Dad does not play nasty tricks upon him. Also if Dad is at the bottom of the stairs looking up, he can see his child because there is light behind the child even though the child cannot see down into the darkness of the cellar. However, the only way in which the child will ever know if the father will indeed catch him is if he fulfils the instruction to jump by jumping.

Similarly, in our Christian lives not one of us discovered whether the claims that Jesus had made about eternal life and friendship with God were true until we made that step of commitment, turned around and decided to give our lives to Jesus, to accept him as the boss. Only after praying some kind of prayer of commitment and meeting with Jesus did we discover that everything that we had assumed could be true was proven to be true in our experience.

So it is with our daily relationship with God. It is a relationship of faith in which we constantly have to leap from the top of those stairs into the arms of the one who loves us and whom we love. It is only once we've leaped into mid-air that we discover whether in fact God is going to catch us or let us crash into the concrete below and mockingly say, 'Fooled you.' This is not the heart and nature of the God we worship, so we can be confident that just as God has brought us to salvation, brought us into a relationship with himself, so he will continue to nurture, nourish and develop that relationship, for he wants good things for his children.

Instead of reducing God's word to the level of our experience, what I would like to suggest (and this is not an original thought) is that we alter our perspective and say, 'Lord, I see what your word says and I ask you to bring my life into line with your word.'

Imagine a pavement alongside which runs a three-foot-high wall. You are on the pavement and a friend is walking along the wall and you are holding hands with each other. Should you want to, you could very easily give your friend's hand a strong jerk and in no time at all he would be joining you on the pavement. However, you could decide to let your friend grip your hand strongly and, with your co-operation, haul you up onto the wall. Obviously it is far easier to pull your friend off the wall to pavement level than to be hauled up onto the wall. It is also evident that you would have a better perspective and panoramic view from the top of the wall than from the pavement.

This basically illustrates the choice that lies before us —the choice we will now need to take. Are we prepared to set aside past experience and ask God to bring our lives and future experience into line with his word? When Katey and I faced this we simply pictured God the Father standing by and offering us his hand. As he did this he invited us simply to place our hand in his hand and allow him to bring our life and experience into line with his word. It might help to picture this in the same way as you make your personal and yet practical response to God.

Consequences

As a couple, making such a practical response proved exceptionally helpful in stimulating our prayer life. The first time we decided to pray believing for specific and practical answers was in response to a news item on the radio. It revealed that a ferocious hurricane was heading directly for an island in some exotic spot and threatened to devastate it and its population entirely. There was neither the time nor the available resources to remove the population, and multiple deaths and severe injuries were forecast.

Horrified as we listened, Katey and I agreed to pray. We didn't know what to pray about but we simply asked God to save the island and its population from this expected destruction. This was done unemotionally and quickly, without much wailing and gnashing of teeth. From then on through the rest of the day we tuned in regularly for news of the hurricane's progress. Each time the voice of the newscaster clinically confirmed the worst fears of earlier bulletins—the island was facing a fatal encounter with an exceptionally violent storm.

As you can imagine, Katey and I felt full of doubt and very helpless, but we stuck to our guns, held on tightly to God's hand and quietly prayed again. I think each of us was constantly firing 'arrow prayers' to God on the island's behalf. In the late afternoon we listened to a further news report and learned to our surprise and joy that the hurricane had 'unaccountably' altered course at the last moment, veered away from the island and spent its force harmlessly in mid-ocean. God had heard our prayers and answered them. We were both greatly encouraged. On this issue our experience had come into line with God's word. Here was a practical, positive consequence from deciding to ask God to bring our lives into line with his word.

From that point on we have made it a principle rule to pray practically and specifically. However, we do not always see our prayers answered. There are issues for which we are praying which to this day remain unanswered; there are others which took a number of months before we enjoyed God's answer in reality; yet other situations met with immediate answers as in the case of the hurricane. The critical point is that for a number of years now we have continued to allow God to prove in concrete terms the truth of his word.

▶ Action stations

You were warned that this was a practical book on prayer. And so here's the place where you can get started. Find time—and now is the best time of all—to sit down with your partner and without any preliminaries pray together and out loud the Lord's Prayer:

> Our Father in heaven:
> May your holy name be honoured;
> may your Kingdom come;
> may your will be done on earth
> as it is in heaven.
> Give us today the food we need.
> Forgive us the wrongs we have done,
> as we forgive the wrongs that
> others have done to us.
> Do not bring us to hard testing,
> but keep us safe from the Evil One.

If you have not done so before, you have just prayed together. Now repeat the same but with eyes open, looking at each other and holding hands—there is nothing spiritual about shutting your eyes or adopting the 'shampoo position' for want of something to do with one's hands! Prayer is all about communication as we will see in the next chapter, and touch is essential to communication.

Finally, tonight before you go to bed pray again. Use the same prayer but this time pray alternate phrases so that while one speaks the other listens and then vice versa.

It wasn't so painful was it?

2

Praying Together Is Fun!

On my weekly trips to the Evangelical Alliance in London I have to take a bus from Victoria to Kennington. This is a tremendous eye-opener, or ear-opener I should say, when I both overhear and become involved in conversations ranging from the state of the weather to the state of the nation. My strangest encounter was with a bus conductor who was convinced that Hitler had been a guy with brilliant ideas whose only crime was to lose the war for which he had been punished with a poor press. It was worth considering that this conductor was not joking when he presented his political perspective to me.

About 90% of the people I overhear or chat to on a London bus are full of gloom and despondency. Life is a burden to be endured rather than enjoyed. Perhaps Alan Herbert was correct when he surmised, 'People must not do things for fun. We are not here for fun. There is no reference to fun in any act of parliament.'

It really concerns me that in a world sadly lacking in good news, those entrusted with the good news to end all news, namely the church of Jesus Christ—that is you and me, appear to be as burdened and impoverished as the world. Clive Calver speaks of a man he met after one service who, while shaking his hand, claimed that he had the joy of the Lord deep down inside. Such was his bearing and the sombre nature of his face that Clive reckoned it was so deep that it required three North Sea oil derricks to get it up to the surface!

So often everything associated with our worship of and work for God is sombre, dull and burdensome. The thought of praying or reading the Bible does not cause the heart to leap but rather to sink and groan. The very practice of all that we believe does not cause us to become overwhelmed with joy and excitement. It is hardly any wonder that the pagan already confronted with problems and pressures and convinced that the world is a place of gloom and doom, gives what he sees of Christianity a wide berth. However, I am convinced that God is a fun-loving God who 'generously gives us everything for our enjoyment' (1 Tim 6:17).

A relationship with Christ is for our enjoyment. I increasingly see God as fun-loving—getting excited and thrilled with the act of creation, setting stars spinning in their orbit, creating the animals. Surely God must have a sense of humour when you take a look at a camel! If that isn't sufficient, cast your eye on his pièce de resistance, that is man.

Many Christians have lost the twinkle in the eye, the sense of exhilaration and fun that God always intended for our relationship with him. Relationships depend upon humour, laughter and merriment otherwise they become cold and pragmatic. There is nothing sadder than a couple joined together through marriage who over the years have allowed the spark that drew them together to be extinguished, and while enjoying the legal status of being married, they have none of the life and spontaneity that enables the relationship to function. Many Christians hold in their hands the legal certificate of marriage to Christ, but any warmth and depth of relationship is all too soon replaced by a formal performance of expected duties.

Obviously this has serious implications for us in our prayer life, both as individuals and with each other. Prayer is ultimately about relationship. It is a means whereby we grow in our friendship and intimacy with God. It is the medium of communication between a people and their God and vice versa. When Moses went in to the presence of the Lord to chat things over, the relationship developed to the point that when he finally emerged he had to cover his face with a veil, such was the radiance of the Lord (Ex 34:29 ff). Indeed, Moses was the one with whom God spoke face to face (Num 12:6-8).

Choosing to relate to God

On reading through the Bible I am particularly struck by the character of Joshua. He is best known to us as the man who took over from Moses to lead Israel out of the wilderness and into the Promised Land. However, I find his personal spiritual journey before his appointment as Israel's leader most illuminating.

We first encounter Joshua in the book of Exodus where he is engaged in conflict with Israel's enemy the Amalekites (Ex 17:8 ff). The story is no doubt familiar. Joshua was directed by Moses to pick an army and engage the Amalekites in warfare. While Joshua battled in the field, Moses retreated with Aaron and Hur to a hill overlooking the skirmish and battled in prayer for victory. As long as Moses kept his hands in the air Joshua and the Israelites gained the upper hand, but

31

when through tiredness Moses was forced to lower his hands the Amalekites seized the advantage in the conflict. Eventually, as the battle raged now one way and then the other, Aaron and Hur decided to hold Moses' hands in the air until sunset and so Joshua overcame the Amalekite army.

Imagine the scene following that victory, one that must have hung in the balance for the soldiers in the field. Tired but exultant the Israelites returned to their camp, maybe cheering their heroic leader Joshua. Naturally, those who had remained behind in the camp, aware that their destiny to some degree depended upon the success of their army, would have welcomed the men home with cheers and shouts, kisses and refreshments, and many would have directed special applause to Joshua their conquering captain in the fight.

At the best of times the Jews found it hard to fully appreciate Moses' leadership and were not above rebelling against it. This man raised by the Egyptians had a unique and awesome relationship with God. He was somewhat hard to relate to and identify with. But now they had a leader they could appreciate, a military man, a man of strength and vigour. You can almost see the mothers calculating how they might arrange a marriage for their daughter with this mighty man of valour—and I guess the dads weren't that far behind!

This was in fact a point of crisis for Joshua. He was a military man; he understood the dynamics of all that was taking place on the battlefield; he recognized that there was something more than military might behind the victory over the Amalekites that day. He realized that at times his army had been all but overwhelmed when suddenly the tables were turned, eventually so completely that the Israelites carried home the honours. I believe that as Joshua was cheered triumphantly back into the camp he caught sight of another small party who were entering the camp—Moses, Aaron and Hur. He saw the lines of exhaustion that marked Moses' face and he grasped the fact that while he had grappled with the Amalekites Moses had grappled with God, and between them faith and works had been combined to the glory of God and the benefit of Israel. Significantly, God required Moses to record this event in writing (Ex 17:14) and commanded him to ensure that Joshua personally heard the story of what he had done and what Moses had done that day. I would like to suggest that at this point Joshua, in the midst of personal adulation, determined to stick close to Moses and get to know this God who worked such powerful wonders. It was a costly decision because he had leadership offered to him on a plate by the celebrating army and camp.

My conjecture is supported from the very next appearance of Joshua in the Scriptures (Ex 24) when we learn that he is now Moses' assistant. Such was his determination to get to know this God whom Moses knew and who had given such a mighty victory, that he had settled for being Moses' servant—a step of some humility from the giddy heights of popular hero to unnoticed attendant. Significantly, it was Joshua and not Aaron and Hur who accompanied Moses up onto Mount Sinai when the covenant was confirmed and the glory of the Lord settled on the mountain. Joshua was growing in his relationship with God.

Joshua was prepared to make mistakes as well as to learn how to be God's man in a given situation (Num 11:28). It has been well said that someone who is not prepared to make a mistake will make nothing. In praying together, Katey and I have goofed and gaffed on numerous occasions. But the fruit of those mistakes has been growth in our understanding of God and of each other and a further insight into the nature and practice of prayer.

As we follow on with Joshua's growth in relationship with God, we discover that whenever Moses went out of the camp of the Israelites to consult with God in the tent of meeting, a place where God met with Moses face to face, Joshua would be close on his heels. Once Moses had done his business with God he would return to the camp, but Joshua did not leave the tent. Joshua learnt what it was to enjoy being with God. The Scriptures do not say that Joshua prayed or that God spoke to him, but we can assume that he enjoyed being in close proximity to God. Joshua learned to recognize when the presence of God was particularly close and he grew to love it and consider it worth remaining in the tent for.

One reason why we often fail to become excited by prayer is because we do not know what it is like to have God around. We know about him but we've not got very far down the road in relating to him. The Bible has a great word for describing this close relationship—'abide'. Jesus used it in John 15 when he called his disciples to abide in him. It literally means to wait, to stay, to remain, to stand firm, to remain true to. Indeed, if we pause for just a moment and consider each of those meanings we get a very full and rich insight into what it means to be a friend of God.

It was while reading John 15 once that I discovered what Jesus was getting at when he said, 'Remain united to me, and I will remain united to you.' I knew just how good it was to have an evening at home with no one to see but Katey. The pleasure it was to prepare a good meal which could be taken at a leisurely pace. To put our feet up and either watch a film or listen to, say, a Bach violin concerto. We didn't need to speak but simply relish the fact that we were together and enjoyed being in each other's presence. Perhaps you can grasp more easily what I mean when I describe to you the isolation of returning home to an empty house, to get a meal for myself and spend an evening watching TV or listening to records alone. This was the situation when Katey was in hospital for ten days and I spent hours in the house on my own. Something was missing, or rather someone, and although I could work through the same pattern it was neither satisfying nor complete. This is why we need to discover everyday companionship with God and the emotional stability and security it brings.

Now I enjoy every moment of every day with God. When I walk the dog, for example, I enjoy God's companionship and we'll laugh together over many things. There are times when I am working flat out that I am reminded that God's around, and I push my chair back from the desk and take a few moments to appreciate what a friendship I have with the Lord. For his part he encourages me, gets me to laugh at myself, my mood or behaviour or just reminds me that I am his son and he thinks I am great. That's not big-headedness by the way, that's the Bible!

Learning to appreciate God can cause a certain amount of embarrassment. I well remember walking the dog around our local golf-course one morning, singing aloud and generally getting very excited at how big God is and yet how personal and practical his love for us is. My mind recalled two or three areas of anxiety that Katey and I had faced which we had eventually (note not immediately because we are slow learners too) prayed about and consequently seen resolution to our great relief. As I chatted with God on my walk, thanking him for this, I was literally filled to overflowing with gratitude and excitement, and as I sang aloud I began to leap around and dance up the fairway. Landing gracefully from a well-executed pirouette I saw someone on the green observing me.

I focused upon them and recognized the steward who was placing the flags in their holes. He looked absolutely stunned and as I resumed a more decorous form of progress towards this same green, giving a friendly wave as I went, he hurriedly disappeared towards his next port of call somewhat perplexed if not a little concerned at what he had observed. Still, I am not the first to be observed 'walking and jumping and praising God' (Acts 3:8)!

On recalling that scenario I can still sense my own embarrassment at the time, caught out as it were in my private devotions. And probably rightly embarrassed because I was communicating the intimacy with my God. I have learned that relating to God involves not only the mind but also the emotions, and certainly as I have broken through emotional barriers such as dance I have discovered a new level of closeness with the Lord himself. We all face a number of personal issues as we develop an active and effective prayer life and each of us will have to decide whether we will face these and press through them. Let's take a few that affect us as couples learning to pray together.

Embarrassment

I have looked at this briefly from a personal point of view but this is also a major area for us as a couple. Somehow it felt silly and unreal saying, 'Let's pray together.' As we adopted our prayerful position, an unhelpful tension and religiosity seemed to overtake us. The voices we used to chat things over with each other assumed an unnatural holy tone and the whole thing was awful. I usually emerged grumpy and critical and poor Katey quietly endured the whole procedure, believing this must be the pain of submission to your husband!

What was even more horrendous was that we were unable to talk the problems through because we wouldn't admit to each other that it was awful.

So all that happened was that we prayed less and less together, lived under a burden of guilt because we weren't a praying couple and when the guilt became intense, set a whole evening aside to pray (to pull back some brownie points on God's great prayer ledger) which was always a disaster. After all, if you can't pray together effectively for ten minutes why should you be able to pray for two hours?

We only began to get this sorted out once we realized that it was false to assume that we knew how to pray simply because we had been told to pray from the moment we had been converted. We had to admit our inadequacy to God and to each other in this department of our lives. We then had to begin to practice being natural in prayer as we were natural in having lunch together, doing the shopping together or walking in the country together. Like Jesus' disciples we came hand in hand and said, 'Teach us to pray,' and from a position of ignorance we began to learn.

▶ *Action stations*

Get together with your partner and take a few minutes, one after the other, to pray out of your love for the other. For example, Katey usually uses the illustration of how she would thank God for my smile by praying, 'Thank you Lord for the smile that you have given Mike, that it is so broad and lights up his whole face. Thank you that he smiles so often and that it is often directed towards me.' You'll find this a heart-warming exercise and full of fun, so enjoy yourselves together.

Tension

Having agreed to do this a whole new area of difficulty opened up. We needed to be real, i.e. honest with each other, and if there is one thing guaranteed to make sparks fly in any marriage it's when your partner tells you a few home truths. However, we were to discover that it was impossible to enjoy God together if we weren't totally honest with each other.

Katey vividly remembers our early attempts to pray together. I would read a passage from the Bible and before praying enter on a long exposition for Katey's benefit. All the while she was sitting there with a demure look on the outside but inside thinking, 'I can do without all this. I know what God has said to me so why can't we cut the sermon?' Once I had finished my homily was it any wonder that prayer fell flat with me expecting some kind of response from Katey while she resented my arrogance in preaching at her. It was a long time before Katey gently told me to 'shut up!'. Being a reasonable fellow I responded by storming out of the room. Such are the delights of marriage!

Once I cooled off I had to admit that Katey was right. This obviously gave her greater courage because she then went on to explain that not only was I preaching at her but assuming a voice reminiscent of a foghorn to do so. I felt quite threatened and sensitive by this assault on what Katey dubs my 'preaching voice', but we had to work through it. Hardest of all was for 'macho Mike' to admit this sense of threat and hurt produced by Katey's honesty.

If we are going to progress in prayer as couples we will have to face and work through the threat we pose to each other and give room for honest criticism and positive response.

▶ Action stations

Get together with your partner. Each of you will need a sheet of paper and a pencil. Now what you must do is write down three strengths that you recognize in your partner. Don't talk, just write.

Once you have written these down, and do take a moment or two to think what you will write, share with each other what you have written down. Men must share first.

Now, having done that write down three weaknesses you recognize in your partner.

Once you have written them down, share again. This time women share first.

This is a lovely way of being able to be honest with each other and we have seen such an exercise bring about real reconciliation between couples.

Remember the purpose of such an exercise is to take some real steps forward in being relaxed and open with each other, so don't neglect to do this regularly with each other. In the next chapter we will look at why men shared the strengths first and women the weaknesses.

Faithlessness

As we've mentioned previously, many of us continue to pray with a long-standing testimony of unanswered prayer. The fruit of this is that we are to all intents and purposes faithless. We do not expect God to act in answer to our prayers, so we perform our duty of prayer but it is no more than a dreary duty. Unfortunately we are not helped here by twentieth-century rationality that can only conceive of things happening if they lie within the parameters of our mental understanding. However, the Bible reveals that God is someone who acts the moment we stop relying on human resources to perform the tasks.

Take the story of the rich young ruler in Matthew 19:16-30. Challenged by his disciples over the impossibility of a rich man entering the kingdom of heaven, Jesus responds, 'This is impossible for man, but for God everything is possible' (Mt 19:26). For us this implies that the moment we exhaust the realm of the humanly possible, God sweeps in and turns our impossibility into his glorious possibility.

For example, when we were going to get married we wanted to buy a house. We were living in Wolverhampton, and friends who were moving offered us their house at £1,000 below the market value. We needed a mortgage. Katey was a teacher with a regular wage, but I had no guaranteed salary. Every building society we approached viewed us as a potential calamity financially and were unable to help. Somewhat discouraged we returned to the BYFC office where I worked and let Clive Calver know our predicament. In characteristic fashion he said, 'What we need here is a miracle,' prayed and sent us out to try another building society. As you may have guessed, this society welcomed us with open arms and gave us a mortgage three times Katey's salary with no guaranteed income from myself.

I learned a lot that day, not least from Clive, about God meeting us at the point at which we exhaust human means and literally taking hold of the impossible and bringing it into existence. This principle is not one by which we can guarantee personal financial prosperity, it is a principle that God moves in response to believing men and women.

▶ *Action stations*

We can encourage each other greatly in building faith

into one another's lives.

Get together again and with a piece of paper and pencil each, write down something about which you want to receive an answer from God. It does not need to be in the material realm. It might be in the area of spiritual development, or it might have to do with an opportunity to speak to a friend or relation. Now, once you have both written something down, join hands and with your free hand hold up the paper to God and ask him to respond to your request.

Do be realistic about what you are asking of God, and remember you are laying building-blocks for growing closer to God and enlarging your faith.

One example of when I followed this practice was the time when Clive and I, having appointed a new secretary, needed to furnish her with a decent typewriter. I told God all about it and then went ahead and placed the order—the total price was £600. It was the day before the bill needed to be paid, and no £600 had appeared. Clive and I were returning from a meeting and we pulled into a service station for petrol. Having filled up I looked down at my feet to discover a £20 note. Bending down to pick it up I found another, then another and finally a thick wad of notes. I put them in my pocket, feeling I was more trustworthy than the petrol attendant.

On returning home we informed the police of the find and they told us to keep the money in the BYFC account while we waited to see if anyone would claim it. After six months no one had, and so the money became the property of the finder, that was BYFC. The total amount? Well, £600 of course—the price of the new typewriter!

If we will co-operate with God we will daily discover that man's impossibilities provide the doorways to God's possibilities. So let's get on with it!

Don't be afraid to go back over the 'Action Stations'

sections and repeat them. The whole point of the exercise is to become natural and at ease in praying together, not just to complete the tasks.

3
Let's Talk About It

Any relationship is dependent for its survival on communication. This is true for every marriage partnership and every relationship between an individual and God.

Throughout the Old Testament God communicated repeatedly with his wayward people Israel to encourage them and correct them and to remind them that they were married to him and therefore had an exclusive relationship with him and he with them. Their disobedience became so great that God refused to speak for 300 years until he made his final statement. This was his Son Jesus. Hebrews 1:1-2 states,

> In the past, God spoke to our ancestors many times and in many ways through the prophets, but in these last days he has spoken to us through his Son. He is the one through whom God created the universe, the one whom God has chosen to possess all things at the end.

That communication between God and his people continues today; his people now being those who know and love Jesus, who have an exclusive attachment to him as he has to them. That communication is vital for the

43

maintenance and development of the relationship between the disciple and God.

Unfortunately, just as communication between a Christian and his God can fall into disrepair and neglect with the stagnation of their relationship, the same can happen between man and wife in marriage. This is a tragedy whenever and wherever it occurs. There is an unspoken assumption today that marriage somehow happens—we are merely passive partners who enjoy the fruit of the relationship. If there is little fruit it is time to change partners, establish a new marriage. The fault is with the marriage not with us. It is little wonder that nationally one in three marriages end in divorce, a figure which according to recent reports will soon increase to one in two. Those of us within the church, however, have little room for complacency or outrage since the failure rate here is reputed to be one in five.

Now I appreciate marriage is no easy matter. We are involved with the premarital counselling of many young couples and few can get their eyes beyond the wedding day and the wedding night! That's no surprise, and it's encouraging that they have such a sense of anticipation. However, unless they can appreciate that the wedding day is just the beginning of a long, exciting and arduous journey, they will make inadequate preparations for encountering the obstacles which may lie before them in the course of their marriage.

The day Katey and I got married was a great day. We were glad when it arrived since the months running up to the wedding were a time of hassle and pressure. The arrangements for the wedding, responding rightly to the families, seeking to prevent the physical relationship from running away with itself (with all the emotional pressure of the wedding the security and stability we found in each other over that period heightened the physical tension).

The day itself, July 29th 1978 (a date later recognized for its quality and utilized by the Prince and Princess of Wales for their nuptial celebration), was boiling hot and filled with excitement. Katey felt hotter than the rest since she had a temperature of 100°, not she assures me at the thought of marrying my good self, but as a result of flu. Everything went fairly well—apart from forgetting to lift Katey's veil at the appropriate moment, so leaving her to swelter still further, and the organist striking up the tune 'While shepherds watched their flocks by night' for the hymn 'O for a thousand tongues to sing'. Strange experience! The service over, it was great to have all the attention of the cameras, making speeches at the reception, saying cheerio to everyone and then clanking off down the road into a lifetime of married bliss.

It was only after the wedding day that reality set in. Seated across the table from Katey at breakfast, I'd ask myself where was that radiant personification of feminine beauty who had swept up the aisle to be joined in matrimony to me? And why was it that piles of junk collected at inappropriate places around the house? And did my trousers really require three creases? Katey of course was contemplating a similar series of thoughts. When would the washer on the tap get replaced? Did I have to pick my nose so publicly? Did we always have to watch war films?

Indeed, the source of greatest frustration between us in the early days of marriage was my nose-picking and the way Katey ate an apple. Pitiful issues, but they assumed great importance to us. And we were poor at communicating in a reasonable way. I'm convinced that communication, or rather lack of it, is a major factor in marriage problems today. It wasn't long before we realized that marriage did not serve us but we have to serve or service it. There was no place for passivity—we had to work actively at relating together. In doing so we learned a number of valuable lessons about communication which have since enhanced our marriage to each other and our friendship with God.

The most important lesson was that what I thought I said was apparently not what Katey heard. For example, Katey turns on the TV. Observing the programme I say, 'I can't stand this!' Katey hears my words but interprets them as, 'I shouldn't have put the TV on,' or, 'How dare he criticize my choice of programme. I have a right to relax too.' Instantly, Katey is grumpy. I get a few atmospherics from the good lady and find myself developing feelings of criticism and alienation towards her for no apparent reason. Result—a rotten evening which has to be worked through before retiring to fulfil the scriptural injunction, 'Do not stay angry all day' (Eph 4:26).

Many were the nights we sat up and talked long and hard in the first year of our marriage; resolving conflicts and misunderstandings; learning to express the way in which we felt hurt by the other and finding a creative and positive way forward. It was only slowly that we discovered that sometimes what we intended to communicate was not reflected to the other by the words we chose. We had to ensure we had been understood, and also provide room for the response of the other, a response that could be positive or negative, without further reaction on either of our parts.

We had to learn to be direct in what we said and not abuse our relationship by seeking to manipulate it. On my part this entailed not taking unilateral decisions and dumping them and their consequences lock, stock and barrel, without giving Katey the right of reply. And for Katey's part, not seeking to choose her moment and line of approach to get round me but rather to state clearly and directly what she was getting at. Many are the games we play in marriage, but the manipulation game should not be one of them. Marriage is a partnership of equals, and as with every partnership the everyday detailed practice needs working at. It is not healthy when we discover ways in which we can achieve our desires and ends through sly manipulation of our partner.

It has been our experience that learning to communicate effectively takes time and energy but pays rich dividends. After eight years of marriage we have not adjusted to each other but become knit together as one, each readjusting where necessary. We have had to learn that we need to take as much care about how we express ourselves as what we express. Previously one of us might have communicated something that was true but presented it in completely the wrong way. Result? A local nuclear explosion of unseemly proportions, in the midst of which the truism was entirely lost. With a little thought and a sense of timing, that which needed to be said could have been outlined without an adverse reaction and with sufficient grace for the issue to be talked through.

This lesson has been vital to our relationship, for in the early days Katey lived in fear of my hot and fiery temper. This had such an effect upon her that she would take virtually any action to avoid stirring me up. The consequence was that areas in my own life which radically required the firm application of the boot were left to continue and fester. Katey was too fearful to challenge me, and I was utilizing my hot temper to keep her and virtually anyone else from levelling with me. I didn't realize it at the time, but I was of course the loser missing out on God transforming my character and making me more like Jesus.

After a number of difficult years, we at last began to

communicate a little more honestly and easily as out-lined above. I gave Katey the right, and requested that she took the responsibility, to tell me when I was being a selfish pig or when I was over-reacting, etc. The immediate consequences of this were that Katey, summoning up all her courage would challenge me and I would refuse to receive what she said. However, I knew I was out of order, and so in our many reconciliations I asked her to forgive me.

We then turned to prayer. I asked God's forgiveness and asked Katey to pray for me. The fruit was that I began to be able to hear her words without over-reacting, and trust her judgements, given for my benefit and out of her love for me. The long-term fruit is that I am now a better adjusted individual: I trust and value Katey's 'input' into my life; I depend upon her keeping a critical eye on my life and my ministry, and I am so much more secure in myself and therefore less vulnerable when with other people and willing to receive honest comment from them. Katey and I are the richer for this. It is a process that we have each had to grow through, and continue to do so, recognizing that it is vital if we are to be effective partners.

Appreciate you are different

Charles Dickens, it is said, had a particularly unhappy marriage, eventually remaining joined to his wife in holy matrimony by word only. In speaking of this unhappy relationship he recalled how once he expressed his in-tention to marry, many of his friends urged him to recon-sider on the grounds that they could see great trouble ahead for such a fiery couple. In spite of the warnings and as well as the constant in-fighting between Charles and his bride-to-be, the wedding took place, the marriage was entered into. It was soon evident to both husband and wife that marriage of itself did not remove any of the problems and difficulties experienced during courtship, and indeed Dickens coined the phrase that rather than reducing areas of conflict, marriage 'magnifies problems'.

This insight—marriage magnifies problems—is absolutely fundamental. Knowing this to be true we can take positive action in response. We begin by recognizing that men are different from women—bright boy you may say, you knew that all along. But, have we really learned to appreciate how different the sexes are, and learned to build with those differences in mind?

The day before our first wedding anniversary we went through the worst crisis of our married life to date. We were having breakfast with friends and I was in the middle of retelling what I thought was a very amusing joke. As I built towards the punchline, Katey leaped in and in a rather pedantic and mocking way pre-empted me with the punchline. At that moment I felt belittled in front of our friends, totally insecure and thoroughly betrayed. Without thinking I responded by throwing the contents of a freshly made, boiling hot cup of coffee all over Katey. With the shock and the heat she rushed out of the kitchen in tears, I immediately regretted what I'd done and felt more stupid than ever, and our friends made a wise and discreet departure. I sought out Katey upstairs, nursing somewhat reddened flesh and began the process of apology and reconciliation. To this day that incident is etched on my mind and still causes me to feel ashamed when I consider it.

In that incident Katey had trodden on the male ego and I had reacted most violently. In our discussions following that incident we began to discover that the make-up of a man is very different from that of a woman.

Think back, if you will, to the exercise in the last chapter where you each identified strengths and weaknesses in each other (page 39). You will recall that when you identified strengths in each other we insisted that men share first. The reason for this is that women are often starved of encouragement. For so long social conditioning has directed women towards a role of subservience that they seldom exercise their gifts and abilities to the full. Therefore husbands have an important role in identifying strengths and abilities in their wives, encouraging them and enabling them to practise and develop such gifts. Too often as guys we overlook the creative touches and very real capabilities in our wives, and fail to provide the nurture they require.

Katey and I are convinced that there appears to be such a dearth of female leadership within the church because even where we have rejected an ecclesiology that relegates women to the role of spectators not participators, we have failed to engage in a programme of providing positive, practical opportunities for women to exercise their gifts. In our marriages, as we firstly encourage our wives through identification of gifts, and secondly provide the practical environment of prayer together for the exercise of those gifts, we can help prepare a whole host of women for leadership roles, for taking over areas of responsibility within the church and society generally. At a time when the feminist agenda is up for discussion, we have the opportunity to demonstrate God's creative perspective through the church.

I first recognized the need for active encouragement for Katey when I discovered she would often 'put herself down' in company or excuse something which simply did not need excusing. As I travelled the country I discovered that this was a common occurrence among the ladies in whose homes I enjoyed hospitality, and that their husbands often seemed unaware of it. The clearest example I can recall occurred over meals. Whenever we entertained, which was frequently, I could guarantee that whatever Katey served up, which was always admirable, she would apologize for, or at least for some part of it. I encountered this same attitude in home after home as meals were set before me. My response was simple; I began to thank Katey for her choice of menu, the quality of the meal and the little touches she had included in setting the table, such as a small vase of fresh flowers as a table decoration. It was glorious to see her flourish under this encouragement and also to develop a greater confidence in hospitality, a subject about which she is now well able to speak on the couples' weekends that we are involved in.

This same principle of encouragement has allowed Katey to develop a speaking role in her own right, rather than shelter behind me and just pop up with the occasional illustration. As husbands we must encourage our wives so that they can fulfil their potential in God. So be a practical encourager.

In the 'Action Stations' exercise in chapter 2 we said that when it comes to identifying weaknesses it is the ladies who should speak first. Often wives know more about their husbands than the husbands realize. Suffice it to say that we men are egotists, with an ego which longs to be applauded and acknowledged.

Wives need to become an anchor point for husbands, and as husbands we need to learn to make room for our wives' valuable input in areas of weakness. We meet so many men who exercise positions of leadership in church life but whose character has sadly never kept pace with the development of their gift. Can there be a sadder sight than a man, mature in years, unable to respond to criticism in any other way than anger? Wives are a godsend because they can actually build character into the lives of their husbands by challenging the weaknesses and precipitating the necessary crises for these weaknesses to be dealt with. Husbands have to develop the humility necessary for this to happen, wives the boldness mixed with much wisdom.

Obviously, wives need their own weaknesses to be identified too, and husbands need encouragement. But it is our experience that encouragement is the place for husbands to start with their wives and weaknesses the place for wives to start with husbands. Of course, none of this can work outside of the security of our relationship with God, and so highlights another vital reason why we must begin to pray together effectively.

Marriage in 3D

In concluding this chapter I want to express our conviction that marriage is supported on three foundational pillars: the social dimension, the sexual dimension and the spiritual dimension. Remove any one of those pillars and a marriage becomes one third more liable to fail to function effectively or even to fail altogether.

The social dimension

When a couple enter into marriage they often assume that they are totally sufficient for each other, so previous friendships are often dropped and very quickly the couple only have one another to socialize with. This is tragic. Katey and I quickly discovered we were not socially sufficient for one another. She still needed to meet up with her girlfriends and do things with them. Likewise I would meet up with my mates for the occasional evening or go off for a day to a sporting fixture or some such event. Furthermore, we needed to develop relationships together with other couples—folk to share holidays with or weekends away. We also discovered that we quickly developed friendships together with single folk, our home becoming an open home. This would mean that I would spend more time with the single fellows on various outings, Katey with the girls, as well as the time we spent together.

We found that very quickly you can get stuck in a rut in marriage and as someone once said, the only difference between a rut and a grave is about 5 feet. We had to be creative about the way we used time off together. Rotting in front of the TV was a dead end. Therefore we began to walk together and explore places. We have recently joined the National Trust so that we can pop into gardens and houses of historic interest and enjoy ourselves in this way. We joined with a good friend and wrote into our diaries weekends visiting various locations. All three of us recently visited Petworth House near where we live and had a really good, relaxing and refreshing day chatting and enjoying each other's company. On a recent speaking engagement Katey and I popped out during the afternoon off and visited some lovely gardens. We were able to reflect on the weekend of ministry and plan for the rest of our time there in the most beautiful and restful of surroundings. So many couples lose this social dimension, only to discover that their relationship turns stale and that they are drifting apart.

This social dimension is absolutely essential and quite possible to maintain. If you are broke financially you need to become creative. Over a period when Katey and I were at our poorest we still found social outgoings. We turned a trip to the opticians (for free eye-tests) into a real day out, and what's more had a very fruitful time of conversation with the Hindu optician.

If you are surrounded by children include them in. I am for ever indebted to my parents who always found something for us to do as a family of five each weekend. We had no car so we would be walked up to the park to feed the ducks, visit the children's zoo, play cricket or hide-and-seek. These form some of my happiest childhood memories, and having since been responsible for entertaining young children I appreciate the effort and cost my mum and dad were prepared to make.

In a recent edition of *Chat* I was struck by the title of an article, 'The family that eats together stays together.'

Identifying something rapidly disappearing from life in our society, the family meal, the paper recognized that family breakdown may well be increased through failure to function as a family. The same is true for couples minus the children as well.

The sexual dimension

The second pillar supporting the marriage is in the sexual sphere. It has been said that if you put a coin in a jar every time you made love in the first year of your marriage you'd spend the rest of your years emptying the jar! Unfortunately there is a grain of truth in this statement. For many couples sex falls into disuse in their marriage as they advance in years. Yet sex is an essential and vital ingredient in every marriage. Paul himself wrote, 'Do not deny yourselves to each other, unless you first agree to do so for a while in order to spend your time in prayer; but then resume normal marital relations. In this way you will be kept from giving in to Satan's temptation because of your lack of self-control' (1 Cor 7:5).

The marriage bed is the place where we learn to lose our inhibitions towards each other, the place where we learn to relax together and laugh together. For all those couples who have puffed and panted their way through various sexual activities the words of St Francis in describing the human body as 'brother Ass' will cause a degree of mirth and agreement. Much is to be learned through our sexual exploits together. The need to give and not to take, to put one's partner's pleasure first, to be unembarrassed in showing one's partner what pleases and to talk honestly and naturally. The learning experience of investigating new positions can be a source of much amusement if not potential physical injury.

Katey and I have discovered that our sexual relationship has grown over the years and benefited through positive communication and learning to be fully relaxed with each other. If you can become totally uninhibited and honest in bed together this encourages and ensures a level of honest communication which services the marriage. It also produces a sense of oneness and dependence which works actively against falling into sexual immorality. Tony Campolo maintained that the average person falls in love seven times before they get married and seven times after they get married! Once you've stopped counting for yourself, remember there are plenty of attractive men and women in the world and none of us is above being tempted into adultery. A positive sexual relationship together as couples is a good protection for our marriages; and if we learn to be at ease with each other then we can express to our partners those members of the opposite sex we find attractive without threatening them. This again acts as a useful deterrent against immorality. Katey knows who I find attractive and I know which male has the sexiest backside as far as Katey is concerned!

The spiritual dimension

So to the final pillar—that which is perhaps best recognized and least practised. The Catholics have coined the phrase, 'The family that prays together stays together,' and there is a great element of truth in that. I love visiting homes of families where prayer is obviously such a natural part of their life together that the children are not in the least nonplussed by it. While staying with one family recently, grace was sung to the tune of 'Thank you very much', obviously a home-grown family version— excellent!

The most difficult nettle to grasp is the tyranny of 'ought'. We all know we ought to pray but don't know how to. The initial thing to do is to sit down and determine when you are going to get started and then start at that agreed point. We shall look at this in the next chapter.

Prayer, like the social and the sexual, provides yet another forum in which we can relate. It includes God much more actively than the other two areas. It is a time for airing hurts and grievances, joys and expectations, and receiving support and encouragement from our partners in the name of God. Katey and I have known anxiety replaced by peace, anger replaced by love and fragmentation replaced by reconciliation as we have prayed together. Indeed, in times of pressure we now actively seek God first of all rather than allowing ourselves to be chewed up by our immediate circumstances. We have also developed a respect and confidence in each other's ability to minister Jesus and have benefited greatly from the practical application of the same.

We will now move on to how we get started, but don't forget our relationships need to function on the social, the sexual and the spiritual planes.

▶ *Action stations*

Get together as couples with pencil and paper handy.

Answer the following questions honestly by writing your responses on your paper.

Social dimension:
    (1) Do I have personal friends with whom I spend
        time at work
        at home
        elsewhere?
    (2) As a couple am I happy with how we use our leisure
        time?
    (3) Would I like to entertain in our home more often?

Sexual dimension:
    (1) Do I feel relaxed enough with my partner to tell him/
        her how he/she could give me greater pleasure
        sexually?
    (2) Am I happy that we make love regularly enough?
    (3) Would I be able to tell my partner if I found someone
        else attractive?

Spiritual dimension:
    (1) Do I want to pray with my partner regularly?
    (2) What is the greatest single factor preventing me from
        praying with my partner?
    (3) Would the children be embarrassed by family prayers?

Now talk through your answers together.

4
Plotting Our Course and Setting Sail

It was said, a little unkindly, of Christopher Columbus, the great explorer who rediscovered America, that he set out not knowing where he was going, arrived not knowing where he was and returned not knowing where he had been—and the whole lot on borrowed money! An entrepreneur of some standing!

For many of us this has been our experience of prayer together. We have faithfully cast off, not quite knowing where precisely we are aiming for. We fire off a few prayers this way and that and finally land, full of dissatisfaction. We then quietly forget about praying together and make out as best we can without it. And what of the borrowed money? Well, we are often stirred into action following a couple's testimony or yet another call to prayer or a wave of guilt, hence acting on someone else's prayer experience instead of investing in one of our own. However, we can all begin our own account at any time and invest in it regularly together.

Before we achieve anything we need to know where we are heading and how we intend to get safely to our destination. Once as a teenager on holiday in Bournemouth I hired a rowing-boat and set off out to sea. I had no idea of where I was going to row to and did not have a watch to tell me the time. I rowed and rowed, thoroughly enjoying the vigorous exercise and letting my imagination have full range—one moment escaping pirates, the next smuggling contraband across the water under the noses of the king's men. I was eventually brought back to reality when I was hailed by a passing yacht. The skipper enquired if I was in need of assistance since they were not used to meeting rowing-boats so far out, but I cheerily said I was fine. Then I realized the pier and coastline were really quite small. Obviously my rowing, aided by the ebbing tide, had carried me a good distance from the shore. I turned the boat about and began the long row in, pausing every so often to peer over my shoulder and get a bearing on the pier for which I was aiming. Three hours—and a pair of very weary arms—later I made shore to be greeted by a rather irate boatman who informed me that he shut at five o'clock (it was now gone six!) and that I had only hired the boat for a two-hour period. I apologized, negotiated a realistic price for my total hiring and went off to find somewhere to get food and drink. The abiding memory is that rowing is not for me and a somewhat jaundiced view of boating generally.

Had I planned properly I could have had a very pleasant afternoon's boating instead of that nightmare—and for many of us this is true of our prayer life. A series of poor experiences prevents us from getting our act together effectively. Katey and I meet so many couples who, in trying to pray together, have set aside a large chunk of time and emerged thoroughly depressed by it— it has been uninspiring and exceptionally boring, and what's more they missed their favourite TV programme. Sacrificing something for God which leaves one feeling disgruntled strikes me as bad news.

We started to add a spiritual dimension to our marriage in a very small way about two years after our wedding. We had both been given copies of *Living Light* on the occasion of our baptisms, and one night we decided to read the verses set aside for that date. It really was no more than reading them through before putting the light out. At the time Katey was teaching in a rather difficult school and one night asked if we could pray about some problem she had to face the following day. Surprisingly enough it worked and we would pray whenever either of us faced a situation needing divine intervention. This developed into a longer time and we decided that perhaps it would be more suitable if we spent time together at the beginning of the day. This we did and also introduced Bible readings. It was not a particularly long time spent in deep Bible study and prayer, but it was a start. *Living Light* had been a good starting-point, providing a loose structure we could easily fit into and eventually leading to Bible reading and prayer at the start of the day.

When we did finally manage to establish a regular, enjoyable and effective prayer life it was only by observing some very basic ground rules.

1. Be practical

So often we imagine we will drift in and out of prayer without a second thought. While I recognize that I am not the most organized of people and Katey probably less so, it soon became evident that unless we took one simple decision our prayer life together would remain in tatters. So the first question we asked each other was, 'When shall we pray?' Initially this was for us last thing at night. Because we made it a priority we achieved it even when tired. Once Katey gave up work we established a time at the start of the day—a nice breakfast together in the company of Radio 4's *Today* programme, or Radio 3's selection, followed by prayer. We noticed an amazing difference once we settled on a time.

Having chosen the time when we would pray, we then agreed on how long we would pray for. Initially we spent ten minutes last thing at night. This grew to around half an hour maximum—a time span we only occasionally extend. We discovered it better to pray effectively for ten minutes than struggle through forty-five minutes of tedium and frustration.

Once we had established the time and the duration, we would take a couple of minutes at the start to identify the people and situations for which we would pray. It's surprising how often our mind goes a complete blank when we start praying. Once we had three or four items for prayer we got on with it. We soon learned not to be anxious if we each prayed for the same person or situation one after the other, or if other previously unmentioned items got incorporated. Our agreed time over we'd finish and go to sleep. We felt really chuffed that we had prayed, fulfilled our target and established a pattern.

▶ *Action stations*

Together decide when you will pray and for how long you will pray. Be realistic. Start small and leave room for growth. Having made your agreement decide when will be the first day you put your decision into action.

2. Be disciplined

One of the rare scientific facts I learned at school (I once scored a miserable 8/100 for a physics paper!) was that a vacuum was a void incapable of supporting life. Unfortunately many of us create a vacuum when we pray together. We adopt the aforementioned 'shampoo position', a holy hush descends and then . . . nothing! Maybe a few mutterings of 'Thank you, Jesus' or a sigh or two, but apart from these nothing.

I well remember when we started praying I would launch out into an all-embracing theological epic and end with a solid 'Amen'. I would then think inwardly, 'Katey, now it's your turn.' Silence reigned. I continued to think Katey ought to get on with it and still she didn't. Then I twigged. Obviously Katey must be in sin and struggling to find the words for a suitable confession. Well I'd wait, and following her confession minister the grace and forgiveness of God (see what I mean about the male ego mentioned in the last chapter?). Still not a word from Katey. Not only was she in deep sin, she must be in outright rebellion as well. This was a task for super-Christian—in other words, me. So with a good dose of condemnation I'd challenge Katey who had been quietly enjoying the Lord and trying to keep in touch with my initial extended prayer, and immediately put her back up. Unable to back down, the prayer time would halt and we would depart our separate ways, grumpy, frustrated and out of fellowship with each other.

We came to learn that our times of prayer needed a helmsman, someone to give a bit of guidance when the going was getting nowhere. We began to break in on the silences by suggesting the other might like to pray for one of the items we had listed, or read a scripture for meditation and then request feedback. It was evident that our times of prayer required a disciplined direction and we each had a responsibility for ensuring this took place. Katey asked if I would carry the ultimate responsibility for this as she preferred not to.

The fruit of all this was that I would act as a sort of chairman and provide a running commentary as and when necessary. If there was silence I would say, 'Let's concentrate upon God's grace for the next two minutes and then give thanks for what we've gained,' or, 'Let's take the next three minutes praying for those we know who are being persecuted,' or, 'Let's bombard God with a stream of short, sharp prayers of thanksgiving' etc. This immediately removed any sense of tension or uncertainty that had accompanied our prayer life together and gave it a very positive framework in which to grow.

▶ *Action stations*

Take time to decide who will carry the ultimate responsibility for keeping your prayer times moving forward in a positive and disciplined direction. Having made your decision, act upon it and stick to it.

3. Be honest

I don't know how many of you have been in those prayer meetings where in the guise of talking to God an individual really communicates what they want to say to somebody else in the prayer group. Frankly, it is one of the most despicable abuses of a time of prayer to have a go at someone under the apparent safety of talking to God. I'm sure God finds this detestable. It may be hard to face up to people with issues, but it's something we have to learn. And it's something we can learn a lot about in the context of praying together.

We are not to abuse prayer by lecturing each other 'in the name of Jesus, Amen'. We are not to pray, for example, 'Lord, I pray that you will deal with Mary's temper. It is obviously an offence to you and no help to her.

Please remove Mary's temper and give her your grace and patience.' As Mary sits and listens to this she is immediately out of fellowship with God and with you. Have the gumption to talk about temper together, not through the medium of prayer. If it is an issue then encourage Mary to have it dealt with through ministry and prayer. Together you can build a framework which will help Mary avoid situations which cause her to lose her temper. You might discover you are a most frustrating character to share the same house with and need to put your own house in order as well. Painful stuff this praying together, but the raw material for effective marriage relationships.

This ability to be able to confront without ultimate offence is essential. I say ultimate offence because in the first instance if I am confronted I will most likely overreact. However, in the fullness of time I will see the error of my ways, the truth of that with which I was confronted and I will want to deal with the situation. If we can learn to do this in the intimacy of our marriage relationships we will become a better person to live with, exercise a greater level of maturity within the body of Christ—able to receive and respond to constructive criticism and encouragement—and a valuable resource to the church in discipling and pastoring others. Sad to say, many in Christian leadership are prepared to demand a level of submission in others which they would never be prepared to receive themselves.

Another issue which surfaced once we started praying together was that of criticism. For no apparent reason I would find myself becoming irritated with Katey over ridiculous things—her prayers, the tone of her voice, the things she forgot to pray. Indeed, I found myself listening intently to every word and missing the purpose of prayer altogether.

There's a story told of a young man who was converted and came from a rough background who was brought along to the mid-week prayer meeting. He found himself in a world he barely recognized. People praying interminably in a language which he thought had died with Shakespeare. However, wishing to communicate with God he opened his mouth and talked with his heavenly Father, briefly and in a language with which he was comfortable. The prayer meeting over he was approached by one of the leaders of the church and taken on one side. He was informed that his prayer was a little inappropriate and not quite what the prayer meeting was used to. Thinking for a moment he replied, 'Well, I wasn't talking to you, I was talking to him up there,' and promptly departed.

It is so easy to forget that prayer is all about a relationship with God. We are not earning points for artistic expression or theological content in the prayers which we execute. We are simply talking to our Father in ordinary ways about ordinary situations. I for my part had to recognize my fault, share it with Katey (not so very easy but a good reason for establishing the ground explained above) and do something about it. In this way I managed to battle through my criticism and Katey hers.

Katey found my need to 'preach' at her very irritating, especially the tone of voice I would employ and my tendency to use any new theological term I had discovered at every possible opportunity. This all had to be talked through and dealt with. However, we still get a good laugh from my 'preaching' voice.

Finally under this heading I can point out that falling asleep while praying is not a sin. It first happened to me at what is called, in shorthand, an O.I.C.C.U. D.P.M. which roughly translated means the Oxford Inter-Collegiate Christian Union Daily Prayer Meeting! I was eagerly looking forward to participating but found that the cumulative effect of the late night rigours of finishing an essay, the easy-chair into which I had slumped and the warmth within the room was one of sleep rather than spiritual warfare. I could only have dropped off for a few moments, but I awoke with a start as my head dropped and immediately pretended that I had been deeply engrossed in prayer. I was acutely embarrassed. Nobody said anything fortunately and I left feeling how dreadfully unspiritual I had been.

Katey and I have nodded off in the middle of praying together. We are no longer embarrassed (the party who fell asleep) nor critical (the party who stayed awake) but just take it in our stride. We see it as the practical outworking of 'snoring in the Spirit'!

4. Dare to be different

If there is one thing that blunts our prayer life it's repetition. We both need to agree to take responsibility to stop our prayer time from getting locked into a set system or form. Here are a few ways to prevent this from happening.

Initiation is important. Introduce a new element into your prayer life. Share a thought that strikes you following your partner's prayer (we will look at this in more detail when we consider the gifts of the Spirit). A preparedness to initiate within the framework of our prayer life will keep the whole relationship fresh and act as a safeguard against creating that 'holy silence' that brooks no interruption.

Indeed, interruption is another important element. We must not be ruled by our time of prayer but rather utilize it practically and effectively. After the style of a well-known scripture, prayer was designed for man and not man for prayer. We often interrupt our time of prayer to offer to pray for the other. This is altogether better than suddenly rising, gliding across the room, clamping hands on your partner and praying. All you need is a few words such as, 'I'd like to pray for you about . . .' and then whatever the issue is. Normality and clarity are important ingredients in our prayer life.

▶ *Action stations*

For this you will need a Bible, pen and paper each, and thirty minutes to sit down together. Don't panic; this is not thirty minutes of prayer but an opportunity to look at and learn from what the Bible has to say about prayer.

Agree how you will tackle the passages. Will one of you look them up and read them? Will you take it in turns? Who will keep their finger in the book and guide the discussion forward? Settle these practical questions.

Having done so, pray together using the Lord's prayer. Now work your way through the scriptures, discussing your own thoughts and noting your conclusions as you go.

Prayer the precursor

A precursor means that which runs before, something which precedes. A quick look at Scripture confirms that prayer always precedes the activity of God.

When Jesus faced the task of choosing twelve close friends to learn from him, he disappeared to pray first (Lk 6:12 ff.). He went out into the hills and spent the whole night praying to God. When morning came he called the disciples to him and chose twelve of them whom he designated apostles. Jesus talked to his Father to discover whom he should gather around him. He wanted to co-operate with God. It was essential that he selected the right people in whom to invest his life (and not simply his knowledge). These folk would be the pioneers of the New Testament church and the Christian message.

Again, we see the place of prayer preceding revelation. Jesus praying in private together with his disciples breaks off to pose a question, 'Who do the crowds say I am?' (Lk 9:18). A number of answers are given, all wide of the mark, when Jesus homes in on the disciples and develops his question by saying, 'Who do you say I am?' (Lk 9:20). This obviously increases the stakes somewhat; no one wants to open their mouth only to put their foot in it. However, before he can check himself Peter blurts out, 'You are the Messiah, the Son of the living God' (Mt 16:16). Jesus does not congratulate him as such, but indicates that that which Peter has expressed was not discerned by any human analysis or computation but had been revealed directly from God. Peter had had a unique revelation; God had spoken directly to him and used him to communicate the unique truth about Jesus.

About a week later this revelation was followed by another entrusted to Peter, John and James. While praying Jesus was transfigured and the three disciples, on the verge of falling asleep, were suddenly totally awake as a piece of high drama took place before their eyes. Bold Peter again opened his mouth but this time let slip a somewhat inappropriate comment. The disciples kept this revelation to themselves, not quite appreciating its meaning at the time.

Briefly looking at Acts chapter 2 we see the disciples were together, no doubt praying for God to do something having convinced them to stay in Jerusalem, probably the most unhealthy spot for any follower of Jesus at that time. The 'something' of God was the outpouring of the Holy Spirit, the person of the Godhead who provided those who had seen the risen Lord with the confidence and power to proclaim as much within a hostile environment.

A little later in Acts 2:42 we find the early church devoting itself to prayer, i.e. seeking to beat in time with the heart of God so that the work of God might flourish, and being ready to take an active part in that.

▶ *Remember*

Prayer always precedes the activity of God. If you do not see much of God's activity around you, pray honestly and stand back, for God will act. We need to be people who hear from God direct; we desperately require unique first-hand revelation. I find it rather sad that so often as I travel I find Christians informing me that what the latest 'big name' preacher has declared is currently the heart of God. I have nothing against what they have preached; my concern is that Christians are getting their revelations second-hand. Many are enjoying God vicariously, i.e. through the experience of another, rather than meeting God face to face themselves.

Take a look at 1 John 2:27—'As for you, Christ has poured out his Spirit on you. As long as his Spirit remains in you, you do not need anyone to teach you. For his Spirit teaches you about everything and what he teaches is true not false. Obey the Spirit's teaching, then, and remain in union with Christ.' God wants to speak to us directly, and we have the capacity to communicate with him one to one, for he has given us his Holy Spirit to enable us to have 'face-to-face' discussion. I believe every one of us should discover what it is to talk with God directly and enjoy personal and unique revelation. As a couple you can do this together; as you get practice in this so your confidence and competence will grow.

Submit to God not to circumstance

In Luke 22:39-46 we read the heart-rending story of
Jesus in the Garden of Gethsemane. As he agonized in
prayer with his Father he was confronted with the way of
suffering which lay ahead and every part of his humanity
recoiled and drew back. However, having poured out his
heart with all the emotion and anguish that he felt, even
to the extent of sweating drops of blood, Jesus agreed to
obey God and serve his eternal and divine will. Jesus had
expressed himself in total honesty before God. There
was nothing super-spiritual about his agreeing to go to
the cross; he didn't gloss over the pain and the anguish
he felt but ultimately determined to place his hand in
God's hand and to hang on tight.

For many Christians calamity or difficult circumstances direct them away from God. They become so full
of the pain and pressure of their circumstances that God
gets crowded out and the relationship falls into disrepair.
Some even choose to reject God himself as the very
source of the problem and direct their anger and bitterness against him. It is very sad when we allow ourselves
to be robbed of a close and loving relationship with God
through the nature of our circumstances. When times are
tough that should be the moment to close ranks with our
heavenly Father. In the face of disaster we should find
ourselves driven into the arms of love waiting to encircle
us.

When Katey and I discovered that we had a less than
1% chance of having a baby we found that we were
driven into each other's arms. We needed each other; we
needed affection and acceptance like there was no tomorrow. We also discovered how much we needed God,
and held tightly in his arms we could express the anger,
pour out the anguish and sob quietly into his chest as he

held us close in arms of unimaginable love and security. We also discovered that instead of being crushed beneath the weight of the problem we were able to develop a godly perspective on it and develop a sufficient sense of proportion to continue functioning in everyday life.

As couples we will find a greater capacity to ride through life when we choose to do so within the arms of God. We need to get used to resting in his embrace and experiencing his love so that we know to whom we can turn if and when circumstances swing against us. Practice getting into God's presence and gaining a godly perspective.

Perseverance

Luke 18:1 informs us to pray and not to give up—and this is sound advice. Muller, who did so much for children in need within his own day and age, prayed regularly for four friends that they might become Christians. During his lifetime he saw three of those friends enter into a relationship with God. However, the fourth one resisted and it was not until after Muller had died that he found the faith Muller had consistently prayed that he would find.

There is much to be said for maintaining prayer for specific situations and not giving up on them. So often we give up partly because we lose heart and partly because we lose originality in approaching the object of our prayer and so become bored. A little thought can ensure that you remain constant in prayer and find new ways to pray for the situation.

For example, when we were praying for one couple over a number of years we began spending time thinking about them and their situation, and although our object was that they should discover the reality of Christian experience for themselves we seldom prayed to that specific end. We began to pray for their circumstances—certain friendships, pressures etc—and all sorts of other obstacles that impeded their perceiving Jesus for who he was and how he related to them and vice versa. This became creative and enjoyable; our faith for them increased and we were able to persevere prayerfully. So remember, if at first you don't see answers—persevere!

5
Worship

The heart of worship

In the early stages of our married life there was one question which consistently stumped me—that question was: 'Mike, do you love me?' Now if I said yes it sounded dismissive and perfunctory, yet if I tried to establish the fact that I did love Katey it sounded rather strained, listing all the ways by which my wife could realize she was loved. In the film *Fiddler on the Roof* Tevye asks his wife whether she loves him. Her response, in song, is to identify all she does for him: 'I cook for you, I wash for you, I clean for you,' all of which is a long way from reassuring Tevye that he is loved.

I'm still faced with the same question today, eight years further on in my married life, and I've learned just how important it is to express frequently and verbally that I love Katey. It is important for Katey to tell me of her love as well. Strange though it might seem, one never grows tired of that little word 'love', and as we express it with our lips we will often demonstrate its reality with a hug, kiss or some similar act of affection.

Sadly, where love is not spoken, the demonstration in the physical realm also falls into disrepair. Remember all we said earlier about the importance of communication.

God longs for a deep and vibrant relationship with people. Having wooed a rebellious people throughout history he ultimately made the final play for their affection and obedience by commissioning his own Son to reinstate a relationship between himself and man that was in a state of extreme disrepair. I can imagine that momentous occasion in heaven when with something of a heavy heart the Father approached his Son and entered into conversation with him. 'Son,' he said.

'Yes, Father,' came Jesus' eager reply.

'Son, I've a task to undertake in which I need your full co-operation. Will you help me?'

'You know I will, Father, it will be a privilege.'

'But wait, let me explain. You know when at the beginning of time we had such fun creating the heaven and the earth and everything on the earth, and how as a finale to all that we created man in our image?'

'Yes, I remember. Marvellous fun!'

'And you remember how having been created as a companion man chose to rebel against us, do his own thing and break faith with us. And how we had to banish him from all this.' God waved his arm in an expansive circle indicating all that the eye could see round about them. 'We lost that friendship we'd enjoyed with him. Well, Son, the time has come to renew that friendship.'

'Father, that's tremendous. I'm thrilled you want me involved.'

'Wait till I've spoken further. I need you to lay aside your royal prerogative and privilege and allow yourself to become a man. To leave this place and live on earth, showing mankind what God is like and living as man was always meant to live.'

'I can do that.'

'Yes, but the men among whom you live will misunderstand your message. They'll begin to hate you. They'll despise and reject you, and even your friends will desert you and leave you alone.'

'Father, hard though that is I would want to do it if it pleases you.'

'Well, these same people will falsely accuse you, they will arrest and abuse you and finally kill you by nailing you to a wooden gibbet in the same way they would rid themselves of a common criminal.'

'That is hard to contemplate, but if it will restore our relationship with man I will go.'

'That's not the worst of it, Son.' And tears began to well up in the eyes of the Almighty as he continued. 'While your battered body hangs suspended on that gibbet I will gather up all the sin and corruption of sin-sick society from its beginning through its present right up to its end and hurl it at you. For the first time in all eternity I will break fellowship with you for I cannot bear to look on sin. Though you cry out to me I shall not answer until the deed is done, sin is dealt with and friendship with man once more a possibility.'

I believe that in the silence that followed, both Father and Son sensed the pain and the cost involved. As we know, Jesus agreed to obey his Father and fulfilled that marvellous unfathomable work of salvation for all mankind. It is in this activity of God that we understand the nature and meaning of love. 'Dear friends, let us love one another, because love comes from God. Whoever loves is a child of God and knows God. Whoever does not love does not know God, for God is love' (1 Jn 4:7-8). Even more remarkable, it was not the lovely but the unlovely that God died for. Mankind was not eagerly demanding a saviour like Jesus, but quite content serving his own interests. Yet love could see beyond this and took action.

What I am constantly thrilled by is the way in which love initiates. God initiated reconciliation and restoration, and so in our marriages the onus is always upon us to take the initiative in reconciliation. In this way, we express our faith in a most practical way. We also renew and refresh our marriage. It may mean swallowing our pride and becoming vulnerable. This is the cost of Christian marriage. Katey and I have learned that the best thing about a bust-up is the getting it back together again. The apology and the renewal of our relationship. Acknowledging and laying aside the wrong in order to give oneself 110% to one's partner again. I for one always find it very hard to say sorry, even when I know I'm wrong and have accepted as much. However, it is the very action that brings about the reconciliation. And this lies at the heart of our worship life together.

The reality of worship

Let's look at Romans 12:1-2. Paul writes,

> So then, my brothers, because of God's great mercy to us [which I've just outlined above], I appeal to you: Offer yourselves as a living sacrifice to God, dedicated to his service and pleasing to him. Do not conform yourselves to the standards of this world, but let God transform you inwardly by a complete change of your mind. Then you will be able to know the will of God—what is good and is pleasing to him and is perfect.

Here is expressed the very nature of true worship—total availability to God. Notice that this condition is reached by the renewal and not by the removal of your mind. We are called to be involved in this process at every level. This text is as appropriate to relating together in marriage as it is in relating to our heavenly Father.

How does worship feature in our marriage? Well, I for one worship Katey and she worships me. I worship her verbally—I tell her I love her, I think she's fantastic, she does me good, I want to do her good, she's the only girl for me. I worship her physically—I kiss her, cuddle her, hold hands with her, make love to her. I think she is worth all of my attention and invite her to make whatever demands she might want to. I am totally available to her—there is no area of my life from which I wish to exclude her, and she has freedom to address me on any issue.

This aspect of worship in marriage is highlighted in the biblical charge to married couples to leave, cleave and become one flesh. The word 'cleave' literally means 'to hold fast to one another' as on a 'glutinous surface'. That's precisely what we must do, both in our marital relationship and in our relationship with God.

When we turn to looking at our worship of God, Paul actually calls us to abandon ourselves to the goodness of God. So often we hold back on giving all to God when he has bought us lock, stock and barrel. He expects us to be totally available to him. Unfortunately, however, because of culture—it's not our custom to leap about; or tradition—we are uncomfortable without someone directing us; or peer group pressure—what will my friends think if I put my hands in the air or if I don't put my hands in the air, we respond to a myriad different voices none of which is God's. We are called to respond to him alone, regardless of the consequences. Indeed, if you are obedient to God the consequences cannot be damaging in the long term.

I well remember when God put me through my paces in this. I was not at all sure about dancing in worship and believed I would feel exceptionally uncomfortable if I did leap around during a time of praise. Although I sensed that God wanted me to dance, my own self-consciousness held me back. However, I was bullied into it through the godly perseverance of Ishmael, one Spring Harvest, and found I did not feel foolish, my inhibitions went and a new sense of liberty and love in my relationship with God was released. This is not to say that everyone should follow suit. This was God's word and way for me. It might be for you too, but you'll know if it is because God makes himself abundantly plain.

A second incident developed from this in that God convicted me about my bad moods. I would walk around at home looking like a thunder-cloud and generating an unhealthy atmosphere. The tragedy of this was not only that I distanced myself from God but also from Katey. She couldn't get close to me even if she wanted to, and didn't know how to approach me without setting off a thermonuclear explosion!

One day God highlighted a verse from the Bible to me—not an especially frequent occurrence. It was 1 Thessalonians 5:16-18: 'Be joyful always, pray at all times, be thankful in all circumstances. This is what God wants from you in your life union with Christ Jesus.' I was not feeling much like praising or giving thanks, and was a little irritated by the way God nudged me and said, 'That's for you and I want you to put it into practice.' I, of course, entered into a long debate with God as to why I couldn't and wouldn't. But he had other plans.

Ecclesiastes 4:12 contains the immortal words: 'A rope made of three cords is hard to break.' It was a verse used at our wedding and roughly translated means that in a Christian marriage there is a partnership of three—the husband, the wife and the Lord. This means, of course, that there is the possibility of a majority decision

78

to resolve any dispute. A husband and wife who choose to neglect God's ways can form an unholy alliance and vote God out of every decision. They are the poorer, but it happens. However, there is also the possibility of the husband or wife teaming up with God to outvote the rebellion and intransigence of the other partner. This is what happened to me.

Somehow Katey discovered what God had said to me about giving thanks in all circumstances. This spelt disaster—there is nothing worse than when your partner agrees you are wrong and you know you are too and are going to have to give in. What happened from the moment the Holy Spirit split on me to Katey was that I would stomp around the kitchen in a foul mood. Katey, in an endearing way, would stop what she was doing and say, 'You know what you've got to do, don't you?' And I would think, 'And you know what you can do, don't you?' but say, 'Yes.' Not content with making me feel uncomfortable she would go on to bully me into praising God! So with a voice empty of emotion and with a touch of cynicism I would say, 'Praise the Lord! Hallelujah! Glory!' By this time Katey had had enough (and God too I guess) and she would give me some VBH (verbal bodily harm), put on a worship cassette and bully me into worshipping.

The most galling thing of all—it worked. Slowly I began to apologize to God and Katey, and started praising God, worshipping him, telling him how marvellous he was, how I was completely his and how I wanted to turn to him in praise and thanksgiving at the first hint of a mood. Best of all, neither God nor Katey exploited their victory but just joined in and we had a smashing time.

We must learn that it is through our worship that we will be conformed to Christ. In a world which seeks to overwhelm us and form us in its image, we need to turn our lives wholly over to God which is true worship. As we serve him and promote his ways then we enable people to see Jesus in us—we become God's highway through a crippled world. C. S. Lewis said that Christians are 'little Christs', and as we abandon ourselves to Jesus we become his effective hands and feet in a world in which people are reaching out to touch him.

Worship, therefore, must form a significant part of our prayer life together as couples. We often pray but do not worship together. The prayerful expression of our worship of God is the love and praise of our hearts expressed with our lips. So infrequently do we really take time to praise God that few people can wax eloquent about the goodness, grace and loveliness of God. When we begin to worship God verbally, concentrating on his love and acknowledging our submission to him, we are released from the self-preoccupation that prevents us from serving our partner and God himself.

We so often seek after God for our own obvious benefit, to get from him rather than to give to him. So often the Sunday worship service is filled with folk all trying to take something from God for their own tattered lives rather than ministering their love to God that he might minister to someone else's tattered life. It seems all wrong that as we gather together Sunday by Sunday we all hope that God will meet our individual needs. Surely we come together to celebrate God, to proclaim that he is alive and full of loving care for us.

We each have testimony to God's goodness during the preceding week. From our fellowship with him and with others within the body, we should come overflowing with praise for him, ready to heap honour upon his name and literally lift the roof with our declaration of his worth. Obviously, there will be the wounded among us. We ourselves may need first-aid, perhaps even major surgery, but we will be all the more able to receive this when we stand among a group of people whose focus is Jesus, whose lives are sold out to Jesus, whose hearts are full of Jesus and hence whose ministry is to bring us Jesus.

Katey and I soon discovered that worship needed to be a key part of our prayer life together. We needed to abandon ourselves to God constantly. We had to recognize that the fruit of self-preoccupation was to become problem centred, and that meant the very life of Jesus was squeezed out of us like juice from a lemon. What was more, we very quickly caught self-preoccupation off one another and so both of us got squeezed dry. This led us away from the Lord, produced friction in our relationship and gave good ground for Satan to stamp all over. We had to practise challenging one another with the goodness and grace and loveliness of Jesus.

In one period of our married life we were skint beyond all skintness. After our outgoings we had the princely sum of £4 per week available for housekeeping. Katey was not at all impressed when I pressed four crisp one-pound notes into her hand at the beginning of the week and told her to bring me the change. Needless to say, we were well provided for by the Lord. However, we did find that the financial situation placed great pressure upon us. It was easy to dwell on it, to grow self-preoccupied and full of envy for everyone else's lifestyle. You only realize what a difference the occasional little treat makes when you can't afford any.

Often, feeling somewhat crushed, we discovered what a release it was to recognize that we belonged to God and that he loved us. Rather like David in some of his psalms, we'd stare at each other confronted by our 'raw deal', focus on Jesus and finish up absolutely amazed by his love. Of course, this didn't always work. We failed, got furious, ranted and raved, but we were able to extract a priceless principle and practise it on several occasions. Indeed, as time passed we got better and better at applying the principle.

If we apply the principle of worship in all circumstances we will fill our Sunday worship with the fragrance of Jesus. Often when we gather together we are empty of things to declare. We have nothing to offer Jesus because we have an impoverished personal experience. In our corporate gatherings we are often challenged and motivated to pray or seek God, only to find that we can never get it together in our personal experience simply because there are no foundations upon which to build. Hence this manual. With an effective and active personal life of devotion we can all gather together with every expectation that each will bring a psalm, hymn or spiritual song (Eph 5:19)—and fresh ones, not ones we have contributed dutifully every week for as long as anyone can remember!

Worship brings us into the presence of God. We can simply enjoy God for who he is. It is essential in enabling us to grow in confidence in the character of God, so that when we run into a time of pressure or difficulty we can fully trust the God who is with us in it. We need to take time to develop that confidence, for it takes time for our intellectual knowledge of God to become established as an experiential knowledge of God. So often when we meet an adversity we have an insufficient reservoir of experiential knowledge of God to give us the confidence within the situation.

When we began to face the reality of childlessness it was hard to do anything more than give grudging assent to the compassion and goodness of God. However, as we have worshipped God regularly it has become easier to entrust him with the situation, knowing he has everything fully under control, he's rooting for us and that he is full of goodness towards us. There is a lightness within us now in this whole area which has proved most creative.

We do not believe that as Christians we can steer a successful course through life unless we are absolutely convinced of the character of God. In these days when it is fashionable to add a qualification to every statement of absolute truth we all too easily find ourselves stepping back from the absolute faithfulness and goodness of God, his omnipotence and omniscience and every other aspect of his character. You cannot have a God whose character is in need of qualification. Either God is God or not God at all. We must accept the absolutes of his character and live in practical recognition of them.

We are a people of certainties in an uncertain world. We are a body of stability when life itself appears to be disintegrating around us. We worship a God who is eternal and whose character remains unchanging through the bleakest of experiences. We find ourselves secure in the palm of his hand as the dust of disturbance which has struck our life settles and we regain a sense of perspective. Our God reigns, and we reign with him. As A.W. Tozer points out in *The Knowledge of the Holy,*

> The most portentious fact about any man is not what he at a given moment may say or do, but what he in his deep heart conceives God to be like . . . The essence of idolatry is the entertainment of thoughts about God that are unworthy of him . . . . The idolator simply imagines things about God and acts as if they were true.

We must at all times beware of idolatry. By active worship, releasing ourselves completely to God, we can both comprehend and develop a complete assurance in his character.

Worship keeps us rooted in God. As Jim Wallis points out in *The Call to Conversion*, 'What roots are to a tree, worship is to the Christian.' We need to retain those roots to draw from the water of life, so sustaining our life and enabling further growth and maturity.

Let's be practical

Having said all this about worship, what is our way forward together? Well, as Katey and I realized the need to take time to focus on God alone we found we shared the same practical problems. Neither of us was musical—I sang somewhat flat, and we both felt embarrassed even at the thought of singing or dancing in worshipful abandon in front of each other. Strange really since we are quite at ease and fairly extrovert in any social gathering of friends. As with everything else in this area of praying together, we had to agree simply to get on with it and see what happened.

When we got together to pray we decided to play a game! One of us would say a word which described one aspect of God's character such as 'grace'. The other would then have to respond by speaking out the first word that came into their head. This was fun, fast and furious. It also pushed any embarrassment to the back of our mind and introduced a very positive element of humour. Any pauses and the culprit would have to sing a chorus which got us launched into singing together without the need of instruments.

Furthermore, sometimes the word one of us spoke out revealed that we had a blind spot or certain reservations about the trustworthy nature of God's character, and so we were able to talk these through together. Sometimes a word might cause us to pause and talk about its particular reference to both God and ourselves. An example might run: grace, goodness, kindness, faithfulness, mercy, justice, love, pain. At which point we would stop to look at pain with reference to ourselves and to God, to reaffirm that in spite of pain God was knowable in the midst of pain. We discovered that biblical references came to mind, for example 2 Corinthians 1:3-5 speaking of the comfort of Christ overflowing in the midst of lives that experience the sufferings of Christ. We would talk about the verse, exchange ideas and maybe meditate upon it before moving on to bombard the gates of heaven with prayers of praise to which our meditation had given birth.

As we became comfortable with this we discovered that one of us did have the courage, if not always the voice, to start up a worship song. Together we would sing and get excited in God. Indeed for a while our whole time of prayer together consisted of worshipping and praising God. It was terrific and provided the source of much practical blessing from the person of God himself.

Having gained a little confidence Katey retrieved her recorder from the loft and bullied me into blowing the cobwebs off my guitar—a memento from the days when as a teenager I had struggled to master classical skills on this instrument—and together we would just play away making music which surprisingly enough was often quite tuneful. The next step on from here was to add lyrics of our own. These were usually spontaneous and forgotten the instant they had been uttered, but they often brought us both very close to the person of Jesus and ministered to us most effectively. The further we progressed the less inhibited we became and the more willing to contribute to larger meetings in which we were involved. We also discovered we had a rich reservoir of God-centred experience to share from, and the more we contributed publicly the less self-conscious we became and the more aware of the Spirit of God. God was blessed, we were encouraged and the body was built up. How very biblical!

We have all been formed in the image of God, and God is a creator. The creative quality of God is in every one of us. Many of us never have the opportunity to express that creativity. Our artistic efforts as children may have been scorned, so we have never developed this area. Yet we can all be creative. In our working together we can experiment with our creativity. We can stimulate and encourage each other. This is both a positive experience and tremendous fun.

▶ Action stations

Hopefully you are both excited by all that we have written above. We suggest you set aside half an hour together for a bit of worshipful fun. Be prepared to enjoy yourselves. Why not start by having a romantic meal together first and then, fully relaxed, take time for the activities that follow. You will need a Bible handy and maybe a song book.

We mentioned above how we got involved in worship by playing the word game. This is the place where you too can start.

Firstly, read aloud Colossians 1:15-23:

> Christ is the visible likeness of the invisible God. He is the first-born Son, superior to all created things. For through him God created everything in heaven and on earth, the seen and the unseen things, including spiritual powers, lords, rulers, and authorities. God created the whole universe through him and for him. Christ existed before all things, and in union with him all things have their proper place. He is the head of his body, the church; he is the first-

born Son, who was raised from the dead, in order that he alone might have the first place in all things. For it was by God's own decision that the Son has in himself the full nature of God. Through the Son, then, God decided to bring the whole universe back to himself. God made peace through his Son's death on the cross and so brought back to himself all things, both on earth and in heaven. At one time you were far away from God and were his enemies because of the evil things you did and thought. But now, by means of the physical death of his Son, God has made you his friends, in order to bring you, holy, pure, and faultless, into his presence. You must, of course, continue faithful on a firm and sure foundation, and must not allow yourselves to be shaken from the hope you gained when you heard the gospel. It is of this gospel that I, Paul, became a servant—this gospel which has been preached to everybody in the world.

Now, thinking about the uniqueness of Jesus Christ, one after the other, and quite rapidly, speak out words or short phrases which spring to mind following your partner's declaration. Wives could start with the words, 'Jesus is supreme,' and then the men respond.

If and when you dry up, break and ask each other the following question in turn: 'What particularly struck a chord with you during that word sequence?' You may remember a scripture, so read it and talk about it. An incident may have been recalled—describe it and chat over why it was recalled. All the time relate back to God.

Having done this, play the word game again, only this time use something from your previous discussion to instigate it—and why not sing a chorus if you are guilty of hesitation?

To end this time of activity, stand up, hold hands and sing the chorus 'I just want to praise you' or another one you know.

In closing may we suggest that if you are musical you

worship God together utilizing your musical skills. Gather the Sunday magazines together and produce a worship collage. You could even adorn your living-room wall with it and it could become a unique talking-point. If you have literary gifts why not contribute a poem to your worship? In all these ways we can discover the reality of the character and personality of Father God and release the love in our hearts to him.

We have discovered the activity outlined above to be one of our most fruitful experiences together, and we know you will too. Let us know how you get on. (You can write to us c/o the publishers of this book, Kingsway Publications.)

6
Discovering the Gifts of the Holy Spirit

It seems that the slightest mention of the Holy Spirit can cause blood pressure to rise, tension to creep in and attitudes to harden. This is very sad since the Holy Spirit is the person of the Godhead who remains here in our world to convict the pagan of guilt and righteousness and to assure the Christian of salvation.

I remember a friend informing me of a particularly sad story he had read in a Sunday supplement. It concerned Percy the Penguin. Percy had been born at a zoo but his mother had taken one look at him and instantly quit motherhood. Poor Percy was now an orphan. However, that gallant band of men we know as zookeepers adopted baby Percy and bottle fed him, ensuring he passed through those critical early weeks and months. The day eventually came for Percy to be returned to the penguin pool to live among his own kind as, naturally enough, a penguin.

The zookeepers gathered around the edge of the enclosure as Percy was introduced to his cousins and they all seemed to get on very well. Greetings over they all filed towards the pool and dived in one after the other—

except that is for Percy. He dutifully shuffled along in the awkward yet orderly line of penguins, but when he reached the edge of the pool he held back and just stared at the water below. Obviously assuming that Percy was overcome at his first sight of water, one of the friendly keepers approached from behind and gave Percy a helpful push into the pool. No sooner had Percy hit the water than he flew like an arrow back onto the side of the pool. He gave the guilty keeper something of an accusing look and would no doubt have accompanied this with a bit of beak had he not been brought up in the best of circles.

A little concerned, the keepers had a brief discussion before advancing on Percy as a body and tipping him back into the pool. Percy once again shot back onto the side. No matter how hard they tried to convince him to swim, Percy was having none of it. The article concluded that Percy was the only penguin in the zoo who detested water.

Amusing though such a story appears, it is sad because Percy had been designed for water. Anyone who has seen a penguin waddling across terra firma recognizes that they are not the most elegant or adept land-based animal. However, place them in water and they twist and turn and perform all kinds of aquabatics revealing that this is the environment for which they were surely designed. Percy, equipped in every way and to a high degree of proficiency for an aqueous environment, refused to experience the life for which he had been designed.

You and I have been designed as containers for the Holy Spirit—God's gift of himself to each and every one of us. Having been born of the Spirit we are to live in the Spirit and keep in step with the Spirit (Gal 5:25). Since the Holy Spirit, despatched by none other than Jesus himself, is the person of the Godhead who takes up residence in the life of the individual Christian, it is little wonder that he is vital to the work of communicating with the Godhead. And since prayer is all about communication, we all need to know, appreciate and cooperate with him.

For many of us our prayer lives have been barren of reality for no other reason than that we have misunderstood, neglected or denigrated the person and work of the Holy Spirit. Now is the time to take a look at who he is and what his work is. Then we will see where this fits into our prayer life together.

▶ Action stations

You will need Bibles, and pencil and paper if you wish to make notes. One of you look up the references, the other read the verses and then together answer the questions. Before we go any further, however, note four very important points:

(1) The Holy Spirit is a him not an it. Look up John 16:7-8 for one reference to this fact.

(2) He always points us to Jesus (Jn 16:14).

(3) He is for every believer—there are no first-class/second-class divides in the Christian family. Peter points out the promise of the Spirit is for all (Acts 2:38-39).

(4) Finally, in Scripture his coming was usually accompanied by evidence of spiritual gifts. Turn on a few pages to Acts 10:46.

Having established those four points we want you now to look together at several encounters with the Holy Spirit. The encounter of Jesus, the disciples, the early

91

church and finally ourselves. Do set aside a useful period of time, say twenty minutes, for this and make whatever notes you feel might prove helpful to refer to later. If you have not got a Bible handy the verses are quoted in full for your use.

1. *Jesus encounters the Holy Spirit*

After all the people had been baptized, Jesus also was baptized. While he was praying, heaven was opened, and the Holy Spirit came down on him in bodily form like a dove. And a voice came from heaven, 'You are my own dear Son. I am pleased with you.' When Jesus began his work, he was about thirty years old (Lk 3:21-23).

Jesus returned from the Jordan full of the Holy Spirit and was led by the Spirit into the desert, where he was tempted by the Devil for forty days. In all that time he ate nothing, so that he was hungry when it was over.

The Devil said to him, 'If you are God's Son, order this stone to turn into bread.'

But Jesus answered, 'The scripture says, "Man cannot live on bread alone."'

Then the Devil took him up and showed him in a second all the kingdoms of the world. 'I will give you all this power and all this wealth,' the Devil told him. 'It has all been handed over to me, and I can give it to anyone I choose. All this will be yours, then, if you worship me.'

Jesus answered, 'The scripture says, "Worship the Lord your God and serve only him!"'

Then the Devil took him to Jerusalem and set him on the highest point of the Temple, and said to him, 'If you are God's Son, throw yourself down from here. For the scripture says, "God will order his angels to take good care of you." It also says, "They will hold you up with their hands so that not even your feet will be hurt on the stones."'

But Jesus answered, 'The scripture says, "Do not put the Lord your God to the test."'

When the Devil finished tempting Jesus in every way, he

left him for a while.

Then Jesus returned to Galilee, and the power of the Holy Spirit was with him. The news about him spread throughout all that territory. He taught in the synagogues and was praised by everyone (Lk 4:1-15).

a) Describe from the passage what happened when Jesus was baptized.
b) Who was it that led Jesus into the desert?
c) How is Jesus described on his return from the Jordan?
d) How is Jesus described on his return to Galilee?

2. *The disciples encounter the Holy Spirit*

When the day of Pentecost came, all the believers were gathered together in one place. Suddenly there was a noise from the sky which sounded like a strong wind blowing, and it filled the whole house where they were sitting. Then they saw what looked like tongues of fire which spread out and touched each person there. They were all filled with the Holy Spirit and began to talk in other languages, as the Spirit enabled them to speak.

There were Jews living in Jerusalem, religious men who had come from every country in the world. When they heard this noise, a large crowd gathered. They were all excited, because each one of them heard the believers speaking in his own language. In amazement and wonder they exclaimed, 'These people who are talking like this are Galileans! How is it, then, that all of us hear them speaking in our own native languages? We are from Parthia, Media, and Elam; from Mesopotamia, Judaea, and Cappadocia; from Pontus and Asia, from Phrygia and Pamphylia, from Egypt and the regions of Libya near Cyrene. Some of us are from Rome, both Jews and Gentiles converted to Judaism, and some of us are from Crete and Arabia—yet all of us hear them speaking in our own languages about the great things that God has done!' Amazed and confused, they kept asking each other, 'What does this mean?'

But others made fun of the believers, saying, 'These people are drunk!' (Acts 2:1-13).

a) What was the day on which the disciples were filled with the Spirit?

b) Where were the disciples?

c) What happened when they were filled with the Holy Spirit?

d) What was the reaction of various groups within the crowd?

3. *The early church encounters the Holy Spirit*

So Ananias went, entered the house where Saul was, and placed his hands on him. 'Brother Saul,' he said, 'the Lord has sent me—Jesus himself, who appeared to you on the road as you were coming here. He sent me so that you might see again and be filled with the Holy Spirit.' At once something like fish scales fell from Saul's eyes, and he was able to see again. He stood up and was baptized; and after he had eaten, his strength came back (Acts 9:17-19).

While Apollos was in Corinth, Paul travelled through the interior of the province and arrived in Ephesus. There he found some disciples and asked them, 'Did you receive the Holy Spirit when you became believers?'

'We have not heard that there is a Holy Spirit,' they answered.

'Well, then, what kind of baptism did you receive?' Paul asked.

'The baptism of John,' they answered.

Paul said, 'The baptism of John was for those who turned from their sins; and he told the people of Israel to believe in the one who was coming after him—that is, in Jesus.'

When they heard this, they were baptized in the name of the Lord Jesus.

Paul placed his hands on them, and the Holy Spirit came upon them; they spoke in strange tongues and also proclaimed God's message. They were about twelve men in all (Acts 19:1-7).

a) What did Ananias do and what did he pray when he was with Saul?

b) What happened when Saul was filled with the Holy Spirit?

c) What baptism had the disciples at Ephesus received?

d) What happened when the Ephesian disciples were filled with the Holy Spirit?

4. *Are we to encounter the Holy Spirit?*

I have told you this while I am still with you. The Helper, the Holy Spirit, whom the Father will send in my name, will teach you everything and make you remember all that I have told you.

Peace is what I leave with you; it is my own peace that I give you. I do not give it as the world does. Do not be worried and upset; do not be afraid (Lk 14:25-27).

But when the Holy Spirit comes upon you, you will be filled with power, and you will be witnesses for me in Jerusalem, in all Judaea and Samaria, and to the ends of the earth (Acts 1:8).

a) What does Jesus promise us when the Holy Spirit comes upon us?

b) What is that power for?

c) What names does Jesus give the Holy Spirit?

d) What two things does Jesus tell us to be?

It should be evident from your Scripture research that the Christian is designed to be a container for the Holy Spirit. It is he who gives us the power to live as Christians and provides the vital communication link with Father God. It is essential that we are filled with the Holy Spirit at every moment of every day. Ephesians 5:18 commands us to 'be filled with the Spirit'. The tense is the present continuous, so the actual meaning is 'go on being filled with the Holy Spirit'. We all need to be full to overflowing with the Holy Spirit if we are to prove effective disciples. Furthermore, communication is two way and God guides us and provides us with privileged information by means of the Holy Spirit. This is so valuable, especially when praying for people and situations.

If you feel powerless or distant from God, pause and take a moment now to invite your partner to pray that you might be filled with the Holy Spirit. There's no need for special language or long prayers. Why not follow the pattern of Ananias and lay hands on your partner and pray simply for the Spirit's fullness. If while you are praying you sense you want to pray a particular prayer for your partner, do so and be a blessing to him or her. It's so lovely when we minister to one another in this way.

The fruit and the gifts of the Spirit

In Galatians 5:22 we read: 'But the Spirit produces love, joy, peace, patience, kindness, goodness, faithfulness, humility and self-control.' In one of our many moves we inherited a garden with a number of fruit trees in it. Being autumn we had no idea what kind of fruit they would bear. However, as the seasons passed and summer returned we were able to identify two apple trees and one pear tree. These trees could be trusted every year to produce apples or pears according to which type they were. We did not expect the apple tree to produce bananas one year, nor did we expect any of the trees to fail to produce.

As Christians the right fruit for our lives is outlined in the passage from Galatians quoted above. If the Holy Spirit is filling our lives then all this fruit should be evident. Where one or more are consistently absent we are in need of a little bit of tree surgery—the acts of the sinful nature need to be chopped off and room made for the Spirit of God to bring forth the crop for which we were originally designed. Since this is the natural fruit of the Christian's life then we do not have to struggle to enable it to flourish. If it is not flourishing then we must ask ourselves if we are filled with the Holy Spirit (if not, pray to be filled yourself or invite your partner to pray for you). If we are filled with the Spirit but still consistently fail to fruit in accordance with the gardener's description, then we need to give a little attention to those things which prevent successful fruiting and apply the correct pesticide. We will see how we do this in the very next chapter.

Scripture makes it very clear that the character of the Christian is marked by the fruit of the Spirit. Therefore if we take the name of Jesus to our lips there is no reason why our lives should not be marked by this fruit. If you are aware of weaknesses or a lack in your own or your partner's life make a note and be ready for 'Action Stations' at the end of this chapter.

God has not only given us the power to produce the fruit of the Spirit, giving our lives their distinctive Christian quality, but he has also empowered us with the gifts of the Spirit so that the church might be effectively serviced, individuals enabled to fruit in greater abundance and the world might be able to enjoy the effective communication of the reality of the love of God. Much has been written and spoken of concerning spiritual gifts, and there is usually a great deal of anticipation surrounding the subject. We have found the context of prayer in our marriage a very fruitful ground in which to discover, experiment with and experience the gifts of the Spirit.

If we turn to 1 Corinthians 12 we discover Paul's great desire that there should not be ignorance about spiritual gifts. We were ignorant of the Spirit for a number of years, let alone the gifts. I remember getting close to turning from Christianity as a young disciple because of my powerlessness and hypocrisy. I was involved in a very active church and participating in evangelism, but while I was smiling on the outside and communicating all the promises of the gospel, I knew that inside I wasn't smiling; inside I wasn't experiencing the reality of those gospel promises. Now one thing I detest is hypocrisy. It was this more than anything else that had turned me into an ardent left-wing idealist when a teenager. I remember walking the streets of Oxford talking to Katey and explaining to her that either Christianity was a deceit or there was a conspiracy of silence about what made it work effectively. Poor Katey, not long a Christian and having to field all my reasoned doubts about the very faith to which I had introduced her.

Getting towards the end of my tether and deciding to make a clean break, we attended a talk one evening about the Holy Spirit. We were both meeting different groups of friends and so got separated at the meeting. It wasn't until after the meeting that we met up again, both waiting to speak to the preacher and discover more about what he had said about the Holy Spirit and fullness. Having spoken to him he offered to pray, but only after we had taken a walk on our own to decide if we really wanted prayer.

As we walked I realized two things—first I felt a tremendous sense of excitement and anticipation, secondly God seemed to be speaking directly and saying, 'My power for your life in its entirety.' I wrestled for about twenty minutes over the decision of whether to go ahead. Although I had little conception of what giving my life in its entirety meant, I knew that the issue was serious and I would have to live with the consequences. I finally decided to ask for prayer, and as the preacher laid hands on me and prayed, after a few moments I saw

Jesus literally reach down and gather me in his arms and give me a wonderful embrace. I am not given to such moving experiences as a rule, but this was tremendous and I was lost in the presence of God, literally 'drunk in the Spirit' for quite a few minutes. For those who feel they have missed something, Katey, who was prayed for at the same time, felt absolutely nothing but just accepted that what you ask for you get (Lk 11:10) and thanked God for her new-found power to live for Jesus.

The gifts of the Spirit

It was not long after this time that we began to discover something of the gifts of the Spirit. When we had our first experience of speaking in tongues we decided it was time to consult the Bible to try and appreciate all that was going on. 1 Corinthians 12:8-10 lists the nine gifts of the Spirit. Paul was obviously comfortable with them, providing instructions for their right use to avoid their abuse which had been taking place within the Corinthian church. (Indeed, in the very first chapter of this letter, in verse 7, he encourages them by informing them that they do not lack any spiritual gift—and neither do we today.) However, our difficulty was that we were coming from a background which did not recognize the gifts of the Spirit, so we had to start from basics. We started by looking at the gifts one by one, and we will do the same now.

Wisdom

This gift is best illustrated by Solomon resolving the dispute between the two women both claiming maternal rights over the same baby (1 Kings 3:16-28). Not an easy task, but with divine wisdom Solomon brought the wrangle to a just and peaceful end. Further evidence of this gift is seen in the life of Jesus when he defused the potentially ugly scene that arose around the woman caught in adultery (Jn 8:1-11). It is evident to most involved in church life today that a mighty measure of this gift is required for the church to function as it should. Who's for wisdom?

Knowledge

When Jesus sat talking to the woman at the well (Jn 4), breaking every social convention and religious custom of the time, he had a clear word of knowledge about her marital situation. He knew she had no husband, that she had had five husbands and her current male companion was not her husband either. Something had been revealed to Jesus that he could not otherwise have known apart from the whisper of the Holy Spirit.

Katey had just such an experience during a recent conference when someone who was praying for her revealed a whole string of personal facts about her background, all of which were known only to her immediate family and a few to me. This is the word of knowledge in action. It penetrates deeply and uncovers vital information for further ministry. It never provides us with the opportunity of becoming some sort of spiritual voyeur into one another's lives. Like all the gifts it is simply a practical tool to bring an individual and God together.

Faith

Obviously every Christian has faith. Ephesians 2:5 tells us we are saved by grace through faith, while Romans 12:3 reminds us that we have each received a measure of faith from God. Yet there are times when we require an increased level of faith. Take for example the story of Abraham and Sarah. In spite of their age, Abraham continued to believe in God and was rewarded (Heb 11:11).

Faith is recognizing the faithful character of God and expecting to see his promises fulfilled in the here and now. Helen Roseveare in her book *Living Sacrifice* speaks of experiencing the peace of God while working as a missionary in the most terrifying circumstances in the Congo. At the appropriate time God met her needs as she continued to place her trust in him. On a more mundane level, recall the provision of the typewriter mentioned on page 41. Although Mike was very concerned about the fast approaching financial deadline, he knew God would act.

Healing

So much has been written on this subject that we do not intend to add another volume. Suffice it to say that healing is one of the gifts of the Spirit given to the church. There are numerous examples in the Scriptures (e.g. Mt 20:29-34), and it is a gift which is of great value within the church today. We have seen a number of people physically healed—and a number who haven't been. We have learned to start with the small ailments and work upwards—save the wheelchairs till you're comfortable dealing with headaches!

While it may seem strange to take a positive stand for healing when we remain childless, some may say unhealed, we can only say that we have prayed for childless couples and they have conceived and produced children, confirming that God is committed to healing in spite of the questions this gift might raise. Questions do not invalidate the gift but rather fuel our prayer and our seeking of God for practical answers.

Miracles

This gift is evident in the Scripture many times. Take the occasion when the sun stood still in the sky while Joshua

was victorious against the Amorites (Josh 10:12-14).
When Jesus fed the 5,000 we see the miraculous provision of food for many mouths, and a good few left-
overs to demonstrate the abundance of God's provision.

Basically a miracle is when natural laws are suspended
and God intervenes directly and supernaturally. Our
twentieth-century minds, conditioned by rationality and
technology, find such a concept extremely difficult to
accept, but we must not let our mental barriers hinder
God's powerful working. This is why it is so important to
appreciate fully the character of God. He is omnipotent
and we must allow him to bring us beyond our reasonable doubts to a level of understanding and faith in line
with his word. We could do with a few more miracles in
the name of Jesus in this land of ours.

Prophecy

This is not simply a *fore*telling but also a *forth*telling. It is
declaring the heart of God in a situation. It will never
contradict Scripture, so we have a means of measuring
prophecy. Since it is given by a human it has a proportion of humanity in it. The one who prophesies is
fully in control of the gift and is not compelled to speak
out their prophecy—'The gift of proclaiming God's message should be under the speaker's control' (1 Cor
14:32).

We have found that often in a time of worship a
prophecy will address a particular issue or an aspect of
God's character using language and illustrations from
contemporary life. The heart of the prophecy is in line
with the tenor of Scripture, yet it is easily accessible because of the nature of the illustrative framework used.
Pastoral images are not that appropriate to an inner-city
situation. When Katey was teaching in such an area she
was responsible for a trip out and on the journey through

the countryside one of the children exclaimed, 'Look, there's a sheep!' to which their companion replied, 'No it's not, it's a cow!' Now one of them was sadly wrong. We worship a God intent on being accessible to people, therefore it is no wonder that he expresses his nature and views in ways that a particular group will easily understand and respond to.

In Matthew 16:17-20 Jesus prophesies about Peter's future ministry. Prophecy has this dimension of foretelling, but the genuine nature of a prophetic word is seen in the fruitfulness of its fulfilment. We should not be so taken up with the practice of the gift that we fail to respond and measure the fulfilment of the word prophesied.

Discernment of spirits

We are involved in a spiritual warfare in which the forces of the enemy lock up and ruin individual lives. These people will not discover freedom and fullness unless the hold of Satan is removed. This is evident in Jesus' dealing with Legion who was ultimately left 'in his right mind' and keen to serve God (Lk 8:26-39). In Luke 13:10-13 Jesus meets a woman crippled by a spirit. Discerning the spirit that had bound her for years, Jesus deals with this demonic hold and she is freed at once.

This gift is vital to our counselling ministry, enabling us to be involved in the effective 'tree surgery' we mentioned earlier in this chapter. As with all the gifts this is a tool for strengthening the body of Christ, both in freeing people from the hold of the enemy and also in identifying positive godly characteristics which are worthy of nurture and encouragement. This latter aspect ensures we identify the people God has chosen for the various essential roles and functions within the church.

Tongues

This gift is best described as a love language to be used in worshipping God (1 Cor 14:2). If your marriage is like ours, then no doubt you have developed a number of phrases which mean something to you but would be meaningless to outsiders. This 'love language' may be intimate, humorous and even apparently stupid, but it is a vital part of your communication with each other. Some couples develop affectionate names for their partners, others adopt almost a whole new vocabulary for use behind closed doors.

Tongues is like this, a language reserved for talking to our heavenly Father. Paul spoke in tongues (1 Cor 14:18) and encouraged the Corinthians to maintain the gift (1 Cor 14:39). It is the only gift which can be used for private benefit as well as for the public purpose of encouraging the body when accompanied by interpretation. Tongues can be used to praise God and to pray earnestly when one doesn't know where to begin praying.

As with all the gifts it is not something we are forced to do by God without any control ourselves, for that is not the character of God. Rather, we choose to speak in tongues, as and when we want to.

Interpretation of tongues

This is the interpretation, not translation, of a message given in tongues in public. It may be expressed as a prayer, a poem of praise, or it may bring a direct word from God to his people.

Other gifts are mentioned in Romans 12:6-8. Take time to look them up now and add them to your existing list of gifts of the Holy Spirit.

The Scriptures urge us to take all God's gifts seriously. We are called to strive for love and set our hearts on spiritual gifts, especially the gift of prophecy (1 Cor 14:1); 'to keep alive the gift that God gave us' (2 Tim 1:6), and reminded 'Each one should use whatever gift he has received to serve others, faithfully administering God's grace in its various forms' (1 Pet 4:10).

However, Katey and I have discovered that though we hear, read and learn much about the gifts of the Spirit we are often sadly lacking in personal experience. In fact, we discovered that our prayer times together provided us with a safe and secure environment to get launched into spiritual gifts and get in some practice. But were we right in practising since we were but two from the body, and could we really claim to be building up the body of Christ through our prayer time together? We believed we could.

Firstly, where two or three gather together Jesus has promised he is there. What is church if it's not where the people of God gather in his presence? We are an expression of church when we pray together. Secondly, as we experimented with and experienced the gifts we were able with a measure of confidence to exercise them within the wider context of our local expression of the body of Christ. This in turn encouraged and enabled others to step out and have a go. If this sounds a little bit unspiritual we can assure you it is not. We worship a practical God who has gifted his church. We need to employ the gifts if we are to obey his word and be what we are called to be in the world today.

The story is told of a very successful and effective managing director who had overseen a large company. His retirement approached and his successor was appointed. Being a man of distinction he visited the retiring managing director and asked him to outline the key to his success in not making wrong decisions. Considering his reply for a moment the managing director simply said, 'Experience.' His successor pressed on and asked, 'How do you get experience?' to which the reply came, 'By making wrong decisions.'(!)

If we are to launch out in using the gifts God has given, we need experience. However, we will make mistakes in gaining that experience, mistakes being a significant part of the learning process. However, God doesn't mind the mistakes if we are sincerely trying to serve and honour him and we recommend you make a good proportion of your mistakes with each other rather than inflicting them all on your local church.

Where to start

We believe the best place to start is with the gifts of tongues, interpretation and prophecy. In 1 Corinthians 14:26-40 Paul outlines the basis for orderly worship, and the instructions he gives about tongues and prophecy give us an indication that the use of these gifts lies within the sphere of human initiative. If God were manipulating mouths for every tongue and prophecy he would not require Paul to give specific guidelines such as, 'If someone is going to speak in strange tongues, two or three at the most should speak, one after the other, and someone must explain what is being said' (1 Cor 14:27), or again, 'You may proclaim God's message, one by one, so that everyone will learn and be encouraged. The gift of proclaiming God's message should be under the speaker's control' (1 Cor 14:31-32). The initiative lies with us and we can choose to go for it or not.

We suggest that together you decide to experiment with these three gifts of tongues, interpretation and prophecy. Stop right now and ensure your partner has read this chapter. Then, if you agree, move into 'Action Stations'.

▶ Action stations

Begin by inviting the Holy Spirit to fill each of you and to fill where you are with his presence. After all, he is a vital personality in the proceedings!

Let's begin with tongues. A number of folk experience some difficulty in getting started with this gift, and this is understandable. I spoke in tongues just a couple of days after I was filled with the Spirit. Katey took about a year to get started. Significantly, Katey had had an inkling she could speak in tongues a while before, but would dismiss the sound which came to mind as something non-sensical which she was making up. It was only as she decided to accept it as God's gift, whether it sounded nonsensical or not, that she discovered her word gave way to a language. Many people we meet have started like this—perhaps you and your partner will.

Nobody has to speak in tongues, but everybody can speak in tongues since it is a gift to be eagerly desired and therefore available to all. If you do want to speak in tongues take a moment to pray, thanking God for his gift of tongues and asking him to release you into it—then wait. That sound, phrase or word that comes to mind is the start of your new love language. Speak it aloud. It may sound nonsensical, but then so does Japanese to me. Partners should encourage each other in the new phrase or word the other is expressing. This is the start. Keep up that phrase or word and more will follow. Don't deny the validity of your new tongue or cease to use it. Rather, as with anything new, use it extensively so that you enjoy it and grow comfortable with it.

Take time to speak in tongues together in praise of God. A lot of folk find it easier to start singing in tongues. Encourage one another and persevere. Praise God with your new-found language. It's been given for that purpose. When you meet a situation for which you don't know how to pray, utilize your new-found tongue. You may well find that the words you use vary—you may identify with Wesley's cry, 'O for a thousand tongues to sing.' There are no limits with God.

We can encourage one another in this gift since one partner may well be a little less confident than the other. I would often take the lead and sing and pray loudly while Katey would draw inspiration from this and follow on but a little more quietly, taking time to build up her own confidence in this gift.

If you are going to exercise the gift of tongues, you will need to ask for the complementary gift of interpretation. It may be that one of you will speak out a short message in tongues and the other will then provide the interpretation. Just pause in the presence of the Lord and speak out the words. As one of you is speaking, the other should stay relaxed, focus on Jesus and simply ask for the interpretation. This may come as a vision in your mind, a sense of what God is feeling, or a clear statement. Once you have an inkling, open your mouth and start speaking.

We can assure you that our early experiences of doing this did not bring forth any earth-shattering revelations, but we found it encouraging and exhilarating to have both been bold enough to participate and to receive simple words of blessing from God through each other. The great thing is to press on with what comes to mind— you may only have a half-formed thought, but express it. You may well embellish it somewhat in an attempt to explain it clearly as you see it; this is our humanity rubbing shoulders with God's divinity. Remember that since the gifts involve human collaboration they will carry a measure of us in them.

The more practice we get, the more comfortable and

confident we will become. And the more comfortable and confident, the more relaxed we are and so the more able to draw upon God's resources and present God's word through these gifts.

We would take the opportunity each time we prayed to incorporate our private love language in praise and intercession, and to give messages in tongues and interpret them. In this way we grew and gained experience. When we contributed in a wider gathering there were others older and more experienced to test the gifts we were utilizing and this acted as a practical safeguard as required.

After you have gained some experience in tongues and interpretation, seek God for the gift of prophecy. Prophecy is similar to interpretation in that as you pray or read Scripture or catch sight of some scene or other you discover that you have a mental picture or clear impression of something to say. It may well not be a complete presentation, but the beginning of something. Only as you speak will you get the whole picture. This is a little nerve-wracking to start with. Many of us have prophesied quite unintentionally in our prayers as we have discharged a burden which we have felt very keenly and which has brought a sense of the presence of God and his perspective to our meeting.

We have found that God has used the gift of prophecy to address us about our circumstances on many occasions. On one occasion God indicated that we were not in an ideal situation from his perspective. One of us had a picture of a fine galleon, sails unfurled catching the wind, but on gazing at the hull it could be seen that the ship was entirely beached and not able to sail before the wind and make for its destination. Not very complicated you say—well no. But in the context of the questions we were asking it spoke volumes and gave us the impetus to put decisions into operation which we felt would refloat the galleon and start it sailing again. Obviously one could interpret the picture in multiple ways, but God had spoken clearly on a specific issue and we decided to be obedient.

Some might object that we conjured up both picture and interpretation since they fitted into the general drift of our thinking at that time. However, God does not play games; just as a father desires no evil for his child, our heavenly Father will not allow us to damage ourselves, which major relocation could do. Also, faith in action takes what God gives and runs with it. So long as it does not contradict Scripture and we are open to chatting it through with other Christians then we can act with confidence.

We have always been ready to communicate what we believe God to be saying with other Christians whom we trust, both because they are friends and because they would not hesitate to say if they thought we were wrong. Often we are so concerned about correction that we stagnate while deliberating about whether God has spoken or not. We have discovered that God finds it difficult to direct stagnant people, but he can more easily govern and guide those on the move as he utilizes their natural momentum. God has always desired a mobile people as the history of Israel in the Old Testament reveals. He will contend with and correct our mistakes while ensuring we reach the right destination.

We are confronted with the challenge of stepping out in faith and experimenting, under God's guidance, with these gifts of tongues, interpretation and prophecy. Utilize your prayer time to gain experience. Perhaps you would like to follow a pattern we adopted for a while. Returning to bed each morning with two steaming mugs of tea. I would revive Katey and then in turn we would each give a message in tongues and an interpretation and then reverse the roles. A very edifying way to start the day! Always remember to retain the ability to laugh and all will be well.

7
Developing a Prayer Life

When we began to experiment with the gifts of the Spirit we discovered a new level of vulnerability. While our marriages do provide a safe and secure environment to gain experience in the gifts of the Spirit, it is amazing just how uncertain one can feel in front of one's partner. This was true for us—we discovered that I felt more threatened than Katey. This boiled down to the fact that as I carefully think everything through, calculating all the options before taking a step forward, I had all my insecurities exposed when I was expected to act on impulse without first checking every final detail out. Katey, however, took to it like a duck to water, being of a more impetuous nature. To this day Katey finds it easier to move in spiritual gifts than me.

However, the vulnerability we experience together is a very positive part of our praying together. Jesus, having died, risen and ascended, promises us three encouragements for our life of discipleship. As we have seen, he gives us his promised Spirit: 'It is better for you that I go away, because if I do not go, the Helper will not come to you. But if I do go away, then I will send him to you' (Jn

16:7). He has also given us his written word, the Bible, which enables us to comprehend more about God and his purposes. In addition he has given us each other:

> I pray not only for them, but also for those who believe in me because of their message. I pray that they may all be one. Father! May they be in us, just as you are in me and I am in you. May they be one, so that the world will believe that you sent me. I gave them the same glory you gave me, so that they may be one just as you and I are one: I in them and you in me, so that they may be completely one, in order that the world may know that you sent me and that you love them as you love me (Jn 17:20-23).

Jesus' prayer, quoted above, reveals that the world will discern our following of him by the quality of the love we extend to one another. Indeed Jesus said, 'And now I give you a new commandment: love one another. As I have loved you, so you must love one another. If you have love for one another, then everyone will know that you are my disciples' (Jn 13:34-35).

Unfortunately we are a very defensive bunch and the very thought of exposure to others causes us to retreat within the castle of ourself, drop the portcullis and lift the drawbridge. However, God is in the business of building practical working relationships. He has established one such between each of us and himself. And he expects to establish the same between us and the other family members who share this planet with us, or more pertinently, our church life with us. While we haven't time to explore this in its wider context, we do need to appreciate its role in our marriages and its place in our prayer life together.

Once we had 'tied the knot' or 'got spliced' or whatever epithet you prefer to use, it slowly dawned on us that we knew very little about the one to whom we had promised to be faithful until death provided a suitable full stop. Perhaps even more intimidating—we each realized how little our spouse knew about us! This posed a problem—in given situations did one behave according to 'expected norms' or was one able to be oneself? We have already looked at this in detail in the section on three-dimensional marriage in chapter 3. Remind yourselves of the practical implications if you cannot remember the content.

Our marriage should allow us to receive counsel and ministry from our partners. We have already said that marriage can be the context in which we are able to encourage our wives to develop experience and confidence in ministry. One way we can do this is let them practise on us men. It is interesting to note that the passage so often quoted to describe the headship of the husband in marriage is immediately preceded by the verse, 'Submit yourselves to one another because of your reverence for Christ' (Eph 5:21). Neither one party nor the other is invited to lord it over the other; each is called to a submissive attitude towards the other. We should each be receptive to whatever God has for us, through whomever he chooses to communicate.

One person we know who has a number of significant spiritual problems and needs has brought God's clear word to us on more than one occasion, and it has been so accurate and to the point that it has made the hairs stand up on the back of our necks. If we have ears to hear, God will constantly communicate with us.

As we progress in getting closer to God, declaring our affection for him and growing increasingly sensitive to his Spirit, we will experience an increased level of vulnerability before each other. When Katey and I were dating there was a diagram much used to describe the male/female Christian relationship. Basically it was a triangle: God was the top corner and we were the two bottom corners, one each side. The object lesson was that the nearer we grew to God the closer we grew to each other, hence intimacy increased and more masks were removed.

We have known what it is to be in the presence of God in worship and then to discover how utterly unclean we are before him. The route forward was to be totally honest with one another over areas in our lives, brought to mind by the Spirit of God, where we were living a lie or exploiting each other. This can be very threatening but also exceptionally enriching. We have verbalized to one another on more than one occasion that since God knows we're rotten anyway and we are only where we are because of his love and grace, why not acknowledge to one another that we are corrupt and helpless as individuals, because in this way we will neither be shocked nor disappointed with one another. We have found that this really takes the pressure off our relationship and means we can be open and honest with no fear that our honesty will be thrown back in our face and our revealed weaknesses exploited at some future date, damaging both the individual concerned and the relationship. As Gerald Coates so eloquently yet economically expresses, 'God will never become disillusioned with us because he never had any illusions in the first place.' We have no right to become disillusioned with one another as a consequence of opening up to each other.

Weaknesses and strengths

While we are not to condemn one another when weaknesses, areas of sin and character deficiencies emerge, neither are we simply to accept them, learning to live with them and accommodating them within our lifestyle.

It was just such a situation that Jesus encountered

when he entered the land of the Gerasenes. These folk had a problem—a guy called Legion. They had tried every means known to them to control or even put an end to his bizarre behaviour, but to no effect. Indeed this character was becoming so well known that had there been travel agents in those days, I've no doubt they would have included him in their brochures as 'local colour'! Eventually he was allowed to take up residence in the graveyard, and the Gerasenes ordered their lives around this frightful and frightening disturbance. By the time Jesus came on the scene they had become so accustomed to accommodating Legion that no one thought to forewarn Jesus or send him a set of directions which avoided the graveyard. As already mentioned, Jesus, when confronted by the man, discerned the spirits and ordered them out, enabling Legion to regain his senses and become an ardent disciple. When the Gerasenes discovered what had happened they were so shocked and disappointed because their whole pattern of life had been reorganized that they begged Jesus to go rather than inviting him for some refreshment and further opportunity to exercise his ministry among them. Read the story for yourself in Luke 8:28-39.

When we discover something out of order in our own lives we are not to push it to the back of our minds and develop a lifestyle and level of Christian experience and service which accommodates it. We are to go up to Jesus, like Legion, and get it dealt with. As Christians we share in the Spirit of Jesus, so we are able to minister him to one another today. This is a vital part of our marital relationship. The sort of ministry to which we are referring is of the tree surgery variety mentioned in the last chapter in the section on the fruit of the Spirit.

One Christmas we were staying with a family and we were amusing ourselves with the children's toys. Katey is convinced that the only reason I want children is so that I can have an excuse to fill the house with toys for my own pleasure. Be that as it may, we had a great time playing with one vehicle which drove across the floor until it encountered an obstacle, at which point it would turn itself over and set off in another direction until meeting some further obstruction when it simply repeated the process. It did this non-stop until it was turned off or the batteries ran out! As Christians we are often confined within borders beyond which we have never explored. The Gerasenes were unable to handle the situation once Legion was set free. The presence and power of God breaking into their well-adjusted lifestyle was too threatening and they asked Jesus to leave, which, being the gentleman he is, he did.

When we pray together and enter into the presence of God, the borders of our own Christian confinement may well be revealed. Areas of weakness, habitual sin and personal difficulty are highlighted, and we need to learn how to minister to one another lovingly and practically. For many of us the plain fact of having to live life in a real and often hostile world has meant that we have learned how to accommodate our weaknesses in order to get through. However, we are very much aware that our lives are anything but peaceful beneath the surface and daily we contend with controlling that turbulence as best we can. Usually it is within our home life, in our marriages, where that turbulence often gives way to a tremendous storm. This is because we feel the least pressure to maintain the mask there or because we think the consequences of such an explosion will not be as damaging to ourselves as in the office or on the shop-floor.

Don't worry when you discover that you are not naturally self-sufficient. All of us bear the marks of our experience of life to date. This has helped to form the people we are. We know a number of areas where we are vulnerable, and should steer clear! We are conscious of weaknesses and work hard at compensating for them. Each of us is also no more and no less than a redeemed sinner, and although the consequences of sin were fully dealt with by Jesus on the cross, we all take time discovering the full extent of our inheritance in Christ as his brothers and sisters. Not only do we need to discover the full extent of that inheritance, we also need to learn how to appropriate it.

We write this in the first instance for mutual assurance. If when you read the section about 'fruit of the Spirit' in the last chapter and concluded that you need a spot of tree surgery, then you have taken a constructive step. We are all in the same boat, Christians saved by grace moving on together and helping one another on as we follow hard after Jesus. It really is the height of arrogance for anyone to believe they are perfect or beyond the need or range of Jesus' ministry. Their position is akin to the Pharisee who denigrated the tax collector in his prayer (Lk 18:9-14). It is Jesus who designates the Father as the vine-dresser or gardener in John 15 and endorses the activity of the gardener as the way to fruitfulness. Ask each other, 'Do you want to be fruitful for Christ?' If the answer is yes, don't be surprised when you discover certain weaknesses or habits becoming highlighted. The gardener is about his work cutting out dead wood that the plant might flourish.

A number of years ago when disaster movies were in vogue a very exciting one was released, fetchingly entitled *The Towering Inferno*. You may have seen it. When we first saw this film at the cinema, Katey virtually crushed my hand such was the intensity of the drama. The film tells the story of a brand-new skyscraper which suffers an outbreak of fire during the opening evening. All the dignatories are enjoying themselves at the very top of the building but by the time the seriousness of the fire is discovered and the 'fireproof' nature of the building proved false, it is too late to leave the building by normal means. The film goes on to show the rescue attempts and the group dynamics of those trapped as individuals seek to ensure that they survive even if it is at the cost of others in the group.

Another plot is also weaved into the film. This gives the reason for the fire in the first place. An enterprising electrical supplier had provided substandard fittings and wiring, well below the original specification, in order to maximize profits. As a result they could not cope with the power demands placed upon them, overheated, shorted and started the fire.

The reason we tell you all this, apart from saving you the cost of the video hire, is that there is an important spiritual principle enshrined in it. The skyscraper did not burn down because of the demands for power placed upon the electrical system. Rather the conflagration was the direct result of an inherent weakness within the construction itself. All that the demand for power did was to expose an inherent weakness, one which eventually led to the destruction of the whole building.

In a similar fashion if we are prepared to walk with God and are committed to spiritual maturity, the Holy Spirit will begin to expose our weaknesses. We may enter a time of great difficulty and pressure. God may appear absent, and the only thing we can focus on is the hurt, the need or the weakness of which we are aware. So often in those times we blame our circumstances or situation when in fact all that is happening is that the circumstances or situation are highlighting an inherent weakness in our life. The route through this is to allow the gardener, God himself, room to remove the weakness and replace it with his strength. We usually require the help, support and prayer of our partner in this since when we expose our weakness to somebody else, as God has exposed it for our consideration, we are less likely either to fail to deal with it properly or to allow it to return to rule our life. God knew what he was about when he left us to one another for our mutual godly benefit. In times of exposure like these we have found that we gain a greater experiential knowledge of the nature of God's inheritance released to us through the death and resurrection of Jesus.

While at Oxford University and attending one of the weekly OICCU Bible readings, we heard a superb exegesis of John 15 given by Ian Barclay. Little did I expect to be working alongside him one day at the Evangelical Alliance. In the Bible study he explained the nature of pruning from a gardener's perspective to help give meaning to the words of Jesus. To this day we remember that the younger the plant and the more vigorously you prune it the more fruitful it will be. A few years later we had a practical demonstration of this when a friend came to tidy up our garden. We had a straggly climbing rose which wandered all over the place. We set off for work that morning leaving our rose in the capable green-fingered hands of our friend. To our shock, on returning home all that was visible was an ugly little stump. To be honest we thought the poor thing was all but dead. We needn't have worried for that summer it flourished and was covered with the most beautiful, pink, scented roses. Do you get the point? We certainly did!

Godly gardening

How does this work out practically in our praying together? We soon discovered that God was more than ready to expose weaknesses in our lives. We then had to decide could we and would we risk levelling with each other and being honest. Fear of rejection and feeling somehow inferior to our partner proved a major obstacle to overcome, but overcome it we did. There was then the question of being able to accept the counsel as well as the prayer of our partner. Prayer is okay maybe, but when we start being corrected and told to repent of certain attitudes by our partner—that's a bit heavy!

All the fundamental lessons previously outlined come into play here. The need to exercise wisdom was paramount in how we broached a subject or an apparent solution, and enabling us to listen without moving onto the defensive or over-reacting. We found that we would often respond by saying, 'I accept that, *but* . . .' and immediately sidestep the point about which the other had challenged or counselled us. There are no 'buts' if we are in a safe and secure environment with someone whom we love and more importantly, in a way, who loves and wants the best for us. We can make mistakes without causing damage; we can learn how to co-operate with God in his gardening activity. It is at this level that the power gifts of the Spirit become very important. Remind yourself of them by turning back to the previous chapter.

One situation in which we discovered something about co-operating with the intelligence God gave us was while selling our house in Leeds. As we prayed Katey had a clear picture of three tall chimneys, the sort one sees at brickworks or being brought down by means of controlled explosion to give a feature for the news! She mentioned this to me and I could see the same in my mind's eye. We prayed on and saw two chimneys come crashing down to the ground. The third remained—a few bricks out from around the base, but not shifting. We asked God to tell us more about the meaning of the picture as we went about our various tasks that week. When we prayed again later in the week we had both recognized the chimneys as obstructions to the sale of our house and the one remaining was symbolic of a materialistic attitude—we wanted to grasp as much from the sale as possible. We repented of the attitude and saw the chimney fall. We celebrated the sale of our house, which had been on the market for several weeks, at that point.

I talked through all that God had shown us with Christian friends. They did not believe that we should drop the price, rather they advised us that selling below market value would be bad stewardship. However, they felt we should be prepared to utilize the proceeds from the sale—all or part—as God directed. We followed this advice and within the week the house sold to someone who had grown up in the road and wanted to get back into it, and we experienced a very loose attachment to the financial proceeds and were able to follow God's instructions cheerfully! The reason for this piece of testimony is to provide an indication of the way God can communicate with us.

When we got involved in 'godly gardening' we discovered God would speak in the same way and we would need to interrupt our prayer times and present, with a measure of grace and diffidence, what we felt God was saying to each other. One incident again concerned the whole area of money. My attitude was one of caution and care. This was healthy up to a point, but did mean that I never had any expectation that there would ever be sufficient finance and lived with a constant tighten-the-belt mentality, always frowning upon, if not forbidding, 'frivolous' extravagances such as a meal out together. Katey identified this one prayer time, receiving a picture of an old, pirate's chest, the lid securely down and sealed. When she had boldly explained this to me she went on to suggest I needed prayer for my lack of expectation and trust in the trustworthiness of God as a provider. This had other implications apart from material ones, Katey was able to minister to me, helping me lay aside my weakness in not trusting God and replace it with a new-found confidence in his practical faithfulness. As if to confirm the reality of the ministry we both had a picture of the lid of the treasure chest open a fraction and the contents beginning to tumble out.

This incident gives some indication of how God can use us to minister to one another, and the way the garden is kept orderly and brought on towards maturity.

We have enjoyed the benefits of ministry to one another in areas of negative attitudes, anger, bitterness and resentment, to name but a few. We have encouraged each other in our service of God and in the particular ways he wants to use us. We have also discovered how to pray for healing for each other with positive results. All this is tremendous fun, and besides being a blessing to us as couples helps us to become a richer resource to the wider body of Christ of which we are a part. As with every area of growing in God, we will have to be prepared to make mistakes and to be wrong. But we will learn through our mistakes. Indeed, as couples we can constructively discuss areas of error or those situations where words don't appear to match up with an individual's experience.

This is the only way we know of becoming familiar with co-operating with God in his gardening duties. It draws us very much closer together and brings a deeper level of security to the relationship. Honesty and openness brings liberty to us as individuals, and when we entrust our weaknesses into the hands of our partners,

we make them fiercely loyal and actively committed to
our spiritual, physical and emotional welfare.

▶ *Action stations*

For all that we have been writing about to become oper-
ative, you will need to sit down together to talk around
and answer a number of questions. As we continually
stress, do ensure you are relaxed and comfortable. Relationships, natural and supernatural, function best
when we are in a state of normality.

Together read then think about each of the following
questions in turn. Discuss your individual thoughts together after each question before proceeding to the next
one.

(1) Am I ready to let God show me who I am and what I'm
really like?
(2) Am I ready to let God show me who he is and what he
requires?
(3) Am I prepared to stop accommodating areas of my life
which are in need of gardening?
(4) Am I prepared to allow the present parameters of my
spiritual life to be extended?

After you have discussed your replies together, asked
each other questions and generally made some decisions,
individually identify any areas in your life—physical,
emotional or spiritual—which require a bit of gardening.
Do both be honest and practical; if your partner produces sixty foolscap pages of how terrible they are, the
basic problem is probably a massive dose of rejection!

Having done this, share your lists with each other and
in turn pray, giving permission and actively inviting both
God and your partner to be involved in gardening in
your life. From now on expect God to speak and act on
what he says together.

8

Spiritual Warfare

The book of Daniel in the Old Testament is the story of a man who knew God, could act as his spokesman within his contemporary world and a hostile environment and practised an effective prayer life. In this chapter I want us to consider Daniel's prayer life, not so that we can all copy his pattern of prayer (we should discover what works for us personally in prayer and not just adopt another person's practice) but to draw out some important principles.

Living in Babylon as one of the thousands of Jews exiled there, Daniel was successful at achieving high office in the king's court through diligence and winsomeness, and in no way did he compromise his faith in God (eg. Dan 1:8-16). (Today we need to see increasing numbers of Christian men and women achieving high office in various walks of life and while not compromising their Christian belief, gaining a positive position to influence contemporary society.)

Daniel was obviously a man who loved God and exercised a regular and meaningful prayer walk with him. In chapter 6, verse 10, we discover that even in the face of government legislation banning prayer, except requests made to the king himself for a period of thirty days, Daniel continued his practice of praying to God three times a day, 'just as he had always done'. This led to his encounter with the lions and the king's encounter with the living God.

Daniel was so used to communicating with God and was thus so familiar with his ways that he was greatly used by God in demonstrating his character—for example, interpreting dreams and deciphering writing on the wall. Basically, he practised much that we have been discovering in our prayer life together in this book. However, Daniel, for all his intimacy with God, still ran into a problem that we will meet too. So let's look at it now.

Turn to Daniel 10:12-14. Here we read how Daniel, having fasted and prayed for revelation for three weeks, finally received the answer to his prayers. He is reassured that his request was heard and answered the moment he first prayed, but that his reception of the answer had been held up because of the spiritual conflict that rages between God with his angelic forces on the one hand and the devil with his demonic host on the other.

We need to appreciate that God's character is always to hear and answer our prayers, but sometimes perseverance is demanded for we are all participants in a cosmic struggle which, while not visible to the naked eye, surrounds us on every side. Jesus himself told his disciples, 'Always pray and never become discouraged' (Lk 18:1). Unfortunately a number of us have not, or maybe will not, develop the stamina required to see God's positive answers released to us in the here and now.

A real war

We noticed in an earlier chapter how the prayerful activities of Moses, Aaron and Hur enabled Joshua to overcome the Amalekites. This was because while Joshua fought within the physical realm, Moses and his party mirrored the conflict but in the spiritual realm. Obviously the devil and his crew were not at all keen for Joshua and Israel to succeed. They were, after all, the vanguard of God's good news and demonstrated within their day and generation to all the nations round about that there was one God worthy of worship and his name was Yahweh.

Although we live in a four-dimensional world, often we never perceive beyond dimension three. This fourth dimension was brought home to us very clearly when we were still an engaged couple. It was summer in Oxford and final exams loomed. Katey was preparing for probably her hardest B.Ed. paper when she developed a chronic migraine the afternoon before the exam. When I arrived that evening she told me of the dilemma she was in. If she took the prescribed medicine she would be virtually knocked out for two days, so she would have to tackle the exam in a state of intoxication. However, if she skipped the tablets then the pain with which she would have to contend, not to mention feelings of nausea and spots before the eyes, was just as likely to cause her to perform very badly in the exam. 'What do I do?' she appealed to me.

Feeling very spiritual at that moment, I suggested we go to God for some guidance. We invited a good friend and just went to God in prayer, saying, 'Help!' As we prayed I found myself thinking about the words in James 5:14-15 about healing, particularly about being anointed with oil: 'Is there anyone who is ill? He should send for the church elders, who will pray for him and rub olive-oil on him in the name of the Lord. This prayer made in faith will heal the sick person; the Lord will restore him to health, and the sins he has committed will be forgiven.' We had nothing except Castrol GTX which I did not feel was very appropriate! Instead I leaped up, got an eggcup, filled it with water and prayed something like, 'Lord, we have no oil but you turned water into wine so I guess you can turn this water into oil. Please do so.' We put some of the water—or was it oil?—on Katey's forehead and I prayed. To my surprise I found myself in the middle of a prayer telling the devil to leave her alone. As I prayed Katey suddenly sprang up and shouted, 'It's gone! It's gone!' We all hugged each other and thanked God and Katey was able to take her exam without the slightest trace of a headache.

We realized, as we talked this incident through, that we had stumbled on the fact that there is a fourth dimension to life. We were called by God to be part of an army. We were at war, not at ease, and it is easy to get duped by the enemy into the heresy of plodding through life awaiting our slice of eternal pie in the sky when we die, or to stoically carry our cross through life, maintaining that this is our lot and we must dutifully see it through to the bitter end. God showed us we were engaged in a real war and that we must fight effectively and continually.

A real enemy

The name 'Satan' actually means 'accuser'. It is one of the names given to the devil by the Hebrew writers of Scripture. To the Jews a name is more than a means of identification, it describes the nature of the bearer of the name. Hence God renames Abram 'Abraham' meaning 'father of a multitude', which certainly describes Abraham's unique place in the purposes of God. It is enlightening to work through the Bible looking at names given to the enemy of God, for in doing so you will discover something of his character and therefore the type of traps he lays and attacks he makes on Christians.

The meaning of the name 'Satan' reveals that the enemy is intent on slandering and accusing God's people regardless of whether they are guilty of the accusation. Many folk we have spoken to express a concern that they feel condemned. When asked why they feel condemned, have they said or done anything they should not have done, they are unable to give a clear answer. So long as they are being honest this suggests that they are being toyed with by Satan—being falsely accused but not of anything in particular. When God corrects us he convicts by his Spirit and his conviction is always specific. Just as when the police bring specific charges against someone when they convict him of an offence, so God will identify the specific issue he wants to deal with; he does not leave us wondering what we should do. Satan knows that if he accuses us and we feel condemned we become totally ineffective for God, which is just what he wants.

Satan may be powerful and devious, but he is in no way an equal though opposite force to God. Films like *Star Wars* have given prominence to a spiritual concept which is gaining increasing credence today. This concept sees the universe as a battleground between two equal and opposite forces. However, this idea is not rooted in Christianity, but is an expression of much Eastern religious thought. Another name for Satan in the Bible is 'Lucifer' meaning 'light-bearer' or 'angel of light', for the enemy of God is no more than a fallen angel. He was one of the three archangels with Michael and Gabriel, but he chose to rebel against God, seeking to be like God (Is 14:12-15).

With his angelic host he mounted an armed revolt but was defeated by Michael (Rev 12:7-9) and was literally thrown out of heaven together with his angelic host who had followed his rebellion. It is this angelic host who now serve him in his work of destruction and death throughout the earth, continuing their acts of terrorism against the righteousness and justice of God whom they hate. In Luke 10:18 Jesus refers to the defeat of Satan in the heavens and his expulsion—'I saw Satan fall like lightning from heaven.' He proceeds to encourage his disciples, among whom we may count ourselves, 'I have given you authority so that you can trample on snakes and scorpions and overcome all the power of the Enemy, and nothing will hurt you' (Lk 10:19).

Satan is a created being, for God declares, 'I am the Lord; there is no other god' (Is 45:5). Satan constantly seeks to convince the world of two things, first that he does not exist, secondly that he is the equal and opposite power to God. However, he is ultimately subject to God's authority. We see this in the book of Job where in the very first chapter we encounter Satan in the presence of God. God points out the quality of Job's faithfulness to which Satan responds by maintaining that Job is only faithful because life is good for him. God then gives Satan permission to bring trouble to Job and his family in order to put Job's faithfulness to the test—but note that Satan could only interfere with God's authority and then only to the degree God permitted. Clearly, God rules over Satan.

A real victory

Furthermore, when Jesus died on the cross he dealt the final blow of defeat to Satan. Until that time Satan, with his great weapon of death, held sway over mankind because of the legal authority granted him through the sin of Adam and Eve. But Jesus, totally man and totally

God at one and the same time, burst into human history to engage in personal combat with Satan.

Satan hurled every temptation at Jesus but he resisted all of them. Eventually by ingenious cunning Satan brought Jesus to death on the cross. No doubt he rubbed his hands together gleefully, believing that once Jesus died he would have him totally in his hands, death being the weapon which he wielded over mankind. However, Jesus, although tempted in every way as we are, did not sin and hence Satan could not claim him. Jesus had kept his allegiance to Father God. As he wrestled on that cross with sin, for the first and only time in all eternity cut off from his relationship with his Father, Jesus was recovering what Adam had lost, the opportunity for personal friendship with God. Eventually he proclaimed those great words of triumph, 'It is finished' (Jn 19:30), referring not to his life but his commission, and then chose to release his spirit back to his Father and died. No one took his life, he gave it up entirely of his own will.

Although Satan and his demonic host must initially have been thrilled at this, three days later, as Jesus broke the hold of death and rose from the dead, a wave of concern passed through the hallways of hell. This turned to panic with Pentecost, the proclamation of the gospel and the rapid conversion of the population and the growth of the church. Since then, Satan has been running scared because God has been rescuing men and women from the ranks of Satan and recruiting them in his own invincible army to do battle in spiritual warfare.

The totality of Christ's victory is declared in Colossians 2:13-15—'On that cross Christ freed himself from the power of the spiritual rulers and authorities; he made a public spectacle of them by leading them as captives in his victory procession.' The picture is one of a Roman general returning from a successful campaign and being granted a military parade through the streets of Rome. He would ride at the head of the procession in his chariot, holding one end of a chain draped casually over his shoulder. Following along the line of the chain one would see the defeated generals in neck-irons attached to the chain, shuffling along in the wake of the chariot. Their defeat and subjugation was complete. They were completely in the hands of the victorious Roman general. In the same way Satan and all his forces are completely in the hands of Jesus.

This brings us to our final point about Satan—he is a personality. He thinks, reasons and employs logic—just look at the way he approached Eve. Because of this he will not lay down his arms and recognize his defeat but rather contests every foot of the ground, constantly seeking to convince people that God is not knowable, not good and not available.

To help explain this point I will use the well-known illustration of D-Day and VE-Day. In 1944 the Allies invaded Europe; the occasion is known as D-Day (Decisive Day). From this point on it was evident that the enemy was defeated, but the fighting didn't stop. The Allies had to fight their way through Europe all the way to Berlin before VE-Day (Victory in Europe Day) was celebrated. So with Satan. He has lost the war but continues to fight a rearguard action. Ultimately God will step in and put an end to his activities and there will be no more battles to fight.

We are on the winning side but can expect to be caught up in battles. Satan is committed to robbing men and women of friendship with God, to neutralizing the church in her effectiveness and to interfering adversely in the lives of Jesus' disciples. The Bible describes him as a prowling lion stalking around looking for someone to maul. We should be on our guard against him, but confident because we are on the winning side and 'the weapons we use in our fight are not the world's weapons, but God's powerful weapons which we use to destroy strongholds' (2 Cor 10:4). We are called to conflict; it is part of our commission. We are in a real war, facing a real enemy but enjoying a real victory!

Prayer and warfare

Since the vitality of our relationship with Father God depends to a large degree on prayer, it is obviously an area where we come under intense pressure from the enemy. Prayer is also the means whereby we make ourselves available to co-operating with God in his purpose of ensuring that his kingdom comes and his will is done on earth as it is in heaven. Hence Satan's resistance to such activity.

We mentioned earlier that some answers to prayer are delayed in coming. This is because we are engaged in a cosmic conflict, the full implications of which we will never understand. As Daniel persevered in prayer—and it was a costly experience—so must we. When we wait for answers that apparently elude us, the voice of the enemy rings clearly in our ears using the same words with which he approached Eve: 'Did God really tell you?' (Gen 3:1). He seeks to create doubt, stir up dismay and cause us to lose heart in the reliability of the character of God.

As many will know, we have a major outstanding answer to prayer. For a number of years we have prayed for children, and to some people's surprise we still expect God to answer. We cannot believe that God has altered his revelation since committing it to paper, as it were, in the Bible where we read that he intends man and woman to be fruitful. If we are to accept our childlessness we will have to break with a conviction in the trustworthy nature of the character of God, and that we cannot do. We are also aware that we share a problem, or as Doug Barnett creatively puts it, 'an opportunity for blessing', which was not uncommon to the great men and women of God spoken of in Scripture. And God rewarded their faithfulness—eventually. Indeed, some laugh when I declare that I will go to my grave still believing that we will have children because God is faithful and true to his word.

However, Satan has been very active in bringing pressure on us in this area. Indeed when we first discovered the situation we were in emotional turmoil and found it very hard to take. Fortunately our marital relationship was such that we could include God in the various moods and verbal exchanges that took place; he was even at the receiving end of some of these. As we began to settle down and gained a little perspective, we very simply agreed to place our hand in the hand of God and allow him to bring our lives into line with his word.

The most immediate consequence was that he revealed to us that we were in a very advantageous position. So committed were we to having children, and so much more convinced in his ability than that of the medical establishment, that he had our undivided attention. Never were ears so highly sensitized to the voice of his Spirit; never were lives more ready to be obedient. We also discovered that God immediately removed our focus from children and redirected it onto ourselves. We discovered we were harbouring resentments towards God and people which provided footholds for the enemy.

Prior to becoming Christians we had been involved in ouija and other occult activities, and also had connections with freemasonry and spiritualism. We repented of these activities, loosing their influence through prayer in the name of Jesus, enabling us to enjoy more fully our rich inheritance given by Jesus at the cross. We have learned to actively wield the weapons of our warfare, putting paid to Satan's attempts to influence our lives.

God also showed us how strongly tempted we were to passively acquiesce to childlessness. Such passivity meant that far less energy need be expended, and we could utilize our childlessness constructively within our married life. But passivity, we have found, is food for the devil. It is the start of simply accepting where one is at and not bothering to push on to maturity. Our names might remain written in the Lamb's Book of Life, but we will not take any new ground from the enemy. No, we need to wage warfare actively and with energy.

Other consequences of warfare, we have found, are wounds, exhaustion and a sense of being overwhelmed. We had to dig deep to find the reserves to continue the fight. Often we are intellectually convinced about spiritual warfare, but when we hit the frontline battle we fall down instantly as if someone has slipped the carpet out from under our feet. The reality of spiritual warfare is that it invades every area of our lives and lifestyle. It costs us and we have to decide daily if we will pay the price. We need to urge one another on—Katey and I are always doing this—and develop the camaraderie of an army at war; an army that has won the war but must still complete the final mopping-up operations.

Don't be caught out when a bomb explodes and scatters shrapnel everywhere. Be aware that we are all on active service. Agree together to wage warfare, to persevere to the end and not to fall prisoner to the lies of the enemy.

▶*Action stations*

God has fully equipped us for spiritual warfare. Turn to
Ephesians 6:10-12. Read this together and take time to
discuss what the passage is saying to you as a couple.

Consider in a practical way where you need to engage
in active spiritual warfare. Invite God to bring to mind
possible chinks in your armour and ask your partner to
pray for you in these areas.

9
Meditation

The great Christian apologist C. S. Lewis was first motivated to write stories through an experience he had on a train journey. Standing on the station he picked up a George McDonald book. As he read this he described the experience as one in which his imagination was 'baptized'. That part of his mind which had been dulled over the years was revitalized and to what a great effect when we consider the books he produced such as the Narnia Chronicles. Incidentally, one of the great ways of sustaining the social dimension of your marriage is to read to one another; if you're a family, read together as a family. We do this, more especially over the winter months, reading a chapter aloud together and enjoying the story. We are especially keen on children's literature, and there is a wealth of material available. This can be most creative and we recommend it for strengthening the family bonds.

Ever since I can remember I have had a problem as a Christian with prayer and Bible reading. We've already said that prayer is a problem, but it should not stay like that. It needs to become a delight and an integral part of our lives. I often felt condemned by books or sermons stressing the importance of daily Bible reading and prayer but I did little about it. I would resolve to read at least ten chapters a day to make up for lost time but would soon 'fall by the wayside'.

This all changed radically when I was introduced to Bible meditation. In these days meditation has almost become a 'dirty word' to Christians. This is mainly because of connotations with Eastern religions which place a strong emphasis on meditation. I had a vivid picture of 'Eastern types' involved in many hours of concentrated naval-gazing which I thought odd and very boring! Christians certainly shouldn't meditate by 'emptying' their minds because the mind is soon filled by the enemy, but we can benefit individually and together as couples by meditating on the word of God and thus filling the mind with thoughts about the character and nature of God.

I looked up 'meditation' in an Oxford dictionary and found the following definition: 'To consider thoughtfully, to purpose, to think on, to revolve in the mind.' When talking on meditation I have often explained it by comparing it to eating and enjoying a good meal. There are always parts of a good meal which are exquisite and deserve to be savoured slowly so that they can be enjoyed to the full. I believe that Scripture contains similar 'tasty morsels' which should be chewed over slowly so that the full meaning fills our minds and can be 'digested' in our lives.

When I was introduced to the art of meditation it really did revolutionize my spiritual life. It was something I could do at any time, and for as long or as little as I liked, without having to set a special time aside. When I realized that I was thinking about the word of God for quite a lot of the time, the guilt feelings I had felt for so long left me. I was thinking on God, Jesus and Scripture far more than I had ever done before, even when I had managed to have a 'formal' quiet time.

I began to notice that meditation was actually affecting my life (this is surely what our times with God should do!). Scriptures which I had been meditating upon would come into my mind at times of delight, stress, boredom and frustration and proved a great encouragement to me. It follows that what you spend most time doing eventually dominates your life. I think this is especially true today of television. It is so easy to get caught up in what we see emanating from the box in the corner and to almost live our lives through the eyes of television characters. This is often a result of boredom, when we have little to occupy our time with. If we are not careful boredom can get out of hand and rob us of meaningful relationships because we begin to fill our lives with anything which is a time filler. Marriage can certainly suffer if one or both partners is seeking just to 'fill time'.

I am not at the stage where I can say that my life is totally centred on Jesus but it is affected by Jesus much more than it was, and meditation has greatly helped in this. Let's take a look at some scriptures which talk about meditation.

> Be sure that the book of the Law is always read in your worship. Study it day and night, and make sure that you obey everything written in it (Josh 1:8).
> They find joy in obeying the Law of the Lord, and they study it day and night (Ps 1:2).
> As I lie in bed, I remember you; all night long I think of you (Ps 63:6).
> I will think about all that you have done; I will meditate on all your mighty acts (Ps 77:12).

Psalm 119 has a wealth of references to meditation. Look especially at verses 15, 23, 48, 78 and 148.

Meditation can be used as part of our worship, individually or together with our partner. If you have never meditated before, try the following exercise. Take the opening verse of Psalm 23: 'The Lord is my Shepherd; I have everything I need.' Now start chewing it over, letting your mind wander around it. You may find it easier to do this out loud the first time you try it. There are no right or wrong answers in meditation. God will use times of meditation to speak to us, inspire us and guide us. As I have meditated on that verse in the past, my thoughts have turned to lordship, what it means and what my response should be. I have also found the whole concept of shepherd very rich in meditative terms. I have found it useful to think around the practical things a shepherd does, such as looking after the sheep, tending the injured and knowing each one individually by name, just as Jesus knows us.

Katey has found it useful to place texts around the place so that she notices them at various times. As a housewife she found she spent a lot of time in the kitchen, especially at the sink, so she would place a text behind the taps which she could think on for a few minutes while washing up or peeling the potatoes. She has found that she never 'uses up' a verse and that there is always more to be gleaned in meditation, but she does change the verses regularly. Another good place to stick a verse is above a light switch. You just glance at it and it then plants a seed in your mind which develops during the day.

Meditation requires a 'sanctified imagination'. By that I mean an imagination which God has got hold of and can use to his glory. We all know of situations where our minds have 'run riot' and not always too profitably. God can take such situations and use them to his glory and to our benefit. When Katey started to meditate she found that her mind would often wander off onto what she considered more pressing matters such as the shopping list and what to cook for dinner tonight. It was a real problem until she asked God to sanctify her mind and especially her imagination. Her mind still sometimes wanders off but Scripture exhorts us to 'take every thought captive and make it obey Christ' (2 Cor 10:5). This is only possible by submitting to God and resisting the devil (Jas 4:7).

Meditating as couples can add variety to your prayer life together. It is good for both of you to be actively involved and to have something positive to contribute and bless one another with.

▶ *Action stations*

Together you are going to meditate on the Lord's prayer. First let's break it up into sections:

(1) Our Father
(2) in heaven:
(3) May your holy name be honoured;
(4) may your Kingdom come; may your will be done on earth as it is in heaven.
(5) Give us today the food we need.
(6) Forgive us the wrongs we have done, as we forgive the wrongs others have done to us.
(7) Do not bring us to hard testing,
(8) but keep us safe from the Evil One.
(9) For yours is the Kingdom and the power and the glory, for ever. Amen.

Here we have nine excellent meditations. If you wanted you could make these the major feature of your prayer life for the next nine days. If it is easiest for you to pray together at the weekends, work your way through the phrases over the next nine weeks.

Following the instructions already given, let the phrases sink into your minds. After about ten minutes, talk through what you have gleaned from considering the phrase. For example, when meditating on 'Our Father' we have found it refreshing to consider how good it is to have a God who is a dad to us. Dads take time with their children; play with them; bring them surprises; cuddle them so that they feel all wrapped up in love and very secure. Our God is just like that.

We discovered that each of us would gain a different perspective with which we were able to enrich our partner's knowledge of God. It also helped us to discover blind spots in our Christian experience—for example, not having any real experience of God as Daddy! We could then invite our partner to pray for us, and could begin a Bible search on the word 'Father' in order to build up a clear picture of the fatherhood of God. Many of us, if we are honest, are not too sure how to read the Bible—and discovering blind spots gives us a purpose for going to the Bible.

Once you've completed meditations on the Lord's prayer, why not start on Proverbs or Psalms? There is a real feast to be had there. Meditating on the Song of Songs will reveal the reality, depth and intimacy of God's love for us.

We have also found that there are many non-biblical sources which can stimulate our imaginations and be a means of directing our thoughts towards God. Take for example the following passage from C. S. Lewis's children's book, *The Lion, the Witch and the Wardrobe* and see how it can become a tool to serve us in our insights into God's work and his world.

He led them up the steep slope out of the river valley and then slightly to the right—apparently by the very same route which they had used that afternoon in coming from the Hill of the Stone Table. On and on he led them, into dark shadows and out into pale moonlight, getting their feet wet with the heavy dew. He looked somehow different from the Aslan they knew. His tail and his head hung low and he walked slowly as if he were very, very tired. Then, when they were crossing a wide open place where there were no shadows for them to hide in, he stopped and looked round. It was no good trying to run away so they came towards him. When they were closer he said,

'Oh, children, children, why are you following me?'

'We couldn't sleep,' said Lucy—and then felt sure that she need say no more and that Aslan knew all they had been thinking.

'Please, may we come with you—wherever you're going?' said Susan.

'Well—' said Aslan, and seemed to be thinking. Then he said, 'I should be glad of company tonight. Yes, you may come, if you will promise to stop when I tell you, and after that leave me to go on alone.'

'Oh, thank you, thank you. And we will,' said the two girls.

Forward they went again and one of the girls walked on each side of the Lion. But how slowly he walked! And his great, royal head drooped so that his nose nearly touched the grass. Presently he stumbled and gave a low moan.

'Aslan! Dear Aslan!' said Lucy, 'what is wrong? Can't you tell us?'

'Are you ill, dear Aslan?' asked Susan.

'No,' said Aslan. 'I am sad and lonely. Lay your hands on my mane so that I can feel you are there and let us walk like that.'

And so the girls did what they would never have dared to do without his permission, but what they had longed to do ever since they first saw him—buried their cold hands in the beautiful sea of fur and stroked it and, so doing, walked with him. And presently they saw that they were going with him up the slope of the hill on which the Stone Table stood. They went up at the side where the trees came furthest up, and when they got to the last tree (it was one that had some bushes about it) Aslan stopped and said,

'Oh, children, children. Here you must stop. And whatever happens, do not let yourselves be seen. Farewell.'

And both the girls cried bitterly (though they hardly knew why) and clung to the Lion and kissed his mane and his nose and his paws and his great, sad eyes. Then he turned from them and walked out on to the top of the hill. And Lucy and Susan, crouching in the bushes, looked after him, and this is what they saw.

A great crowd of people were standing all round the Stone Table and though the moon was shining many of them carried torches which burned with evil-looking red flames and black smoke. But such people! Ogres with monstrous teeth, and wolves, and bull-headed men; spirits of evil trees and poisonous plants; and other creatures whom I won't describe because if I did the grown-ups would probably not let you read this book—Cruels and Hags and Incubuses, Wraiths, Horrors, Efreets, Sprites, Orknies, Wooses, and Ettins. In fact here were all those who were on the Witch's side and whom the Wolf had summoned at her command. And right in the middle, standing by the Table, was the Witch herself.

A howl and a gibber of dismay went up from the creatures when they first saw the great Lion pacing towards them, and for a moment even the Witch seemed to be struck with fear. Then she recovered herself and gave a wild fierce laugh.

'The fool!' she cried. 'The fool has come. Bind him fast.'

Lucy and Susan held their breaths waiting for Aslan's roar and his spring upon his enemies. But it never came. Four Hags, grinning and leering, yet also (at first) hanging back and half afraid of what they had to do, had approached him. 'Bind him, I say!' repeated the White Witch. The Hags made a dart at him and shrieked with triumph when they found that he made no resistance at all. Then others—evil dwarfs and apes—rushed in to help them, and between them they rolled the huge Lion over on his back and tied all his four paws together, shouting and cheering as if they had done something brave, though, had the Lion chosen, one of those paws could have been the death of them all. But he made no noise, even when the enemies, straining and tugging, pulled the cords so tight that they cut into his flesh. Then they began to drag him towards the Stone Table.

'Stop!' said the Witch. 'Let him first be shaved.'

Another roar of mean laughter went up from her followers as an ogre with a pair of shears came forward and squatted down by Aslan's head. Snip-snip-snip went the shears and masses of curling gold began to fall to the ground. Then the orgre stood back and the children, watching from their hiding-place, could see the face of Aslan looking all small and different without its mane. The enemies also saw the difference.

'Why, he's only a great cat after all!' cried one.

'Is *that* what we were afraid of?' said another.

And they surged round Aslan, jeering at him, saying things like 'Puss, Puss! Poor Pussy,' and 'How many mice have you caught today, Cat?' and 'Would you like a saucer of milk, Pussums?'

'Oh, how *can* they?' said Lucy, tears streaming down her cheeks. 'The brutes, the brutes!' for now that the first shock was over the shorn face of Aslan looked to her braver, and more beautiful, and more patient than ever.

'Muzzle him!' said the Witch. And even now, as they worked about his face putting on the muzzle, one bite from his jaws would have cost two or three of them their hands. But he never moved. And this seemed to enrage all that rabble. Everyone was at him now. Those who had been afraid to come near him even after he was bound began to find their courage, and for a few minutes the two girls could not even see him—so thickly was he surrounded by the whole crowd of creatures kicking him, hitting him, spitting on him, jeering at him.

At last the rabble had had enough of this. They began to drag the bound and muzzled Lion to the Stone Table, some pulling and some pushing. He was so huge that even when they got him there it took all their efforts to hoist him on to the surface of it. Then there was more tying and tightening of cords.

'The cowards! The cowards!' sobbed Susan. 'Are they *still* afraid of him, even now?'

When once Aslan had been tied (and tied so that he was really a mass of cords) on the flat stone, a hush fell on the crowd. Four Hags, holding four torches, stood at the corners of the Table. The Witch bared her arms as she had bared them the previous night when it had been Edmund instead of Aslan. Then she began to whet her knife. It looked to the children, when the gleam of the torchlight fell on it, as if the knife were made of stone, not of steel, and it was of a strange and evil shape.

At last she drew near. She stood by Aslan's head. Her face was working and twitching with passion, but his looked up at the sky, still quiet, neither angry nor afraid, but a little sad. Then, just before she gave the blow, she stooped down and said in a quivering voice,

'And now, who has won? Fool, did you think that by all this you would save the human traitor? Now I will kill you instead of him as our pact was and so the Deep Magic will be appeased. But when you are dead what will prevent me from killing him as well? And who will take him out of my hand *then*? Understand that you have given me Narnia forever, you have lost your own life and you have not saved his. In that knowledge, despair and die.'

The children did not see the actual moment of the killing. They couldn't bear to look and had covered their eyes.

[Taken from C. S. Lewis, *The Lion, the Witch and the Wardrobe*, Geoffrey Bles 1950, Collins/Fontana Lions 1980, pp 135-41, and used by permission.]

It is, I am sure you will agree, a very moving passage and gives a whole new angle on the crucifixion of Christ. We can have our own spiritual experience expanded by drawing upon the imagination of others in this way. Familiar stories can gain fresh meaning and move us again and often at a deeper level. When Katey and I compared thoughts after this passage we discovered that our eye and mind had been drawn to some of the details of the crucifixion as never before. We were able to have an extended and fruitful period of prayer as a result.

Finally, meditation can help us in our prayers for others. Consider the following poem:

> Lord, how is life for him? Keep a watchful eye,
> Lest that bare cubby-hole apartment drive him to madness.
> Make his pain a dark secret and lend to his face a light
> Meant for two, so the world shall perceive adversity mastered.
> With a lifted cup I salute the force of Your will
> (See the ease of that gesture—my hands held high without trembling.)
> But with Being's radiant armor, protect his soul
> From the jeers of the rabble.
> Unlike him in obscurity, I have a road so plain,
> Polished smooth by the multitudes, memorizing each pebble.
> I can manage this task—just watch me! But please keep him safe.
> From the nooks of insane asylums with spider webbing.
> Do not dispossess him, depriving him of Your strength,
> Do not let Your hand fall carelessly from his shoulder.
> From eternity's alloy of spirit and truth
> Let him fashion a chain and manacles for our sorrow.
> When we stand in Your presence in the next life,
> Asking nothing—except a companionship past all fractures,
> Past the power of angelic trumpets or rending knives,
> We will look at You, ready to give You our answers.

This poem was written by a Russian Christian who until recently was imprisoned for her faith and serving a sentence in a labour camp. By reading her thoughts we will find plenty of fuel for prayer both for her, her husband and others in similar situations. A very fruitful meditation could result from pondering this poem.

Postscript

As you approach the end of this book you are only just beginning an exciting journey of praying together. We hope that the previous chapters have proved both readable and a stimulus to action. However, once you have worked through the book, what then? Will you have the ability to continue to develop an enjoyable prayer life together? Maintaining prayer is always a challenge.

We are convinced that if you continue to put into practice the principles outlined in this book you will establish your own unique and effective life of prayer. Having participated in the 'Action Stations' you have in fact already launched out into praying together. All you need now is to find the time and dive in. As you do this you will establish a personal prayer experience.

Do remember at all times that prayer is for your benefit. So often it exercises a tyranny over us causing us pangs of condemnation. We are not slaves to prayer, rather it is a God-given gift for our welfare. Prayer is our servant, deepening our relationship with our Father and bringing his will and purposes into reality on earth.

It would be unfair to pretend that Katey and I, having

discovered the lessons written about here, have found prayer plain sailing. We have struggled to keep up our practice of prayer. There are even times when we have ceased praying altogether, but at such times we don't beat ourselves or each other with a club of guilt but simply sit down and re-evaluate our situation. The process of overcoming embarrassment with regard to praying together has enabled us to talk the situation through calmly, draw conclusions and take practical decisions to move us forward.

So often we seem to establish a pattern for prayer and no sooner having done so we grow uncomfortable with it or just plain bored. At other times we have to recognize that the framework we have been using has grown stale and so our praying together has become mechanical and lifeless—a duty maintained and little more. One way to combat this is to take the positive steps suggested by us to keep prayer alive, fresh and vibrant.

In one of his books Juan Carlos Ortiz recounts the day he decided the prayer meeting had grown stale. Seated in a room with a group of hallelujah hearties he decided to break the mould once and for all. It was as if the affirmations of 'Thank you Jesus', 'Amen', 'Glory' etc. which regularly punctuated the prayer time were simply tumbling from people's lips through habit. Ortiz took everyone out of the room and into the open air. He then encouraged them to keep their eyes open, move around and praise God for the many glorious evidences of his creation. The expressions of praise were to be clear vocal declarations—and so the fun began. The lesson is not to troop out into the back-garden and do likewise (although you might like to give it a go), rather it is that we need constantly to discover fresh ways of praying that prevent us from stagnation.

We often pray when out walking the dog. As we stroll

along the beach we spontaneously thank God for the many good things around us or for how good it is to be related to God and to each other. Such spontaneity is itself a creative stimulus for each partner and in no time at all a praise meeting has broken out on the beach— well, two of us getting excited and a bemused dog looking on.

When visiting friends some of my most pleasurable moments have been when their children, having looked me over carefully for some time, have all of a sudden crossed the room with arms uplifted in a silent request for a good cuddle, demonstrating that I've been accepted by them. There is something very heartwarming about such spontaneity. I believe we need to find ways of releasing that kind of spontaneity within our worship as churches whether our liturgy be formal or free.

When walking the dog it is not just praise and worship that flows from our lips. We also pray for specific situations as we walk along, breaking into our conversation with an appeal to God about what we have been discussing before resuming our conversation once again. I personally find a walk very helpful in talking through all the things on my mind and Katey proves a most helpful sounding-board. As we express all our concerns and dreams and consider the plight of various individuals and groups it seems only natural to pray there and then. Our prayer is increasingly and effectively woven into the everyday fabric of our lives.

But what if . . .

We have learned over the years that the biggest impediment to action is one small three-letter word—'but'. It seems that for every proposal someone can be relied upon to find an exception. Few will accept this as the exception which proves the rule.

Often the exceptions pinpointed relate to circumstances. We need to recognize that there are some circumstances that we cannot change; however, circumstances always contain the capacity to change us. It is in this area that some of our greatest apparent difficulties may emerge.

(1) But what if we've young children?

Since we cannot speak from experience, we have chatted with couples with young children and noted their wise counsel.

As with all 'what if' questions, there has to be the desire and commitment to look beyond the problem to a solution. Obviously time is at a premium and opportunity to pray very limited. That is where spontaneity is more helpful, and why establishing an effective pattern of prayer from courtship onwards pays dividends. For example, why not chat to God while bathing the baby or feeding the youngster. Recognizing that evenings are rest and recovery periods for Mum, seek to ensure a time of worship over breakfast. If this happens to coincide with the baby's feed-time at 6 a.m., so be it. Or if it entails bringing a tray of tea and toast upstairs to the bedroom, then do it. The arrival of children demands a reordering of lifestyle, including spiritual life. Perhaps Dad could find a short verse at the start of the day for both to meditate on during the day and then talk over the fruit of that meditation as you sit facing each other in the bath at 8 p.m. that night! Just a suggestion.

(2) But what if I'm on shift work?

You could try the meditation principle suggested above and talk it through when you link up. If you are not going to see each other, leave a verse on a postcard ready for your partner along with the other special treats which help keep romance alive. When you both have a day off together, give yourselves time as a couple to go for a walk or out for a drink and talk and pray as you go. Try to ensure you have a word of encouragement or a prophecy for your partner for when you are together. If work means being apart for a long time agree beforehand targets to focus prayer on each day while separated. When I travelled a lot with BYFC Katey and I would agree what part of the Bible we would read, keep to it as best we could and expect to have a feast to enjoy together when reunited.

(3) But what if I give up?

The simple answer is don't. The practical reply is start again, maybe utilize this book once more as a springboard to action. Don't become a slave to your past—shrug it off and have another go. As a Christian you have all the resources you need to overcome hindrances in prayer. Once you recognize that, make the necessary allowances then get started at a level at which you feel comfortable. You will then discover how enjoyable and effective the whole business of prayer is.

We urge you from this point on to begin your own unique journey and establish a personal testimony of praying together with your partner.

Classics from Arthur Wallis

by Arthur Wallis

The complete text of three bestselling titles from
Arthur Wallis.

- *Living God's Way* provides a course specially
  designed to disciple new Christians. With a clear
  and straightforward approach it covers the Bible's
  basic teaching so that the new Christian can gain a
  thorough and practical understanding of Christian
  commitment.

- An ideal follow-up to *Living God's Way*, *Going on
  God's Way* is designed to help you ensure that
  spiritual growth is a reality in your life and your
  church. Practical, relevant and biblical, it is ideal for
  individual or group use.

- Becoming a Christian is to join forces with God
  against the powers of darkness. *Into Battle* shows
  how victory over the enemy can become an
  increasing reality in every part of our lives – starting
  with repentance from sin, faith in the saving
  power of God and then baptism in water and the
  Holy Spirit.

ARTHUR WALLIS was internationally renowned for his
Bible teaching ministry, especially through his many books.

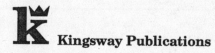

Kingsway Publications

Classics from Floyd McClung

by Floyd McClung

The complete and unabridged text of three of the best loved titles from Floyd McClung.

- *The Father Heart of God*   Many people suffer from deep emotional hurts and fears. Time and again it has been the discovery of God as Father – perfect and reliable, unlike any human parent – that has brought healing and liberty.

- *Loving the God Who Loves You*   God is committed to you. He longs for your devotion and service, but even more he is looking for your love. Your friendship. This book shares how to know God – as Saviour, Friend and daily companion.

- *Learning to Love People You Don't Like*   Whether it's a colleague who irritates you or a leader who's become heavy-handed; or you simply need to forgive someone who has wronged you – this book will give you practical steps to bring harmony and reconciliation into all your relationships.

FLOYD McCLUNG lives with his wife Sally and their two grown-up children at Mission Village in the Colorado Rockies, where they direct Youth Explosion, a ministry to train the leaders of tomorrow.

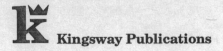 **Kingsway Publications**

Preface

In the cold, black night of Christ's betrayal, his disciples could not tarry one hour with him in prayer. In the Garden of Gethsemane, while Jesus earnestly prayed in such agony of spirit that his sweat became like great drops of blood falling to the ground, his disciples, ignorantly oblivious to the eternity-shaping events about to transpire, slept.

Jesus, heavy and sorrowful in spirit, awakened his sleeping disciples and asked, 'Could you men not keep watch with me for one hour?' (Matthew 26:40).

Mirrored in that tragic scene is the plight of the church today. Jesus, our interceding High Priest, is praying; his disciples are sleeping; and Satan is winning contest after contest by *default*.

It would be impossible to calculate the failures, the ruined reputations, the defeats, the broken homes and the other multiplied tragedies that could have been avoided if believers had prayed. It would be impossible to measure the destruction that could have been turned and the judgment that might have been averted if only God's people had taken the time to pray. I am guilty, and so are you.

But I didn't write this book to send anybody on a guilt trip. I wrote it because I know what it's like to be haunted by the call to pray, and because I know what it's like to let interruptions, fatigue and pressures drown out that call. You see, God haunted me for six years with the call to pray before I finally obeyed his plea to tarry with him one hour each day in prayer. But when I did so, my life and ministry were revolutionised.

I want to make you a promise: something supernatural happens when you pray an hour a day. It does not happen overnight, but slowly, almost imperceptibly, the *desire* to pray becomes firmly planted in the soil of your heart by the Spirit of God. This desire crowds out the weeds of apathy and neglect, and matures into the *discipline* to pray. Then one day you discover that prayer is no longer just a duty or drudgery; instead, the discipline of prayer has borne the fruit of *delight*. You find yourself eagerly longing for your daily time with God.

The supernatural work of prayer continues and begins to possess and reshape every area of your life. You notice that your heart is no longer devoid of the presence and promises of God. You discover how to set, maintain and pray God's priorities in your life; you learn how to appropriate God's provision for your needs. Life moves into a new dimension as you begin to experience greater joy and fulfilment in your relationships with people.

And as you begin to walk, not in the realm of the flesh, but in the realm of the Spirit, you discover how to move in the power of God and stand in the victory Jesus has won for you.

How do I know? I know because that is what happened to me as I obeyed the call to pray. I know because that is what happened to the believers after Christ's ascension.

Think about it: what transformed the slumbering disciples, disheartened believers and vacillating followers pictured in the final chapters of the gospels into the determined, driving, unified army of the book of Acts? What made them into a mighty, spiritual army that seized difficulties and turned them into opportunities; an army characterised by clear-headed, incisive decisions instead of foggy thinking and confusion; an army that, in one generation, turned the world upside down for Jesus Christ?

Prayer. Prayer that unleashed the power of God and tapped into his infinite resources.

What will transform the slumbering disciples, disheartened believers and vacillating followers today into a mighty, marching army with deliverance as its song and healing in its hands?

Prayer. Prayer that snatches the victories Jesus won for us out of Satan's greedy clutches. Prayer that storms the gates of hell.

If you do not consistently pray one full hour every day but would like to learn how, take the prayer secrets the Holy Spirit has taught me on my knees and begin to practise them. As you learn to pray the way Jesus taught us to pray, your prayer life will no longer be a frustrating, hit-or-miss experience; instead, tarrying with the Lord an hour in prayer will actually become easy and natural.

Won't you bow your head right now and pray: 'Jesus, plant in my heart the desire to pray. Enable me to develop a daily, consistent time of prayer. Transform prayer from a duty to a delight. Make me a mighty warrior in your prayer army'?

Did you pray that prayer? Did you mean it? Then you had better get your uniform out of mothballs, polish those brass buttons and shine your boots because, soldier, God's army is getting ready to march.

Larry Lea